Rugby League Re...
Number 2

Edited by Dave Farrar and Peter Lush

London League Publications Ltd

Rugby League Review
Number 2

© Articles copyright to the contributors.

The moral right of the contributors to be identified as the authors has been asserted.

Cover design © Stephen McCarthy. Photographs © the photographer or contributor of the photograph. No copyright has been intentionally infringed.

Front cover photo: To mark the great success of Catalan Dragons in 2008, their centre Adam Mogg is given our front cover spot (Photo: David Williams, rlphotos.com). Back cover photo: Warrington versus St Helens Recs in the Challenge Cup in 1926, Ben Jolley (Warrington captain, right) and Jack 'Tot' Wallace shake hands. The referee is the Reverend Frank Chambers (Photo: Courtesy Eddie Fuller & Gary Slater)

This book is copyright under the Berne Convention. All rights are reserved. It is sold subject to the condition that it shall not, by way of trade or otherwise, be lent, resold, hired out or otherwise circulated without the publisher's prior consent in any form of binding or cover other than that in which it is published and without a similar condition being imposed on the subsequent purchaser.

A CIP catalogue record for this book is available from the British Library.

First published in Great Britain in September 2008 by:
London League Publications Ltd, P.O. Box 10441, London E14 8WR

ISBN: 978-1903659-41-0

Cover design by: Stephen McCarthy Graphic Design
46, Clarence Road, London N15 5BB

Layout: Peter Lush

Printed and bound by: Biddles Ltd
King's Lynn, Great Britain

About our authors

David Ballheimer went to Craven Cottage mainly out of curiosity during Fulham's first season. His second match - the shock John Player Cup defeat of Leeds - hooked him and he has been a regular fan ever since. He has reported on the London clubs since the mid-1980s and is probably the only journalist to have written regular reports on Fulham, London Crusaders, London Broncos, Harlequins and London Skolars. He reports for *League Weekly*, *The News of the World*, the Press Association and local hospital radio as well as many regional newspapers and is an occasional guest on BBC London 94.9's *Rugby League show* and has seen the London clubs' home games at more venues (21) than anyone else.

Garry Clarke was born into a rugby league family, the son of former Warrington, Leigh and Liverpool City player Doug Clarke, one of four brothers to have played professional rugby league, Garry is a Warrington supporter, former chairman of the Supporters Club, and is a follower of the game at all levels watching amateur games on park pitches up to the World Cup Final which he will be attending in November.

Pete Cropper was born in the year the Challenge Cup first came to St Helens and he has supported Saints since he saw his first match against Wakefield Trinity in 1965. He wrote *From Great Broughton to Great Britain: Peter Gorley - Rugby League Forward* which was published in 2004), and he has recently been contributing regularly to the 'The Way I See It' fans' page in the St Helens programme. He hopes to have his first novel, *Bowing Out*, published this year. He is married to Josephine and lives at Horwich near Bolton.

Gordon Derbyshire was born and brought up in Widnes. He watched the Chemics from the late 50s, played for Simms Cross Primary School and then much later had a couple of years playing on the wing for Widnes RLFC from 1969 to 1971, playing around 30 first team games.

He spent a year in Australia a bit later, and coached secondary school teams in Widnes alongside Mick Naughton, Robin Whitfield, Roger Harrison and Mike Findlater in the 1980s. His work then took me to the West Country where he met up with Lionel Hurst, Ruth Sigley and Stephen Rigby and later led to some involvement with the RLC. In 2000 he moved to France and now lives in Carcassonne. He watches league the year round the famous Canaris of ASC XIII in the winter and now the Catalan Dragons in the summer.

Neil Dowson is the finance manager at Warrington Wolves and has been at the club for 11 seasons. A season ticket holder at Warrington before joining the staff, Neil has been watching rugby league for over 45 years. He managed the club's development of The Halliwell Jones Stadium and move from Wilderspool. Neil was involved in the setting up of the Warrington Wolves Supporters Trust and still serves as the club representative on the Trust Board. He has written a book about the history of Warrington RLFC *End of an Era – Wilderspool 1898 to 2003* and is also involved in the Warrington Wolves heritage project Wire2Wolves. Neil played rugby union for Leigh RUFC for 26 years.

Sean Fagan is an Australian sports historian, author and journalist, specialising in rugby league and 19th century rugby. He has written articles for national daily newspapers, RL1908.com and numerous sports magazines. His most recent book is *The Master - The Life and Times of Dally Messenger.*

Robert Gate is Britain's most prolific and distinguished rugby league historian, and was formerly the RFL archivist. His groundbreaking work on Welsh players in the 1980s has been followed by biographies, including Brian Bevan and Neil Fox, and club histories, and most recently a history of Great Britain's rugby league test matches. He lives in West Yorkshire and until the start of Super League watched Halifax. These days he is more likely to be found watching Siddal.

David Hinchliffe was a hooker in amateur rugby league for many years and is a life-long supporter of Wakefield Trinity RLFC. He served as the Labour MP for Wakefield from 1987 to 2005 and was secretary of the All Party Parliamentary Rugby League for most of this period. His Sports Discrimination Bill in the early 1990s drew national attention to rugby union's treatment of those who had also played rugby league. Away from sport, David has had a longstanding interest in health and social care. He was shadow Health Minister from 1992 to 1995 and chairman of the Commons Health Select Committee from 1997 to 2005. Since his retirement from Parliament he has been a director of an NHS trust and his continued involvement in rugby league includes serving as a trustee of the RFL's Benevolent Fund. He lives with his wife Julia in a converted barn in the West Riding Pennines.

Ian Jackson has a longstanding fascination with the heritage of rugby league whilst following simultaneously the fortunes of Swinton Lions RLFC. He writes regular articles in the Swinton programme and is currently researching rugby league players who fell in World War One. Also, he is an active member of the Swinton Supporters' Trust and is helping to co-ordinate a local history project known as Lions' Tales together with Supporters' Direct and the Federation of Stadium Communities to record the memories of Swinton players, officials and supporters past and present.

Stuart Leadley was born in East Yorkshire, where he lives with two cats and lots of books, and is a Hull supporter. He studied history at Durham University but now works for the NHS. He is attempting to compile a comprehensive bibliography of rugby league; for more information about this email: stuart.leadley@dunelm.org.uk

Geoff Lee first learned to write at Knowsley Road School in St Helens just after the end of the war. A draughtsman for most of his working life he began writing a novel called *Tales of a Northern Draughtsman* in 1988. It was later changed to *One Winter* and has been followed by another three, all set against a strong rugby league background: (www.geofflee.net). He is secretary of the RLSA and manages the distribution of its magazine TGG for which he also writes.

Bill Lythgoe, like most people who are born in the no-man's land between Wigan and St Helens, grew up to love one and hate the other. He has written for *Open Rugby*, *TGG, League Express* and was a regular contributor to *Our Game*.

Dr Richard Mawditt played rugby union at wing forward (flanker it's now called) at a modest junior club level in Bristol and Brighton for some 600 games before finally falling over and finding it difficult to get up again. Having moved to Bath (university administrator and academic) the support and following of Bath Rugby ultimately led him to become chairman of Bath RFC for eight years from 1994 at a time of the great transition during which he was a member of the RFU Commission producing the report into the future of rugby football in England. His sporting connections have included being a member of the Executive Board of the European Youth Olympics and for 22 years a governor of Millfield School.

Phil Melling is a reader in American Studies at the University of Wales, Swansea and a visiting research fellow at the University of Havana. He is an author of plays and biographies on rugby league, including *The Day of the African* and *Man of Amman*. He was co-editor of *The Glory of their Times*. Since 1978 he has been at the heart of the development of the game, particularly in the universities and colleges, and in Wales. He is a former chairman of Swansea Valley Miners RLFC and former vice chairman of the Wales Conference.

Michael O'Hare freelances as a rugby league writer and editor although he does have a 'proper job' at *New Scientist* magazine. He is the author of that publications' science question and answer books which include *Why Don't Penguins' Feet Freeze?* He was brought up as a staunch Huddersfield supporter but a long exile in the south of England has, he hopes, beaten the parochialism out of him.

Huw Richards writes on both codes of rugby for the *Financial Times* and on cricket for the *International Herald Tribune*. He is a former Fulham RLFC programme editor, contributed to Dave Hadfield's *XIII Winters* and to numerous London League Publications books including *Tries in the Valleys* and *I, George Nepia*.

Glyn Robbins played rugby union for 20 years. His main club was Old Bealonians in Ilford, now defunct (a victim of professionalisation). He represented Sheffield Polytechnic in the 1988 British Polytechnics Cup Final (thrashed by the Welsh) and also played for Sheffield, London Jewish (under the name Robinski) and finally, Hackney.

Alex Service is a Saints' fanatic since being taken to Knowsley Road by his father in 1960. Alex is the club historian at St Helens RLFC and has written nine books about the club and its players. He has been a regular contributor to the club's programme since the early 1980s and has compiled a number of Testimonial brochures for players such as Paul Loughlin, Keiron Cunningham and Sean Long. Having accepted early retirement from Broadway High School in Thatto Heath in 2006, Alex began to research the history of the St Helens / Pilkington Recreation team. He is naturally devastated that both the Recs and Saints will lose their spiritual homes over the next few years – a sad time for true devotees of the rugby league game in the town.

Gary Slater was born and bred in Warrington and saw his first Warrington match in 1972 at the age of 10. He was a pupil at Penketh High School and graduated from Imperial College, London, in 1982. He is a former deputy sports editor of the *Warrington Guardian* and *Birmingham Evening Mail* and is currently a senior production journalist and news editor on the *Daily Telegraph* sports desk in London. He, too, has been a regular contributor to the Warrington Wolves matchday programme.

Hendrik Snyders has been involved with rugby on club and provincial level for 30 years both as player and administrator. He represented Velddrif RUFC and the University of the Western Cape at club level and the West Coast Rugby Union – an affiliate of the former Western Province Country Rugby Union and South African Rugby Union - on sub-union level. In addition he served as secretary of the West Coast Rugby Union before and after the rugby unification process. Currently he is the chairperson of Velddrif RUFC and has recently been elected as the chairperson of the newly established Cape West Coast Rugby League Province with its base in Saldanha Bay, the home town of Green Vigo.

Ray Warburton has been a clinical scientist in the NHS for 40 years. He is a supporter of Manchester United, Lancashire CCC and, more importantly, Salford City Reds. He saw David Watkins make his debut for Salford in the late 1960s but didn't see another game of rugby league until Great Britain versus Australia in the 1980s; around the same time he saw Widnes play Canberra Raiders in the World Club Championship at Old Trafford and became hooked. He then started watching Salford regularly and has been a rugby league fanatic ever since. He often writes letters to the weekly and monthly league papers. Finally, he says that Salford will be in their new ground in 2010 and will get crowds between 10,000 and 12,000 in the first season there.

Denis Whittle cut his oval ball teeth within the fertile breeding ground for stars that is St Helens. He was educated at Lowe House School and has supported Saints' since World War Two, when he carried the team changes board around Knowsley Road. Denis met his late wife Margaret on the half-way line at Saints and he would like his ashes scattered there, even if the hallowed turf is redeveloped. Now 75, he spent 30 years with the *St Helens Reporter* and 10 with the *St Helens Star*. He was privileged to be a close friend of the late Eric Ashton. Then a teenager, Whittle was involved with the launching of the four-page hot-metal *Rugby Leaguer* in 1949.

Gavin Willacy has been involved in rugby league for less than a decade but in that time has thrown himself into it. He has reported on games at all levels for the trade press, national newspapers and radio; been press officer for St Albans Centurions and Scotland; managed Southgate College and Scotland 'A'; helped London Skolars in whatever way he can; became a qualified coach; and written a book, *Rugby League Bravehearts*. His second book, *No Helmets Required*, about attempts to launch the game in America in the 1950s and the adventures and calamities that ensued, will be published very soon or else he will find himself single again!

Graham Williams has been following rugby league in general and Leeds in particular for over 30 years. For the last 20 years or so he has been delving into areas of the game's history, especially its attempts at expansion and its struggles with both football and rugby union. In that time he has contributed articles to a number of club programmes, to magazines such as *Open Rugby*, *Rugby League Journal* and the original *Code 13* as well as collaborating on a couple of books with Peter Lush for London League Publications.

And finally

Dave Farrar, born in Salford, has been watching the game for 45 years. He has been following the game in London since Fulham's first season and is the official timekeeper at the Skolars. Dave has been writing about the game since participating in the *London Calling* fanzine 15 years ago. He founded *London League Publications* with Peter Lush in 1995 and has done occasional match reports for the *Evening Standard* and the *Yorkshire Post*. He has also appeared on the BBC Radio London 94.9 Thursday night rugby league show and writes a regular column in the London Skolars programme.

Dave works as an electoral consultant in local government, with occasional forays into IT.

Peter Lush was introduced to rugby league at Fulham in 1980 by Dave Farrar. With Dave and Michael O'Hare he wrote *Touch and Go – a history of professional rugby league in London* in 1995, the book that saw the creation of London League Publications Ltd. Since then he co-edited *From Fulham to Wembley* and *Tries in the Valleys* with Dave Farrar, co-wrote *Rugby's Berlin Wall* and *Peter Fox – The players' coach* with Graham Williams and co-wrote two guidebooks to rugby league grounds and two cricket grounds guide books. He also co-edited *Our Game* magazine with Dave Farrar, and *Rugby League Annual Review 2007*. He is now working on a history of rugby league and South Africa with Hendrik Snyders, and has recently completed a history of Hendon Football Club with David Ballheimer. He has also written for *Rugby League World*, *League Express* and the London Broncos club programme. He is director of a small training charity in central London.

A great new book from London League Publications

Peter Fox
The players' coach

Peter Fox was involved in professional rugby league for almost 50 years. After playing for Sharlston Rovers, he had a 13 year playing career with Featherstone Rovers, Batley, Hull KR and Wakefield Trinity, he became one of British rugby league's most successful coaches. Highlights of his coaching career include:

- Coaching Great Britain and England, including beating the Australians in 1978
- Winning eight matches with Yorkshire
- Winning the Challenge Cup and promotion with **Featherstone Rovers**
- Winning the First Division title in 1980 and 1981 with **Bradford Northern**
- Winning promotion with **Bramley**
- Winning the Premiership, Yorkshire Cup and John Player Trophy

With a foreword by David Hinchliffe, this authorised biography, published in June 2008 and based on extensive interviews and research, gives the inside story of Peter's at times controversial rugby league career. It includes how he developed the teams he coached, and the players he signed. Every rugby league fan will find it of great interest.

Special offer for readers of this book: £14.00 post free (cover price £14.95). Credit card orders via www.llpshop.co.uk or from PO Box 10441, London E14 8WR (Cheques payable to London League Publications Ltd)

The book can also be ordered from any bookshop at £14.95 (ISBN: 9781903659397)

Contents

History
Spreading the gospel by Gavin Willacy	1
Rugby League in Runcorn by Garry Clarke	4
Early tours, cricket and rugby by Sean Fagan and Ian Jackson	12
Warrington – between the wars and the Hall of Fame by Neil Dowson	24
Northern Union rugby in 1908 by Garry Clarke	29
Eddie Waring by Huw Richards and Peter Lush	33
Wayne English: Swinton's number one by Ian Jackson	39
All local lads! The famous St Helens and Pilkington Recreation by Alex Service and Denis Whittle	42

League and Union
Just because you're paranoid... by David Hinchliffe	45
Wigan versus Bath by Michael O'Hare and Richard Mawditt	51
Ok... It is boring! by Glyn Robbins	58
'That's entertainment' says David Watkins	60
London's Oldest Rugby Clubs reviewed by Gavin Willacy	61

Features
Rugby league in Cuba by Phil Melling	63
Get rid of the video referee by David Ballheimer	66
The Co-operative National Leagues: The Future by Ray Warburton	69
The rugby league press by Peter Lush and Gary Slater	74
The RFL Benevolent Fund by Tim Adams and Stephen Ball	81
Rugby league worldwide by Garry Clarke	84

South Africa
The history of rugby league and South Africa by Peter Lush	85
Green without Gold – The Green Vigo story by Hendrik Snyders	89
Between the Springbok and Ikhamanga by Hendrik Snyders	97

Book Reviews — 112

Obituaries by Robert Gate — 132

Grubber by Steve Spencer – see page 73

Editor's note: As this book went to the printers, it was announced that Don Fox had died. Don was one of the great players of his generation, for Featherstone Rovers, Wakefield Trinity and Great Britain. RFL chief executive Nigel Wood said: "Don Fox was a tremendous player with great skill. As a Great Britain international and a Lions tourist and a Championship winner and a recipient of the Lance Todd Trophy, he achieved the highest accolades in the sport. He will be regarded as being among the greatest ever players to represent both the Featherstone and Wakefield clubs."

About this book

The origins of *Rugby League Review Number 2* are in the magazine, *Our Game*, which we ran from 2000 to 2006. After seven years we felt the magazine format was exhausted, and decided to publish a book, with similar material on current issues facing the game, history, book reviews and obituaries.

The format of this book is similar to *Rugby League Annual Review 2007*. We dropped the word 'Annual' as we may not publish every year in future, depending on other work, and the year, as the articles do not relate to a particular year.

So we hope you enjoy this book. We would like to thank everyone who contributed articles and photographs, Steve McCarthy for designing the cover and the staff of Biddles Ltd for printing it.

Dave Farrar and Peter Lush
Editors, *Rugby League Review*

Rugby League Annual Review 2007 is available from London League Publications Ltd at the special offer price of £5.00. Visit www.llpshop.co.uk to pay by credit card or send a cheque for £5.00 to London League Publications, PO Box 10441, London E14 8WR.

London League Publications: 50 books

This is, just about, our 50th book. We set up the company in 1995, to publish our history of rugby league in London, *Touch and Go*. So it is worth spending a few lines on how we have developed since then. Although the main emphasis of our work is on rugby league, we have also published books on cricket, football, boxing, judo and bottle collecting. The latter is out of print, in case any readers are curious.

Biographies or autobiographies have included Brian Bevan, Neil Fox, Doug Laughton, Trevor Foster, Paul Newlove, Duggie Greenall, George Nepia, Ces Mountford, Peter Gorley, Kevin Sinfield (a dairy of the 2003 season), journalist and broadcaster Keith Macklin and most recently Peter Fox. There's a decent team in there, although we need a scrum-half and a winger.

Club histories have included three more books on London, two on St Helens, one on Keighley Cougars and earlier this year one on Warrington.

Historical or general books on the game include *Rugby's Class War* by David Hinchliffe, *A Westminster XIII*, Maurice Bamford's *Play to Win*, *Champagne Rugby*, *Snuff out the Moon*, *Rugby's Berlin Wall*, *The Rugby Rebellion*, *We'll Support You Evermore*, *Beyond the Heartlands*, *The Sin Bin* and the 2007 *Rugby League Annual Review*. There have also been histories of the game in Wales and Scotland, three novels, two by Geoff Lee and one by John Vose, and two guidebooks.

And there are titles in the pipeline, including Liverpool City, St Helens Recs in 2008 and more booked in for 2009.

We would like to thank everyone who has written books, had books written about them, provided photographs, sub-edited, lent us material, laid out covers and printed the books. We look forward to the next 50.

Dave Farrar and Peter Lush

Spreading the gospel

Gavin Willacy reflects on the extraordinary experiences of the Americans who took up rugby league in the early 1950s.

Many rugby league folk will have heard of the 1953 tour of Australia and New Zealand undertaken by a group of Californian college American Football players under the guise of the 'American All Stars'. Far fewer will know much of their second excursion, a tour of France over Christmas that year and in to 1954. And if you knew that it spawned a clutch of rugby league-playing high schools around Los Angeles in the 1960s then I would be astonished. A brief recap:

When tour Svengali Mike Dimitro returned from down under in late August 1953, he had lost much goodwill – if not a bit of money – and had to recruit an almost entirely new squad for his next expedition to Europe. It was a similar mix of college American football and rugby union players from around Los Angeles as the All Stars Mark I.

Although the schedule was nowhere near as draining as that in Australia, when the All Stars clinched their first win over a Provence Selection in Avignon on New Year's Day 1954, it was their fourth game in 12 days.

Among the try scorers that day at Stade de Saint-Ruf were player-manager-tour operator-move-and-shaker Dimitro, Pepperdine graduate Bob Lampshire – who also kicked two goals – and another player who scored twice. His name was Hilgenberg, according to the French papers. But they also called him Helteberg, Hildenger and Hildenberg. He was and still is the mystery man of the All Stars.

No one knows who he is now and it seems no-one really knew who he was then either. In researching my book *No Helmets Required* (to be published imminently) every other player in the squad has been accounted for, contacted personally or their life story recounted by a team-mate.

"It could have been Hildenberg," claimed the otherwise superbly adroit Landon Exley. "I think he was one of the Pepperdine guys. If not, he'll have to be 'The Unknown Soldier'."

Two days later, on 3 January 1954, a Combined Nations XIII were due to play France in Lyon as part of the French Federation's 20th anniversary celebrations. Several of the All Stars had shown enough promise to be invited to represent the USA in the Selection Internationale. With only the small matter of the inaugural USA international to come six days later against France at Parc de Princes, it seemed an ideal opportunity for some of the Americans to experience what the greatest team on earth had to offer.

Full-back Bob Lampshire, three-quarters Leon Sellers, Exley and Larry Marino; second rower Tony Rappa; and props Willie Richardson and Xavier Mena were all called up. They were in illustrious company in the international XIII: Huddersfield's awesome Australian try machine Lionel Cooper – his 441 senior tries put him sixth in the all-time British records; Scottish loose-forward Dave Valentine would captain Great Britain to World Cup triumph later in the year; Warrington's Gerry Helme also won a World Cup medal; Ernest Ward was one of the leading players and personalities in the world game; Welsh hooker Phillips had won four GB caps; and Salford's Tom McKinney, born in Ireland but brought up in Scotland, was a regular Great Britain prop.

Come game day, Sellers and Lampshire paired up on the right wing with Ernest Ward at full-back and Aussie duo McLellan and Cooper on the left. Banks and Helme were the half-backs with Phillips at hooker, Welshman McNally and Italian Vigna in the second row, American Richardson alongside McKinney at prop and Dave Valentine at loose-forward.

Exley, Marino, Rappa and Mena were on stand-by in case any of the other stars based in England failed to make it. Warrington winger Naughton and the yet to be capped Leeds star Stevenson didn't travel but it was Don Lent who got a late call-up to the bench.

They were up against arguably the best team in the world. Many of the side had played in the victorious and stunning romp through Australia two and a half years before, a team that shocked world rugby and introduced a new brand of the handling game. Many of them would, four months later, return down under to prove it was no fluke, beating the Kangaroos in another test series on their own patch. In November 1954 they then would beat Australia and New Zealand at the inaugural World Cup in France before losing the final 16-12 to Great Britain in Paris.

France, led from the back by the majestic Puig-Aubert and featuring Bastianelli, Rey, Cantari, Jiminez partnered Joseph Crespo in the halves with stand-off Rene Duffort at hooker, predictably won against a scratch side, but only by 19 points to 15. Banks, McKinney ands Vigna touched down for the internationalists, Wards kicked three goals. Everyone was happy. Especially Don Lent.

"Dimitro chose me to be an alternate and I suited up for the game along with Lampshire, Sellers and Richardson," recalls Lent. "As far as I can remember, I believe I got in a little at the end. The rest of the team watched from the stands without suiting up. It was a very impressive game with some high-powered athletes."

That evening the whole party were invited to the Anniversaire dinner at Restaurant Nandron in Lyon. For starter: caviar. Then escargot, patte, fromages. Then the main course. And to finish? Vermouth, cassis, champagne and liqueurs de France. Nine courses. The Americans slept well when they eventually found their beds.

"There must have been 500 people there," reminisces Landon Exley, a quarter-back from University of Southern California in Los Angeles. "All of the French players would come and talk to us – we couldn't communicate at all but they would say, 'You guys are very fast and very strong'. They kept telling us 'Rugby league as a game is not boom, boom but finesse, finesse'. They would always preach that to us but then the next game we would just go out and bang the hell out of them again and... lose! We were always in the game but then all of a sudden they would just go racing past us.

But we hadn't even seen a game before and to have those guys pull off some of that really slick stuff that they did... But apart from not knowing all the nuances of the game, we thought we could beat them because we were better athletes, or at least we thought we were."

They never got the chance to find out. There were no more games and just a single member of the squad remained involved with rugby league. The rest were lost to the sport.

"I never played rugby ever again," says Exley. "Never before and never after. There weren't many opportunities. I think most of us would've done it again, done another trip, but it never happened."

Tony Rappa spent two years in the Army and then a life dedicated to his parents' seafood restaurant in Monterrey. He swears he hasn't seen another game of rugby since either. "That was the last time most of us played football or rugby. I wish that I'd spent all that time playing golf or tennis or something that you could do the rest of your life."

"I never did play rugby league again," admitted Sam Grossman, "although I really enjoyed the game much more than football. I haven't seen a match since." Grossman is now one of the biggest property developers in South-West United States, building shopping malls and Sheraton, Marriott and Hilton hotels. He is a multi-millionaire and has been linked with bids to buy the Washington Redskins for $600 million in 1998. Rugby league let this man go!

The one exception, bizarrely, was Don Lent. Having graduated from Pepperdine University with a teaching degree, Lent spent time with NFL franchise the LA Rams and played in the Canadian FL with his pal Bob Lampshire at Vancouver before they both returned to Southern California to coach and teach high school and college football.

It was Lent who kept the rugby league flame flickering in the most unlikely places. While every one of his team-mates gave up the game immediately on their return from France, Lent decided his school football players could learn from rugby league – and enjoy it.

"The rugby experience influenced all of us very much," insists Lent. "Rugby league was a tough sport and I never liked rugby union. So when Mike Dimitro and I coached together at Elsinore High School in Wildomara for a couple of years, we incorporated some of the plays into our football programme.

"Later, when I was head coach in high schools and college I had all my teams learn to play rugby league in the off season. I taught rugby league at Elsinore, Anaheim High, Magnolia High in Anaheim, Newport Harbor High and at Cal Poly University at Pomona. It was good for keeping our players in good condition and in competition as well as toughening them up without pads."

This extraordinary development has never been revealed before. Some English magazines and newspapers spoke of league been played in Californian schools but there was no evidence and this was dismissed by league historians as a figment of some missionary's imagination, a work of propaganda.

In 1986, Don Lent had a heart attack. On his hospital bed he had a vision. The following year he was ordained as a minister and formed the Timothy II Ministries in Orange County. The man who took rugby league to the OC is now called Timony II.

Hard to believe but it is all true.

If you want to read more about the All Stars' adventures on and off the field – their flights, fights, flings and stings – watch out for Gavin's book *No Helmets Required*.

Editor's note: 'Football' in this article is American Football, not soccer.

Rugby league in Runcorn

Garry Clarke looks at the long history of the game in Runcorn.

When Runcorn Vikings made their debut in the Rugby League Conference in 2005 to many it was seen as another example of the summer competition expanding the game into another new area. However, what many people may not have realised is that rugby league in Runcorn dates all the way back to the birth of the game in 1895.

The first rugby team in Runcorn was formed in 1876 as a section of the Runcorn Young Men's Christian Association Athletic Club, which took up a variety of sports and found that "football played under rugby rules" attracted the largest number of spectators. They first played at Greenway Road, a venue that was later covered by the Runcorn Soap and Alkali Company. Fields were also used in Moughland Lane and behind the water works before a move was made nearer to the town centre on land that again was taken over by the soap and alkali company. In 1878-79 the club shortened its name to Runcorn Football Club and played part of the following season on the Runcorn Cricket Club field, which was said to be in the occupation of the Runcorn Recreation FC.

In 1879-80 the club moved to a new ground near the town centre situated in Irwell Street, later renamed Canal Street. Over the next few years many improvements were made to the ground as the two pitches at the site were enclosed and the club being one of the first to install turnstiles at a rugby ground.

The club's original colours were amber and black, however in 1893 a change of club colours to myrtle green and yellow was made giving the club their nicknames of the Myrtle Jackets and the Linnets.

Runcorn soon became a stronghold of the game with 19 junior teams, with exotic names such as Runcorn Jockeys, Runcorn Waterlily and Runcorn Tam O'Shanters, playing in the town by 1886, while the senior club became one of Cheshire's most successful rugby clubs and was well represented at county level and also supplied nine players to the England international team.

During the 1885-86 season Runcorn took part in rugby's first ever knock out cup competition – The South West Lancashire and Border Towns Cup and with it the first points scoring system to determine winners and avoid so many inconclusive games. Prior to this in rugby the number of goals, of any type, kicked, decided games. A touchdown only earning a 'try' at kicking a goal. For this competition a goal placed from a try was worth 8 points, a goal kicked from the field 6 points, a try 4 points and all types of minors to score 1 point each. The only proviso being that the winners had to have at least a margin of 3 points to secure victory.

Runcorn defeated Sutton (70-1), Leigh (31-17) and Wigan (46-0) to set up a semi-final clash with near neighbours Warrington at Widnes. A controversial game, played before a then ground record crowd of 9,000, was abandoned with score at 2-2. A fight resulted in each side having a player sent off. The referee had to abandon the game when the Runcorn side walked off it protest at the referee's refusal to allow the dismissed player to return and replace an injured team mate. The cup competition committee decided the tie should be replayed at Southport where Warrington won 29-14 in a game played in four quarters of 20 minutes each.

Although not represented at the historic George Hotel meeting on 29 August 1895, Runcorn applied to join the Northern Union, and following the withdrawal of Dewsbury were accepted as founder members of the new organisation. The first round of fixtures were organised for 7 September with Runcorn welcoming their neighbours, from across the River Mersey, Widnes to Canal Street. The Linnets won their opening game 15-4, recording the highest score of all 20 teams taking part in the opening weekend end of Northern Union fixtures.

The *Bradford Observer* carried reports of all 10 games played on that historical first day, the report from Canal Street read: "At Runcorn in splendid weather. Being local clubs there was much excitement. Moores scored after good passing among the home backs and Dunbavin improved. Jolly, soon afterwards, got hurt and Warder filled his place at back. Robinson also got over and Dunbavin converted. In the second half play was fast and exciting Runcorn having rather the best of matters. From a throw out Farmer obtained possession and scored. Dunbavin again doing the needful. Widnes got into the Runcorn half and Rispen dropped a goal."

Runcorn, winning 24 games and drawing eight, finished the first Northern Union season in a highly respectable third place with 56 points from 42 games. They were just 10 points behind champions Manningham. The Linnets ended the inaugural Northern Union season with silverware. Having finished joint top of the Lancashire Senior Competition with Oldham, both teams gaining 28 points from 20 games, Runcorn defeated Oldham 6-5 in a play off at Broughton Rangers. On their return to Runcorn with the cup they were accompanied by a torchlight procession from the railway station through the town.

The Northern Union's first season was so successful that many more clubs crossed the great divide and to accommodate these new clubs the Northern Union split into two separate leagues, one covering Lancashire and the other Yorkshire. As Cheshire's leading side Runcorn were placed in the Lancashire section. Runcorn were always near the top of the table in the early years of the competition. Although maintaining a high standard the club suffered several setbacks, with the death of J. Langshaw the long serving and enthusiastic secretary and the refusal of some leading players to turn out for the club. Seemingly, it was alleged, Warrington had made tempting offers for a number of star players to transfer. The problem was resolved in time for the start of the 1899-1900 season which saw Runcorn crowned Lancashire League champions winning 22 of their 26 league games they finished three points ahead of second placed Oldham, who they beat by a try to nil in front of a record 15,000 crowd (gate receipts of £360) at Canal Street to clinch the title on 10 March, earning gold medals for the team and a place among the elite for the club. Throughout the whole campaign only seven tries were conceded. Runcorn also reached the final of the South West Lancashire and Border Towns Cup where they lost to St Helens.

When Runcorn were playing away from home the result of their game would be displayed in a shop window on Bridge Street, as this was the quickest way for fans to find out how their team had got on in the 19th century. Such was the interest in the team children would be sent to the shop on Saturday evenings just to find out the score.

In 1901 Runcorn were one of fourteen clubs that resigned from the two county leagues to form a new Northern Rugby League, a Super League of its day. Despite having two points deducted for breach of professional rules Runcorn finished the 1901-02 season in third place.

For season 1902-03 the Northern Union changed its league structure introducing two national leagues. Placed in Division One, Runcorn finished the first season of divisional Rugby in a creditable fourth place before slipping to 16th the following year. They then finished bottom of the table at the end of 1904-05 but were spared the embarrassment of relegation as the league set up was once again changed as the two divisional system was scrapped with all clubs being placed in a single league.

Under the single league format clubs from the same county all played each other and arranged inter county fixtures, because not all clubs played the same number of games positions were calculated on a percentage basis. Under this single league system, Runcorn's best season was 1906-07 when they finished third in the table and qualified for the top four play off which had been introduced for the first time to decide the championship. They lost 11-3 in the semi-final at Oldham, but gained a little consolation by heading the six club South West Lancashire League.

New Zealand

Runcorn provided one of the stiffest opponents to the 1907-08 touring New Zealand All Golds being the only team to prevent the tourists from scoring, winning 9-0. The victory won Runcorn wide spread acclaim and reports suggested that local player Johnny Moran outpaced the legendary Dally Messenger on his way to the try line. Runcorn half back and captain Jim Jolly also played against the New Zealanders in all three test matches for Great Britain kicking a goal in the first test and scoring a try in the third. The following season the Australian touring team visited Canal Street and won a close game 9-7 watched by 3,000 spectators. Runcorn prop forward Bob Padbury also faced the Australians in the third test match.

The Australians returned to Runcorn in January 1912 as part of their 1911-12 tour of Great Britain, winning 23-7 in front of a crowd of 2,000. The two sides had already met on Christmas Day 1911 in an exhibition game played in Southport, which is not recorded on the official tour programme. The Kangaroos completed a double over Runcorn winning 54-6 in the seaside town.

Such was the club's reputation in the early days of the Northern Union it was said that any player from Runcorn was gladly given a trial by the big clubs as it was taken for granted that a Runcornian knew a good deal more than the rudiments of the game. Players such as Jack Faulkner, described as the most subtle half back of his generation, and Sam Houghton were, along with Jolly and Padbury, among the stars of the Runcorn team, but the town's most famous rugby player never played for his home town club.

Born in Runcorn in 1880, Jackie Fish was one of the game's first superstars. Starting his career with Lostock Gralam, he joined Warrington in 1898. A flying winger with fantastic acceleration and a tricky swerve, he could also stop dead in his tracks whilst running at full speed leaving many would be tacklers flying into touch. An inaugural member of the Warrington Hall Of Fame, Fish played 321 games for Warrington scoring 215 tries (bettered only by Brian Bevan) and kicking 262 goals before retiring in 1910.

Runcorn reached the semi-final of the Lancashire Cup in 1908 losing to Oldham, but they tried to claim a replay as they said a spectator interfered with a Runcorn player attempting to prevent a try being scored by Oldham. Their appeal was rejected as although it was accepted that a spectator did interfere it was after the try had been scored.

However, the golden era of rugby league in Runcorn was coming to an end as the club started to struggle usually occupying a position in the bottom half of the table, as clubs with more money were able to attract better players.

The Canal Street ground at the time was not equipped with changing rooms, players and officials changing in the Wilson's Hotel in Bridge Street and walking to and from the ground. In November 1902 the ground was suspended by the Northern Union and Runcorn were ordered to play three home games at Birkenhead. This followed an assault on the referee after Halifax had ended the Linnets unbeaten home record. After a similar demonstration against a match official in January 1911 the club were ordered to build dressing rooms on the ground. That same season Runcorn paid a deposit of £200 against a purchase price of £1,600 for the ground.

For many years a superb oil painting hung on the wall of the Royal Hotel in Runcorn depicting a Northern Union game at the turn of the century, when the sloping pitch ran east to west.

Towards the end of the 1912-13 season Runcorn beat Broughton Rangers at Canal Street, but the Manchester club lodged a complaint to the Northern Union claiming the pitch was too short. Runcorn admitted the pitch was indeed short but could do nothing about it until the end of the season. The game was ordered to be replayed on the same short pitch and Broughton agreed not to protest again.

During the summer of 1913 a major reconstruction and improvement programme was undertaken at Canal Street, intended to increase ground capacity and improve facilities. From the mid 1880s the pitch remained virtually undisturbed, running parallel to the old Brick Works boundary fence. There was very little in the way of terracing or cover for the spectators, and visiting teams were often heard to comment on the slope and narrowness of the pitch. The major alteration to the ground was the turning around of the playing area from its original east west axis so the pitch ran from north to south, but still with a pronounced slope.

New ground

The first game at the newly laid out ground was the opening game of the 1913-14 season against St Helens on 6 September, when Runcorn intended to display the results of their summer labours to a hoped for record crowd. The gates were opened at 2.15pm with the local territorial band entertaining the arriving spectators before the intended kick off time of 3.30pm. But while the townsfolk were streaming in eager to inspect the new facilities, the visiting St Helens team were enacting a drama of their own. Although there were special football trains running direct from St Helens to Runcorn, the Saints players and officials chose to travel to Widnes and across to Runcorn via the Transporter Bridge. Unfortunately, as the carrying platform was crossing the gantry wall it stopped and all efforts by the bridge engineers to get it restarted were to no avail. Time was passing and the 3.30pm kick off time loomed ever closer.

The problem was solved by a resourceful St Helens official hailing a near by tugboat. After some manoeuvring the players descended a ladder on to the tug and were put ashore on the Runcorn side of the canal in time to start the game at 4.05pm. The events surrounding the game were to provide a better storyline than the game itself. In the press box the auspicious occasion had drawn many of the best-known northern sportswriters of the day, but the Transporter mishap had already provided them with memorable cover for the day. The Runcorn team caused something of a surprise themselves, turning out for the first and last time in a royal blue kit. St Helens won 10-5, but the Runcorn officials had the consolation of a crowd of over 8,000, the highest to watch the Linnets for over 14 years.

Season 1914-15, the last before fixtures were suspended for the duration of World War One, saw Runcorn finish bottom of the pile picking up just one point from their 27 league games. This proved to be the club's last season, as they did not return after the war ended. During 1918 the Canal Street ground was sold to the owner of the Highfield and Camden Tannery, a soccer enthusiast who stipulated in the lease that in the future the ground would only stage association football.

The disbandment notice published in the *Widnes Weekly News* paper on 9 August 1918 reported: "The Runcorn Football Club has succumbed to the strain of wartime. An organisation that won, and for a long period held, fame in the world of sport is no more. The news will be received with great regret by lovers of football in all parts of the country, for the Runcorn club's gallant fight against the odds of "complete" professionalism has been watched with sympathetic interest by many who recall another day."

The disbanding of a football club may seem a matter of small moment in these times. But the Runcorn club was unique. It rose from a humble beginning to be one of the most famous congregations of rugby players in the country. It proved to be one of the greatest nurseries for players in the Kingdom, and its character for the discovery and development is excelled by no single town of any size in the country. The early successes of the team turned the minds of the town to the game, and for an amazingly long period of years the material was forthcoming for the maintenance of a side that could hold its own with the best of Yorkshire, Lancashire, Cumberland, Wales or the Midlands."

The news of the end of the venerable club – there are few, if any, that date back so long – is more regrettable than surprising. Since the advent of "complete" professionalism, financial difficulties have cropped up. In football, as in most things, a long purse has grown to be a matter of vital importance. Runcorn, with its local players, found in the town and trained in the town, had to meet in competition clubs with much greater wealth, organisations which could boast of receiving sometimes in a single Saturday as much gate money as the whole season would produce at Irwell Lane. Promising players found monetary inducements to go elsewhere. Those who were loyal found themselves pitted against players transported from all parts of the country and even men from the Antipodes, men playing the game for high wages.

For a decade the end has been in sight, but a gallant struggle was made to avert it."

Over the years several amateur clubs tried to keep rugby league alive in Runcorn, but none survived for long. The earliest of these was Runcorn Recs who played at Heath Road for a number of years around the same time as the Linnets and in 1899 played against the senior side in the Challenge Cup, with the professionals running out winners 70-4. Six years later a team called Runcorn Highfield were one of 40 amateur clubs who entered the 1907 Challenge Cup competition.

In the 1930s Ship Canal carried the flag for the town, but despite boasting Widnes legend Tommy McCue in their ranks for a time they did not last long. Neither did Runcorn White Star who played in the 1940s, based at the White Star pub they played near Picow Farm Road.

A more recent side were Runcorn Amateurs who played at Haddocks Wood in the 1980s and 1990s. Based near Canal Street they provided their professional neighbours Runcorn Highfield with several players, but folded soon after Highfield left Runcorn.

Professional rugby league had returned to Runcorn in 1984, when after an application to the Rugby Football League for a new club to play at Canal Street was withdrawn,

Runcorn Highfield versus Widnes 19 August 1984 (Photo: Mike Haddon)

Huyton decided to take up residency at Canal Street. The club which started life in 1922 as Wigan Highfield had left their Alt Park ground after giving up the constant battle against vandalism, renamed themselves Runcorn Highfield and hoped the club had found its final home after more than 60 years of wandering.

The first game of rugby league played at Canal Street in 70 years was a pre-season friendly on 19 August 1984 when, as in 1895, Widnes crossed the Mersey. The move to Canal Street revitalised the club as their fortunes took an upward turn after many years of struggling to survive they finished their first season a respectable 14th out of 20 clubs in the Second Division and reached the second round of the Challenge Cup for the first time in over a decade. Two seasons later they managed to reach 11th place, but struggled to attract the crowds in a town whose sporting scene was dominated at the time by one of the country's most successful non-league football clubs.

However, their improved fortunes were not to last much longer. As most struggling clubs do, Highfield suffered from having a constant turnover of players, fielding many trialists, sometimes from rugby union, but more often than not from amateur sides from surrounding areas, these players usually being listed as the world famous AN Other on the team sheet.

Of all the players who turned out for the club during their time in Runcorn the most unusual was Australian stand-off Kerry Gibson, who was quite a talented player despite the notable handicap of having only one arm. Gibson had been born with a left arm that ended before his elbow, but could still pass the ball with power and accuracy. He was persuaded to join Highfield by one of the club's greatest players, John Cogger. Gibson was named as a substitute for a league game at Springfield Borough on Good Friday 1988. An Australian film crew showed up at Springfield Park to report the story of the one armed rugby league player. Unfortunately for them, they did not know which player was Gibson. The team had been tipped off about the filming and as the players got off the coach each player had tucked his left arm into his jumper. Each one smiled at the camera and nipped into the changing room. Needless to say, the film crew were baffled.

During the 1988-89 season Runcorn Highfield were drawn at home to Wigan in the John Player Trophy. This game was seen as an ideal opportunity to promote the game in the town and persuade the people of Runcorn to give rugby league a try. However, the club's directors switched the game to Central Park, in exchange for a fee from Wigan, claiming the Canal Street ground did not have the capacity to stage the game. The players, seeing the club would receive more money from a game at Central Park, asked for a greater share. The directors' refusal led to a players strike, leading to head coach Bill Ashurst having to field a scratch team of local amateurs to fulfil the fixture. The first team players attended the game, along with supporters who had boycotted the club's official transport, voicing their disapproval at the stand-in players and change of venue.

The game started badly for Runcorn. Ashurst, who came out of retirement to add experience to the team, was sent off after just 11 minutes for violent conduct, head butting Andy Goodway. He was later banned for four games and fined £100 for bringing the game into disrepute. Highfield lost 92-2.

The club had introduced an 'A' team at the start of the season playing at Haddocks Wood in Norton Village, but due to lack of players failed to fulfil its fixtures.

The club never recovered from the defeat at Wigan going on to lose every game the following season, finishing eight points adrift at the bottom of the table. When in 1990 the football club increased the rent, the nomadic club once again hit the road after six seasons in Runcorn, moving to the Hoghton Road ground of St Helens Town FC, and then to Hope Street in Prescot before folding in 1996.

A year after Highfield left, Runcorn Schools under-11s were selected as the Development Area team to play in the curtain raiser at the 1991 Challenge Cup Final. Through the work of the area's development officer, along with a hard working band of teachers helped by several Widnes players, rugby league was on the timetable at most junior schools in the area. Twenty out of 29 schools were playing a modified game in a Participation League, which allowed children to play at equal ability levels. The team, which performed on the big day before the St Helens versus Wigan match was drawn from 11 schools, but were unable to match their opponents from Halifax who won 22-0.

Rugby league was briefly played at Canal Street in season 1994-95 when Widnes played four games there while Naughton Park was being redeveloped. However, the Canal Street ground, which had been one of the sites under consideration for a new stadium to house the proposed Cheshire Super League Club (Super League's original plans called for Warrington and Widnes to merge) closed its doors in May 2001. Severe financial constraints, brought on by the cost of maintaining a ground, which had been badly damaged by storms and a fire, forced Runcorn FC to sell it and share the Halton Stadium with Widnes Vikings. The site is now part of a housing estate called Linnet Park.

Rugby league lay dormant in Runcorn until 2005 when the Runcorn Vikings were formed as part of the successful 'Vikings in the Community' programme. Widnes Vikings had been re-introducing the game into schools in the Runcorn area. However, after leaving school these new players were being lost to the game. The idea was that these players could join Runcorn Vikings. The club was set up by Widnes Vikings in the Community staff who helped establish a committee to run it. Former Widnes legend Ray Dutton, having played for a previous Runcorn amateur side, became club president.

Based at the Gentlemen of Moore Rugby Union Club on the outskirts of Runcorn, the new club entered the Rugby League Conference and being on the fringes of the games heartlands were placed in arguably the strongest RLC regional divisions. Rather than provide players from established BARLA clubs with games during their off season, they recruited a small nucleus of Widnes based rugby league players, the majority of the squad being local rugby union players, youngsters from Runcorn schools and players with no previous rugby experience. In their division were teams from Rochdale, Warrington, Widnes and Wigan, while even teams from development areas such as

Crewe, Liverpool, North Wales and Ormskirk all had a core of experienced rugby league players to call upon. Because of the more experienced side in their division Runcorn struggled to make an impression. However the team, which at the start of the season consisted of total strangers, improved each week becoming more competitive, even in defeat, and ended the season with two wins.

The improvement continued in the following season, when after two early season home wins against stronger and more experienced opponents they found themselves facing former professionals, BARLA internationals and National League Three players as opponents boosted their ranks when playing Runcorn. Two more victories later in the season saw Runcorn challenging for a place in the Divisional play-offs. The talent in the Vikings' ranks was recognised when three of their players were selected for the Conference's North West Representative side that beat their South East counterparts.

The establishment of the Runcorn Vikings first team was just the first step in setting up a thriving amateur club with sides at all levels. 2006 saw teams made up of local school children representing the club at under-16 and under-18 levels, while the club also fielded under-12 and under-13 girls teams in local rugby league festivals.

Prior to the start of the 2007 season a new chapter in the long and varied history of rugby league in Runcorn was opened when the club declared independence, breaking away from the Widnes Vikings, aiming to establish themselves as a rugby league force in Halton in their own right. Dropping the Vikings tag, they changed their name to Runcorn Rugby League Club, adopted the town's coat of arms as their crest instead of the Viking's head logo and reintroduced the traditional green and yellow colours.

Throughout 2007, as the club, now run by an independent committee, developed off the field, the team continued to improve on it. Recording several good wins over strong opposition during the regular season, for the first time Runcorn qualified for the RLC Cheshire Division play-offs. Reaching the final they lost 42-16 in a hard fought game at league leaders Macclesfield Titans. Another significant event during the 2007 season was on Saturday 14 July when the club staged a game in the town of Runcorn for the first time, when they hosted North Wales Coasters at The Heath Specialist Technology College, which is now their permanent home. They decided the best way to continue their development was to change their home ground and be based in the heart of their home town. This change was just one of several exciting initiatives announced by the club prior to the 2008 season. The link between Runcorn RLC and the school has seen The Heath become an accredited RFL centre for coaching and match officials.

Development and expansion of the game in the borough is important to the club and a lot of emphasis has been placed on bringing on some of the talent in Runcorn, which will involve working with the Widnes Vikings community team. Widnes have for several years been running coaching sessions in the town, and now there are more young people playing rugby league in Runcorn than ever before.

The club hope to start an under-12 team, and over the next few years progress to under-14 and under-16 levels. It is expected that The Heath College will provide most of the players as they run teams at all age groups. To develop these teams, there is the O2 Cup for secondary schools in Runcorn, in which The Heath will be challenged by St Chad's, The Grange and Hatton High. These four schools will generate a Runcorn Town team which will compete in the North West Counties League, eventually as Runcorn RLC.

Over the years many have tried, and failed, to restore the game to the town where it was so successful in the early days of the Northern Union but now the future of rugby league looks very bright in Runcorn thanks to one of the game's newest clubs.

Early tours, cricket and rugby

Sean Fagan of RL1908.com looks at the influence of cricket in establishing rugby league in Australia, while **Ian Jackson** looks at the famous 1888 tour.

Cricket's ashes gave rise to rugby league down under

In the early years of the 1900s Australian cricket was in the midst of a battle - not with England, but with itself. The fight between the fledgling Australian Board of Control, and the country's top cricketers, produced an unexpected off-spring - Australian rugby league. Cricket's first Ashes contests were driven by money, as promoters, prominent cricketers and English clubs organised the tours and shared in the gate money among themselves. Barely a decade after the first test between Australia and England, at the MCG in 1877, thoughts turned to the possibility of organising similar contests between football players.

An ambitious plan to take an Australian 'football' team to England - combining rugby union players from Sydney and Australian rules footballers from Melbourne - came tantalisingly close to fruition in the early 1880s.

The first international rugby tour came about in 1888, when a British rugby union team journeyed to Australia and New Zealand. The tour was organised by English cricket professionals Arthur Shrewsbury and Alfred Shaw, who were looking to recover financial losses from their 1887-88 Ashes cricket tour down under.

The two men recognised though that bringing out a rugby union team to play solely in Sydney and Brisbane would not be profitable. They were well aware of the large crowds attracted to Australian football's club matches in Melbourne, and decided that their team would play both codes.

Given the team was set to play Australian football as well as rugby union, and was clearly a money-making exercise for the players and promoters, the English RFU were particularly reluctant to endorse the tour. The mainly upper-class RFU officials were especially fearful of the tour's effects upon the growing trend towards professionalism in their sport - something they were hell-bent on keeping out of rugby union after having witnessed association football overrun by working class men once they allowed payments to players.

The RFU's concerns were well founded. The majority of the team were from the mills and mines of Yorkshire and Lancashire in Northern England - the region that gave birth to professional rugby league barely seven years later. Many of the men played for clubs that became some of rugby league most famous entities.

It was not until 1899 that the next British rugby union team came to Australia - this time there would be no matches against VFL clubs in Melbourne, and the team was comprised entirely of amateurs.

After the first test match against Australia, the rugby communities of Australia pondered, as had happened in cricket, the possibility of sending a team to England. Unlike in cricket, where professionals and amateurs played alongside each other, the RFU forbade any form of payment to players - the birth of English rugby league in 1895 had made them even more determined to follow the path toward pure amateurism.

As Australia's best rugby players were working men, it was obvious that no representative team of substance could be banded together – to take part in such a tour a man would have to absent himself from work for nine months. Of more pressing concern for those that were married, was who would look after their family financially while they were away playing football?

Sydney's major sports newspaper, *The Referee,* astutely offered, "This makes a problem to be tackled by football legislators of the future, so let it pass on to them." However, even *The Referee* did not foresee how soon that 'problem' would come to erupt.

Through the 1890s Sydney rugby union had been dominated by a handful of socially-based clubs. Long before salary caps and player drafts, the strongest of these clubs touted for the best footballers on offer - not only the city's finest rugby players, but also from New Zealand, Queensland and country teams in New South Wales. The top footballers gained lucrative benefits, while the rank-and-file got nothing.

In an era where labour issues and a fair-go for all prevailed among the working class in Australia, a call began to grow to follow the lead of cricket, which had been 'democratised' in 1894 via the introduction of residentially-based district clubs to Sydney cricket.

Aware of the increasing signs of discontent, in 1900 the NSWRU followed suit, disbanding the old clubs, and giving birth to districts with names and colours now synonymous with rugby league: South Sydney, Balmain, North Sydney, Western Suburbs, Newtown and Eastern Suburbs.

By 1905 'district football', which engendered local rivalry and tribalism, had revolutionised Sydney rugby union. The code began to enjoy greater popularity with the city's sports fans - a timely happening for supporters of the English game, as Sydney was then on the cusp of falling to Australian rules football.

Cricket had indirectly provided the template to reinvigorate Sydney rugby union, and was cited as a game where men of all classes were treated fairly. However, the summer sport would soon have a more direct impact on rugby union across Australia.

The NSWRU continually suffered criticism for raking in large profits (gate-receipts) from the unpaid labour of their footballers. In comparison, Australian cricket teams and their tours to England were organised by the players themselves and their financial backers - they alone shared the often spectacular profits. Cricketers such as Victor Trumper, who toured with Australian teams to England in 1899, 1902 and 1905, did particularly well financially.

A former rugby union player himself, Trumper played full-back in a representative match at the SCG in 1898 alongside Dinny Lutge (who later captained rugby league's first Kangaroos) and 'Jersey' Flegg (ruler of the NSWRL for its first 50 seasons). Trumper was also a friend of Dally Messenger. It was not lost on Sydney's best footballers how unequal the financial rewards and opportunities to tour England were between the sports.

Trumper though, and Australia's other prominent cricketers, were facing a battle to hold onto their control of Ashes tours. Ironically, it was this cricket dispute that gave rugby league the financial backing it needed to get up and running.

In 1906 the NSW and Victorian cricket associations began moves to wrest control of Ashes tours from the players and their promoters. The newly formed Australian Board of Control (ABC) issued an invitation to London's Marylebone Cricket Club (MCC) to send an England team to Australia for the 1906-07 summer. On the advice of prominent

Australian cricketers, and the Melbourne Cricket Club, the MCC chose to ignore the ABC, instead opening their own negotiations for the tour.

The Melbourne club and its contacts in Sydney secretly signed the best cricketers, including Trumper and M.A. 'Monty' Noble, to form an Australian team to play England. Trumper and other senior cricketers were not keen to simply let the ABC put an end to player-controlled tours.

Aided by Sydney entrepreneur James J. Giltinan, and the Melbourne Cricket Club, *The Bulletin* claimed the cricketers were making a determined effort to, not only secure the 1906-07 Ashes series, but to permanently grab control of the summer game and run it as a professional sport.

The Melbourne Cricket Club denied that the latter two objectives were part of their plans, however, ultimately it didn't matter as the challenge against the ABC failed, and the players lost control of international tours.

Australia's top cricketers were reduced to receiving allowances in the same manner as their rugby union counterparts, while the ABC began to build up financial reserves from test match income.

To be fair, the plight of the cricketers was not as poor as that of the rugby union players - the 3s (15p)-a-day doled-out by the NSWRU to Waratahs players on NSW's tours to Queensland wasn't enough to get them through one round of beers if they were called on to 'shout' in a Brisbane pub.

Unlike in cricket though, two organisations controlled rugby in England, giving the Sydney footballers a choice - the amateur RFU, and the professional Northern Union (rugby league). Giltinan and Trumper, inspired by the financial success of the 1905 All Blacks tour of Britain, which made a profit of more than £10,000 for the NZRU, turned their attention to rugby. Through Trumper's rugby connections they were aware of the considerable dissatisfaction amongst Sydney footballers over their tour allowances, and poor compensation for injuries and time off work.

While it is clear Giltinan and Trumper were on the look-out for financial opportunities, they also had a desire to aid the working-class footballers in their fight for a fair share of the income from the gate-takings at their matches (a NSW game in 1907 attracted over 52,000 to the SCG - a century later, that figure is still yet to be repeated by the Waratahs).

Both men genuinely believed in the principles that they were fighting for - that the preference of the NSWRU to stay bound to the English RFU, and its strict abhorrence to paying footballers for time away from work for tours and injury, was totally unrealistic in working-class Australia.

Giltinan and Trumper had the foresight to see that the sympathy of largely working-class Sydney would side with the footballers, and the uprising had every chance of succeeding. Secret meetings were held with leading footballers, and their political and financial supporters, at Trumper's Sydney sports store - a business he operated in partnership will Halifax-born (Yorkshire) test cricketer Hanson Carter, and then later with Giltinan.

In mid-1907 the rebel group made contact with similar-minded counterparts in New Zealand, and aided them in the preparation of the 'All Golds' rugby league team, readying itself for the first professional football tour of Britain. They sent to the Kiwis a contract from one of Trumper's English cricket tours, which they adopted as a template for their tour agreement. Trumper and Giltinan also convinced the New Zealanders to include rugby union's star player, Dally Messenger, as a member of the team.

When the 'All Golds' arrived in Sydney, their leader Albert Baskerville was at great pains to point out that his touring party was going to England under the same 'share-and-share-alike' terms of Australian cricket sides, and that the footballers were no more professionals than the nation's cricketers had been.

Giltinan (secretary) and Trumper (treasurer) became the founding fathers of rugby league, the first professional football code in Australia, and oversaw the NSWRL's inaugural season in 1908. Without their involvement and organisation, rugby league arguably would not have been formed so soon. Indeed, rugby league may never have established itself at all, as links could just have been made with association football in England or Australian rules in Melbourne, which adopted professionalism in 1911.

As it was, rugby league quickly took hold of Sydney, and Messenger became the star attraction of the sport. By the end of the winter of 1910, after the visit of the first British rugby league tourists, rugby league had usurped rugby union and Australian rules from controlling NSW and Queensland.

Many of cricket's traditions were quickly taken up by rugby league, the most notable being the establishment of a regular exchange of Ashes tours between Australia's Kangaroos and Great Britain's Lions - though, with cricket in mind, the Australians couldn't help but always call them England!

© **Copyright 2007 – Sean Fagan / RL1908.com**

Photo: Dally Messenger wearing the New Zealand kit from the 1907-08 tour.
(Photo: courtesy Sean Fagan)

Pocket-money Professionals

Ian Jackson recalls the extraordinary British rugby union tour to Australia and New Zealand of 1888.

The 1888 rugby union tour by a British team to Australia and New Zealand is one of the most extraordinary episodes in the entire history of sport. There is an array of strange adventures, bizarre events as well as no shortage of mystery and tragedy. At the centre of the story is a group of mainly working class footballers who embarked on the first overseas rugby tour from Britain but without the consent of the governing body. The tour was organised by two professional cricketers who used their connections and influence to arrange the tour in the first place and then subsequently avoid any repercussions after the return home. In the process of becoming pathfinders, the tourists played two codes of football and defied the odds by almost certainly being paid as professional footballers in an era of strict amateurism in rugby.

    The origin of all rugby expeditions can be found in cricket tours dating back to the 1860s. In many ways cricket is a natural game to be played periodically on overseas tours since it tends to be more leisurely than any code of football. Nevertheless, the 1887-88 cricket tour by England to the Southern Colonies, as Australasia was then known, convinced two prominent cricketers that a rugby tour would be a good idea, too. The men in question were two Nottinghamshire cricket professionals, namely Arthur Shrewsbury and Alfred Shaw (in addition another England cricketer, James Lillywhite was involved from time to time with the tour). From the beginning, the aim was to model the tour on the cricket trips down under and in the process make money principally for the organisers who were already successful businessmen in their own right and well versed in the profit motive. This approach was destined to involve paying some of the players on tour which was contrary to the stringent rules of rugby which forbid acts of professionalism in the late Victorian era. Regardless, Shrewsbury and Shaw organised the tour along the lines of cricket which in broad terms involved players (professionals) and gentleman (amateurs).

Professionalism and the tour

As far as the governing body, the Rugby Football Union (RFU) was concerned there were two main problems with the proposed tour. Firstly, the nature of the trip would result undoubtedly in members of the tour being paid for playing rugby even as compensation for loss of wages. Secondly, the itinerary of the trip included games of football under Australian rules. So, a full seven years before the formation of the Northern Union in 1895, the RFU was taking a hard-line stance against both alleged professionalism and games of football not under the auspices of the rugby union code. However, writing in 1892, the Reverend Frank Marshall who was a leading referee and chief advocate against professionalism wrote: "The only objectionable feature of the tour was the arrangement of matches under Australian rules." And yet, just prior to tour, it was the threat of professionalism that reportedly vexed Roland Hill, the Secretary of the RFU. He alleged that: "Some of the men, who are going for expenses and a cheque for pocket-money, are professionals." Therefore, at worst the RFU was actually ignoring their own evidence concerning professionalism on the tour; and at best, the authorities subsequently had a convenient change of policy regarding the payment of the tourists, even for money to cover loss of income.

Whatever the reasons for the RFU ignoring this evidence, the members of the tour were never deemed professionals before, during or after the tour, except one. Jack Clowes, a Halifax and Yorkshire forward was found guilty of being a professional by the RFU before the tour had set sail for accepting a £15 clothing allowance indirectly from Shrewsbury (and even this decision appeared to be part of a long-standing feud between Halifax and Dewsbury). Of course, there are numerous possible reasons why the other tourists were not expelled from the game for professionalism. First, the RFU accepted apparently the word of the men who signed sworn affidavits on their return claiming no existing RFU rules regarding professionalism had been contravened on tour. Secondly, the tour party was so far away and absent for so long that is could hide all the true facts which confirmed subsequently forms of professionalism under the RFU laws of the day. Thirdly, the RFU were dealing in part with certain people of their own social standing, namely university-educated members of the middle-classes from the south of England, such as cricket and rugby international Andrew Stoddart (who joined the tour in Australia) and not wayward Northern folk from the working classes. Finally, the sporting success of the tour (and lack of financial success) could have won the rugby authorities over. In other words, the very idea of a tour was appealing, professionalised or not. In fact, later the same year in 1888, Joe Warbrick from Auckland brought a team of New Zealand Maoris to Great Britain and played many of the leading Rugby Union teams. This particular tour including a match against England at Blackheath on 16 February 1889, which in an ironic twist was refereed by Roland Hill. Nevertheless, whatever the future held, the RFU refused consistently to officially sanction the 1888 tour to Australasia before and during the trip.

Shrewsbury and Shaw may have been smart businessman with an eye for an opportunity but their sport was cricket and not rugby. As a result, the tour party was quite difficult to assemble not least without the patronage of the RFU. Indeed, the actual organization of the tour was not without sizable problems either. Specifically, the third partner at various stages, James Lillywhite who was a Sussex and England amateur cricketer, failed to contribute his share of the financial burden. Also, many leading players who were invited did not agree to tour for whatever reason. Notwithstanding, the tour party itself featured representatives from across the British Isles including players from England, Scotland and Wales, plus one from the Isle of Man and another who was born in Ireland. Even so, most of the players were from the North of England and a majority came from future Northern Union clubs. The *Manchester Times* noted in March 1888 that "Though by no means representative, the team is very powerful, especially forward."

Unsurprisingly, Shrewsbury and Shaw looked to the North and Lancashire in particular to form the backbone of the party. Rugby in the Manchester area for instance was very strong in the late 1880s. There was a relatively large number of successful clubs such as Swinton, Salford, Broughton Rangers and Manchester who were based then at Whalley Range. On the tour from Swinton was full-back Arthur Paul, half-back Walter Bumby and forwards Tom Banks and tour captain Robert Seddon who had recently transferred from Broughton Rangers. From Salford there was Jack Anderton in the three-quarters and forwards Harry Eagles, Tom Kent and Sam Williams. All these eight players had Lancashire county caps with Seddon having represented England three

The touring party (Courtesy Ian Jackson)

times in 1887. Tom Kent was destined to be a future England player from 1891 to 1892; and Harry Eagles had also been selected to play for England earlier in 1888; however, the game never took place due a dispute with the other home nations although Eagles did receive an England cap and jersey.

Of course, Yorkshire was the other great powerhouse of English rugby at the time. Although there were players on the tour from Batley, Bramley, Dewsbury and Halifax the suspicion of professional loomed large over the White Rose County and many leading players from the area decided not to take part in the tour including Bradford's Fred Bonsor and Dewsbury's Dickie Lockwood. The suspicion was apparently well-founded as Jack Clowes had been declared a professional prior to departure and although he travelled on tour he never played a game (much to the chagrin of Shrewsbury and Shaw who in effect paid for the return passage of a non-playing spectator). It is likely that other players received the £15 clothing allowance that was the downfall of Clowes. The *Leeds Mercury* reported on the 8 March 1888: "The Rugby Football Union decided on the evidence before them that J.P. Clowes is a professional within the meanings of the laws. On the same evidence they have formed a very strong opinion that the others composing the Australian team have also infringed those laws, and they will require from them such explanations as they may think fit on their return to England." Hence, all the available evidence suggests that many of the tourists were 'pocket-money professionals'.

Of the other players on the tour there were the Burnett brothers and Laing all from Hawick in Scotland and William Henry Thomas the only Welshman who had to take leave of his studies at Cambridge University. However, the fact remained that most of the players were from northern gate-taking clubs who presumably could not afford to support themselves and their family for 36 weeks of unpaid absence. Meanwhile, Shrewsbury sent a cheque for £50 to Stoddart as a retainer to secure his services. There is no evidence that Stoddart ever returned this money and it can assumed that he kept it for the purposes it was given, that is an advanced payment for participating in the tour. Incidentally, Stoddart was in Australia already with the England cricket tour of 1887-88 and it was agreed that he would join the rugby tour along with Shrewsbury, Lillywhite and two other cricketers George Brann and C. Aubrey Smith, the latter two being renowned association footballers for Swifts and Corinthians, respectively.

The 1888 tour to Australasia

The players and officials were instructed to assemble in Nottingham. In early March 1888, the eight Lancashire players met at the Central Station in Manchester to take a train to Nottingham where they would meet-up with the tour organisers and the other players. A Manchester newspaper correspondent reported that a huge crowd of several thousand had gathered to witness the departure of the players. The Midland train company provided a special saloon attached on the Nottingham Express for the player's comfort. The scene was chaotic for the players due to the enthusiasm of the crowd. It was reported that: "One of them, Seddon, nearly missed the train; another, Eagles, had to jump into the guards' van." The departure of this train with everyone on-board proved to be fateful for both Seddon and Eagles, since there were contrasting fortunes for these men on the tour. At the same time, the Yorkshire players departed from Leeds to Nottingham and eventually all those selected arrived in time to depart by another train on this occasion bound for the south coast of England and the next stage of the epic journey. The tourists departed aboard the SS Kaikoura bound for New Zealand and immortality as the first British rugby tourist to Australasia. On 23 April 1888, the players arrived at Dunedin with Seddon elected unopposed as captain of the tour.

As for the games on tour, the team first went to New Zealand and then to Australia. In total, 35 games were played under Rugby Football Rules winning 27 and losing only two with six drawn. In a strange twist, as many as 19 games were played in the state of Victoria under Australian Football Rules, but only nine of these games were won. It is recorded that Stoddart in particular excelled at the Australian code of football, perhaps illustrating his genuine all-round sporting prowess. However, according to Shrewsbury in a letter to Shaw, who remained at home throughout the tour, the elder Burnett brother and Laing "don't have the slightest idea how to play" the Australian Rules code.

Part way through the tour, tragedy struck. Bob Seddon, who had helped establish the Broughton Rangers club in 1877, drowned on the Hunter River in Maitland, New South Wales on 4 August when his outrigger capsized. In fact, Seddon was an expert swimmer and a member of the Broughton Amateur Rowing Club, but his feet were strapped to the bottom of the vessel and he could not free himself in time. Seddon left a fiancée and parentless sisters and a younger brother. He was one of only four men on the tour not to take-out an insurance policy against losing his life. He thought taking chances was part of life. In direct contrast, Harry Eagles, who had played originally for the Crescent Football Club which had its base at one time in Peel Park, near Broughton became an ever-present player throughout the entire tour. It is with some irony that away from rugby and back home Eagles was awarded the Salford Hundred Humane Society medal for rescuing four people from drowning.

The influence of cricket was everywhere on the 1888 rugby tour. Arthur Shrewsbury, who John Arlott described as a "legend" and Alfred Shaw were established cricket tourists. In fact, Shrewsbury, who was W.G. Grace's predecessor as England cricket captain relied heavily on Stoddart during the tour, who was subsequently W.G. Grace's successor. According to the plan, the amateur England and Sussex cricketers George Brann and C. Aubrey Smith were to join the tour (the latter becoming a famous Hollywood actor in later years). Even so, Shrewsbury was not impressed by these two fellow cricketers who between them were costing him far too much money and fast becoming a bad influence on the other footballers in terms of expenses. Eventually, Brann and Smith left the tour. Furthermore, one unnamed player was allowed by Lillywhite to become overdrawn by between £60 and £70. The mystery remains but the suspicion falls heavily on Stoddart as the culprit, who as a fellow England cricketer was one of a few on tour that was the social equal of Lillywhite.

The aftermath of the tour

The majority of the tour party returned to Britain by November 1888 and went their separate ways. It was widely reported that three members of the tour remained in Australia to begin a new life. They were the older Burnett bother, Angus Stuart and Harry Speakman from Runcorn who went on to play rugby for his adopted Queensland.

In all, the members of the group were very talented sportsmen and still had bright futures. However, the question remained whether there would be any sanctions upon their return. As it happened, the players did not need to worry, because no formal action was taken against anyone. Overall, there remains a mystery surrounding why the RFU was so eager to whitewash what was in fact a professional tour. Indeed, as early as 22 November 1888 Clowes had been reinstated and able to play again for Halifax. This action by the RFU in effective closed the book on the affair as far as the rugby authorities were concerned.

Back home the players received a heroes welcome. John Nolan, who scored 16 tries on tour, was greeted by a brass band and several thousand people when he arrived back in Rochdale. Swinton organised a banquet at the Bulls Head pub in the town for their returning players Tom Banks and Walter Bumby; whilst Arthur Paul remained in London amid rumours that he was to pursue a cricket career. In fact, he returned to the play for Swinton later in the season, but Tom Banks picked-up a serious shoulder injury on tour and only played once more for the Lancashire club. Walter Bumby remained a stalwart of the Swinton club and after retiring from rugby ran the Bridgewater Arms pub in neighbouring Pendlebury. As for Arthur Paul, he fulfilled his unique sporting career.

Having excelled at rugby football for Swinton and Lancashire, he played county cricket for Lancashire from 1889 to 1900 and then association football for Blackburn Rovers in 1899. He passed away at his Didsbury home in January, 1947.

Eventually though, the unfortunate end that befell Robert Seddon in Australia was not the end of the tragedy for some of the other tourists. Some years later in 1903, Arthur Shrewsbury shot himself when he became convinced that he had an incurable illness and the fact that he knew his outstanding cricketing career as a player was over. Four years later, Shaw passed away, too after a long illness. In the same year, John Nolan was killed in an accident at work after an eventful and turbulent life. In 1915, Stoddart became the second member of the tour to commit suicide when he shot himself after the collapse of the Stock market during the First World War had left him ruined financially. As noted in his obituary in the *Wisden* cricket almanack: "A brilliant career thus came to the saddest of ends."

Conclusions

There are some events in the history of sport that are genuinely extraordinary. The 1888 rugby tour is one such episode and all of this occurred against a background of a pioneering spirit and a true sense of adventure. How two English cricket professionals organised a rugby football tour to Australia and New Zealand and ended up playing Australian Rules football is bizarre. How the Rugby Football Union subsequently waived claims of professionalism given there was strong evidence to support the accusations that some of the tourists were paid pocket-money and expenses is inexplicable even from this distance in time.

Significantly, the events unfolded when the national sport, namely cricket, was beginning to accept the role and scope for professionals to participate at specific levels of the game. The question is why did rugby football not accept likewise this role for the professional within its ranks? Only a matter of seven years later, the resolve against professionalism by the RFU was so strong again that it forced the Great Split and the formation of what became known as Rugby League. However, perhaps this outcome was as much to do with a power struggle between the clubs in the North and the authorities in the South as it was to do with payment over broken time and professionalism.

Revisiting the events surrounding the 1888 tour provides a glimpse into the sporting issues of the day. As a result of the whitewash after the tourists arrived back home in Britain, it may be that the Rugby Union authorities continued to ban professionalism in spite of the 1888 tour rather than because of it. Whatever the case, players from clubs such as Batley, Halifax, Rochdale Hornets and Swinton have now been accepted retrospectively as a recognised part of the British Lions Rugby Union heritage.

The Tour Managers and Organisers
Alfred Shaw and Arthur Shrewsbury (Nottinghamshire and England Cricketers)
James Lillywhite (Sussex and England Cricketer)

The players

Full-backs
J.T. Haslam	Batley, Yorkshire and North
A. G. Paul	Swinton and Lancashire

Threequarters
J. Anderton	Salford, Lancashire and North
H. Brooks (Dr)	Durham and Edinburgh University
H.C. Speakman	Runcorn and Cheshire

Half-backs
W. Bumby	Swinton and Lancashire
W. Burnett	Hawick and Roxburgh County
J. Nolan	Rochdale Hornets

Forwards
T. Banks	Swinton and Lancashire
P. Burnett	Hawick and Roxburgh County
J. P. Clowes	Halifax and Yorkshire
W.H. Eagles	Salford, Lancashire and England (non-playing cap)

A.J. Laing	Hawick and Roxburgh County
T. Kent	Salford and Lancashire (future England player 1891-92)
C. Mathers	Bramley, Yorkshire and North
A.P. Penketh	Blackheath, Kent Rovers and Douglas, Isle of Man
R.L. Seddon	Swinton, Lancashire and England (Captain until August)
A.E. Stoddart	Blackheath, Harlequins and England (Captain from August)*
A.J. Stuart	Dewsbury and Yorkshire
W.H. Thomas	Cambridge University and Wales
S. Williams	Salford, Lancashire and North

* Joined the team in Australasia after an England cricket tour

Umpire

J Smith (Dr)	Corinthians, Swifts and Edinburgh University

Rugby Union Results

Opponents	Result	F	A
In New Zealand: first leg			
Otago	W	8-3	
Otago	W	4–3	
Canterbury	W	14-6	
Canterbury	W	4–0	
Wellington	D	3-3	
H. Roberts XV	W	4–1	
Taranaki Clubs	L	0-1	
Auckland	W	6-3	
Auckland	L	0-4	
In Australia			
New South Wales	W	18–2	
Bathurst	W	13–6	
New South Wales	W	18–6	
Sydney Juniors	W	11–0	
King's Sydney School	D	10–10	
Sydney Grammar	D	3–3	
Bathurst	W	20–0	
New South Wales	W	16–2	
University of Sydney	W	8–4	
Newcastle	W	15–7	
Queensland	W	13–6	
Queensland Juniors	W	11–3	
Queensland	W	7–0	
Ipswich	W	12-1	
Melbourne	W	15–5	
Adelaide XV	W	28–3	
In New Zealand: second leg			
Auckland	W	3–0	
Auckland	D	1–1	
Hawke's bay	W	3–2	
Wairarrapa	W	5–1	
Canterbury	W	8–0	
Otago	D	0-0	
South Island	W	5–3	
South Island	W	6–0	
Taranaki Clubs	W	7–1	
Wanganui	D	1–1	

Source: Thomas (2005: 18-19).

A contemporary account of the death of Robert Seddon as reported in the *Western Mail*, Cardiff 18 August 1888.

Fatality to an English Footballer: RL Seddon drowned

According to a *Sporting Life* telegram from Newcastle, New South Wales, RL Seddon, the well-known member of the Swinton Football team and now touring with the English team in Australia, was drowned on Wednesday in the River Hunter near Maitland, New South Wales, by the capsizing of an outrigger in which he was sculling.

Seddon, first distinguished himself in England in the ranks of the Swinton club, and also rendered yeoman service for Lancashire. The last match of importance he played in England was North v. South at Blackheath on February 4 of this year. He was 26 years of age, 5ft. 11in. high and weighed 12 stone. His untimely end will be greatly deplored by all Rugby Football players with whom he was exceedingly popular.

Author's note: Robert Seddon was actually 27 years of age and he first distinguished himself at Broughton Rangers, a club he helped to form in 1877. Seddon was known locally as the

"Broughton Steam Engine" such was his reputation as a strong forward. He joined Swinton in October 1887 and was almost washed overboard on the outbound journey of the tour. In a letter home, he wrote: "I don't think I was born to be drowned."

Bibliography
Arlott, John (1897) *Arlott on Cricket*.
Collins, Tony (1998) *Rugby's Great Split*.
Delaney, Trevor (1984) *The Roots of Rugby League*.
Delaney, Trevor (1993) *Rugby Disunion Volume One: Broken Time*.
Dunning, Eric and Sheard, Kenneth (1979) *Barbarians, Gentlemen and Players*.
Green, Benny (1986) *The Wisden Book of Cricketers Lives*.
Griffiths, John (1982) *The Book of English International Rugby, 1871-1982*
Marshall, Frank, (1892) *Football: The Rugby Union Game*.
Thomas, Clem (2005) *The History of the British and Irish Lions*.
Wild, Stephen (1999) *The Lions of Swinton*.

Newspaper Sources
Leeds Mercury: 8 March 1888
Leeds Mercury: 26 September 1888
Manchester Times: 3 March 1888
Manchester Times: 17 November 1888
Reynold's Newspaper, London: 19 August 1888
Western Mail, Cardiff: 18 August 1888

Warrington – between the wars and the Hall of Fame

Neil Dowson reviews a new book on Warrington, and reports on three additions to the club's hall of fame.

So Close to Glory
Warrington Rugby League Football Club 1919 to 1939
By Eddie Fuller and Gary Slater

So Close to Glory is the third collaboration by Gary Slater and Eddie Fuller. The book follows on from their successful *Warrington Rugby League Club 1970–2000* and *100 Warrington Greats* and adds to the growing library of Warrington history books.

Daily Telegraph sportswriter Gary Slater and award winning photographer Eddie Fuller, who have both followed the fortunes of Warrington RLFC for 40 years, have written a book that demonstrates their support and passion for a club that is close to their hearts. *So Close to Glory* has been published by those prolific rugby league book publishers London League Publications.

So Close to Glory tells the story of Warrington RLFC between the two World Wars. In this period the club reached three Challenge Cup Finals, including two at Wembley and three Championship Finals and lost them all. Prior to the First World War Warrington had appeared in five Challenge Cup Finals and won the trophy twice.

The book forward is by Fred Higginbottom, the only surviving Warrington player from before the Second World War. Fred a centre threequarter was signed from local amateur side Rylands in 1937 for a sign on fee of £75. Fred remembers many of the Warrington heroes from the 1930s including Jack "Cod" Miller, Billy Dingsdale, Dave Cotton and Jack Arkwright. He even recalls the Germans bombing Thames Board whilst relaxing in the Wilderspool bath following a war-time match.

Each of the 20 seasons between the wars has its story retold taking the reader back into that period of hard times, but ones in which Warrington RLFC prospered. There are also chapters on the club, its fortunes and those of some of its players during both World Wars.

Those heroes who gave the ultimate sacrifice for their country in the "the war to end all wars" are remembered. The story of Welsh forward George Thomas is told along with that of his nine playing colleagues who also died in the First World War.

One person whose own career, all be it a non-playing one, runs throughout the book. Bob Anderton became secretary after the war and for 50 years he became the greatest and most energetic administrator in the club's history. He was responsible for the revamping of the official programme into an informative production, the extensive development of Wilderspool into a first class stadium and the signing of world class players. He also found time to make two tours of Australia as England manager.

The story of each season is told, together with wonderful pictures of the day, and pieces on Wilderspool heroes and Warrington's heroes. Included in the Wilderspool heroes are Billy Dingsdale, Billy Holding, Dai Davies, Bill Shankland, Jack Miller and Jack Arkwright. Whilst the Warrington local heroes are Olympic athlete Chris Vose, champion jockey Steve Donoghue, England cricketer George Duckworth, Channel swimmer Sunny Lowry, world boxing champion Peter Kane and footballer Fred Worrall.

These tales of the sports personalities of the time help to give the reader a better idea of what it was like for people in this tough era. It was a time of hardship and mass unemployment and sport was the relief from those pressures that people sought, as demonstrated by the vast increase in Wilderspool's gates over the period. Wilderspool acted as the focal point for the local community and the stadium development enabled more people to take advantage of watching Warrington.

The successes of four Lancashire Cup victories and a Lancashire League title are detailed. However these 20 years were a frustrating time, as Warrington lost six major finals. Today's Warrington Wolves supporter will be able to sympathise with those of 80 years ago as in the Super League era the club have failed to reach a major final or consistently make the Play-offs.

Just like any era in any sport there are tales of hard luck and misfortune. Injuries to Billy Kirk in the 1928 Challenge Cup final and then Dave Brown and Billy Holding 1937 Championship finals, did little to improve Warrington's hopes of success. This was all at a time before substitutes and so Warrington had to finish the finals with less than the thirteen players they started with.

There are plenty of wonderful short tales relating to the exploits of the players, such as the player sent off twice in the same match, the captain who talked golf with the king, the four players sent off on Christmas Day, the giant Welshman who wanted to be a boxer and many more.

For those who like their statistics there is a section at the end of the book that details the playing records of all 229 players who played in those 20 seasons, those who gained representative honours and the scoring records of the period.

The book which is available from the Warrington Wolves club shop, Wolfware for £12.95, is a great read not just for Warrington supporters but all those interested in the history and development of rugby league.

So Close to Glory was launched in conjunction with the Warrington Past Players Association in April when they inducted the three latest members to the Warrington Hall of Fame. On the evening Gary Slater and Eddie Fuller gave an enjoyable double act presentation of the inter-war period and finished up with an interview with Fred Higginbottom. Fred still had clear memories of the players and his time at Warrington. He stills speaks to school children as part of the Warrington Wolves Foundation and Heritage Wire2Wolves programmes.

Warrington Hall of Fame

Jim Tranter, Ray Price and Derek Whitehead were the three new inductees to the Warrington Hall of Fame. This brings the total to 28 players elected by their peers to the Hall of Fame. On the evening, a delighted Lance Todd Trophy winner Derek Whitehead told of his time at Wilderspool.

Derek Whitehead played his first game on 4 October 1969 and his last on 13 May 1979, he made 245 appearances plus a further 29 as a substitute, scoring 17 tries, kicking 713 goals and 21 drop goals 6, for a total of 1,516 points.

Derek became only the second Warrington player to win the Lance Todd Trophy as man of the match in the Challenge Cup Final. His seven goals in 1974 helped Warrington to defeat Featherstone Rovers 24-9 to lift the cup.

A man of the match performance by Derek had seen Warrington win the Captain Morgan Trophy, he kicked six goals and a try against Rochdale Hornets in the Players No.6 Trophy success and two more goals in 13-12 victory over St Helens in the Club Championship final. This rounded off a great season for Derek who equalled Harry Bath's club record of 162 goals in a season and finished with four winners medals. He returned to Wembley the following season only to lose to Widnes.

Whitehead joined Warrington in September 1969 from Oldham. He joined the professional ranks at Swinton from Folly Lane, before moving on to Oldham. At full back he stood 5ft 10in and weighed 13st, a butcher by trade, he would "carve up" many a defence with his classic sidestepping attacking runs.

While at Warrington Whitehead played three times for Great Britain, scoring a try and six goals, he also made five appearances for Lancashire, scoring a try and fifteen goals.

In 1979-80, whilst on the coaching staff at Wilderspool, Derek was awarded a well deserved Testimonial.

Jim Tranter played his first game on 16 November 1911 and his last on 26 December 1928, he made 439 appearances scoring 120 tries and 6 drop goals 6, for a total of 372 points.

Tranter who hailed from Longford, signed for Warrington as an eighteen year old in 1911, receiving £5 as did his amateur club Newton. He made his debut in the second row in an 8 all draw at Ebbw Vale. The following season he played centre in the Challenge Cup Final opposite Harold Wagstaffe, in a 9-5 defeat to Huddersfield's "Team of All Talents".

Jim, a big man at 6 feet 1 inch and weighting 14 stone 7 pounds who was a deadly tackler famed for his "Tranters Hook" tackle, which was reserved for opponents who had been dishing it out! In the modern game this would be classed as a high tackle.

Tranter was in Warrington's first Lancashire Cup winning side of 1921, when Oldham were defeated 7-5. He captained the 1926 side that lost in the Championship final to Wigan and received a second Challenge Cup runners-up medal in 1928.

Jim made his 439th and final appearance in a 12-7 victory at Rochdale Hornets on Boxing Day 1928. A strict teetotaller and a model professional he was six times Warrington's leading try scorer. In 1924-25 his loyalty was rewarded with a shared testimonial with Arthur Skelhorn.

Tranter played twice for England and made 8 appearances for Lancashire, scoring three tries. When the club suspended operations during the First World War he guested for Runcorn.

Ray Price played his first game on 29 August 1953 and his last on 27 April 1957, he made 113 appearances scoring 23, for a total of 69 points.

Welshman Ray Price joined Warrington in August 1953 from Belle Vue Rangers in exchange for Jim Featherstone and an undisclosed cash sum. He made is debut in a 16-4 win over Rochdale Hornets. So began, with Gerry Helme the most successful of Warrington half-back partnerships. Price was a rugged, resourceful and ferocious tackler, who was the perfect foil for Helme.

Price and Helme were at the heart of the Warrington Challenge Cup and Championship double winning side of the 1953-54 season. Price was injured and missed the final when Warrington retained the Championship title the following season.

Ray had been captain of Abertillery RUFC before moving north joining Belle Vue Rangers in 1947. While at Wilderspool Price played nine times for Great Britain, twice for Wales and twice for Other Nationalities. He went on the 1954 tour of Australia and

Left: Jim Tranter
Middle: Derek Whitehead
Bottom left: Ray Price
Bottom right: Gary Slater and Eddie Fuller with Fred Higginbottom

(Courtesy Neil Dowson)

New Zealand, with his half-back partner Helme. He was also selected for the 1957 World Cup in Australia, but an injury in a warm-up match kept him from tasking part in the tournament.

He was transferred to St Helens in 1957 for £ 1,500. Ray put Tom Van Vollenhoven over for a try on his rugby league debut. On retiring from rugby league he returned home to Blaina and died aged 64 in 1988 after suffering a brain haemorrhage.

The Warrington Hall of Fame was instigated by the former Past Players chairman the late Derek 'Nobby' Clarke. The 28 members are Jack Arkwright, Willie Aspinall, Harry Bath, Brian Bevan, Ernie Brookes, Jim Challinor, Billy Cunliffe, Billy Dingsdale, Jim Featherstone, Eric Fraser, Jack Fish, Laurie Gilfedder, Parry Gordon, Mike Gregory, Gerry Helme, Albert Johnson, Ken Kelly, Jack Miller, Albert Naughton, Harold Palin, Ray Price, Bob Ryan, Bill Shankland, Frank Shugars, George Thomas, Tommy Thompson, Jim Tranter and Derek Whitehead. They are all remembered with a picture and a citation in the Hall of Fame Lounge at The Halliwell Jones Stadium.

Published in 2008 by London League Publications Ltd at £12.95
ISBN: 9781903659373

Neil Dowson

Northern Union rugby in 1908

Garry Clarke looks at highlights in rugby league, or Northern Union rugby, 100 years ago.

Hunslet
Hunslet made rugby league history in 1908 by becoming the first club to win all four major trophies in the same season. Having beat Halifax 17-0 to win the Yorkshire Cup at Headingley in December 1907, they finished nine points clear of the Thrumhallers to win the Yorkshire League title. Then having finished second behind Oldham in the Northern Rugby League table with a success rate of 79.82 percent, the top two met in the Championship play off final at Salford on 2 May. In front of a crowd of 14,000 the two sides fought out a 7-7 draw. The replay held at Wakefield on 9 May played before a crowd of 14,054 was won by Hunslet 12-2. Two weeks earlier on 25 April Hunslet had won the Challenge Cup for the first time in their history beating Hull 14-0 at Huddersfield.

Other domestic winners
Having finished top of the Northern Rugby League table with a success rate of 90.62 percent only to lose to Hunslet in the Championship final, Oldham ended the 1907-08 season with two trophies. Having won the Lancashire Cup in November 1907, beating Broughton Rangers 16-9 in the Final, the Roughyeds finished seven points clear of their Manchester rivals to win the Lancashire League title. Both Oldham and Hunslet reached their respective county cup finals in 1908, but neither was able to retain their trophies. Wigan winning the Lancashire Cup final 10-9 at Broughton and Halifax the Yorkshire Cup final 9-5 at Wakefield.

England versus Wales
The first ever international between England and Wales was played on 20 April 1908 at Pen-y-graig, Tonypandy. The Welsh ran out victors 35-18 in front of a crowd of 12,000. The return game at Wheaters Field, Broughton was played on 28 December with England winning 31-7.

New Zealand tour
Having arrived in England on 30 September 1907, the New Zealand 'All Golds' were two-thirds of the way through their historic first tour as 1908 dawned. New Years Day 1908 witnessed the first ever rugby league international game as the New Zealand tourists met Wales in Aberdare, the home side winning 9-8. During the 1908 segment of the tour New Zealand played 11 games including three test matches against the Northern Union. Despite losing the first test 14-6 at Headingley, New Zealand won the series 2-1 beating the Northern Union 18-6 at Stamford Bridge, Chelsea and 8-5 at Cheltenham.

Australia tour
The first Australian touring team arrived at Tilbury on 27 September 1908. They were nicknamed the Kangaroos, no doubt because they had brought a Kangaroo with them. The tour opened in Wales on 3 October when the Australians beat Mid-Rhondda 20-6. Of the 45 games played on the tour, which ended on 8 March 1909, 24 were played in 1908

including the first Great Britain versus Australia test match. Played in front of a crowd of 2,000 at Park Royal in London on 12 December the game ended in a 22-22 draw.

Crowd trouble
There were several instances of crowd trouble at Northern Union games in 1908:
*At the end of the Huddersfield versus Broughton Rangers game in February there was a demonstration against the referee. He eventually left the ground disguised as a policeman but as he was not wearing regulation trousers and boots his disguise was seen through and he was pelted with snowballs. At a subsequent league meeting the referee, Mr Smirke, said that he had not made an official report because he did not consider the matter serious enough.
*After their game against Rochdale Hornets in March, Merthyr Tydfil were ordered to post warning notices and play their next home game at least five miles away.
*In the Hunslet versus Merthyr Tydfil game the referee was kicked by a spectator who received a court summons for the offence. Hunslet were ordered to post warning notices and pay the court costs. In court, after hearing that the man claimed the kick was accidental and that he had apologised to the referee and shaken hands, the magistrate suggested the summons be withdrawn. The prosecution agreed.
*On 9 April Bramley were ordered to play their next two home games away from home because of stone throwing.
*On 14 April a special league meeting was held to consider two reports of disorderly conduct at Hull. It was decided that they were not of a serious nature and Hull were ordered to post warning notices and consider moving the officials dressing rooms to a place less likely to come into contact with the public.
*Runcorn lodged a protest against the result of their Lancashire Cup semi-final at Oldham on the grounds that a spectator interfered with a Runcorn player attempting to tackle Dixon who scored a try. After hearing evidence the committee decided that a spectator did interfere but after Dixon had already scored and the result would stand.
*In September Widnes were ordered to post warning notices after a demonstration against a referee and were advised to provide a dressing room under the grandstand.
*Also in September, at Huddersfield magistrate's court a youth was fined 10 shillings for throwing stones at the Wigan team's wagonette as they were leaving the ground and injuring a player. The mayor said that the practice of throwing missiles as football teams or officials must be stopped.

Northern Union / Northern Rugby League AGM
The accounts showed that although £316 had been paid in grants to junior and school football the balance in hand was still over £1,000. The chairman congratulated Hunslet on winning all four cups, and regarding the tour he said that the visit of New Zealand had been an undoubted success and had done an immense amount of good to the game. Proposals put to the meeting were to amend the committee, for Northern Rugby League clubs to pay £5 to a junior club when signing a player and to ban studs in boots and only allow bars. All three proposals were defeated. Bramley and Ebbw Vale were re-elected to the Northern League and Bramley and St Helens were re-elected to their County Leagues. Three proposals agreed were that the Championship Final would be played in the county of the club with the best percentage, an official list of referees would be compiled for league games and junior clubs would be paid for players signed on. Mr J. Nicholls was elected president and Mr J. Platt was re-elected secretary.

Welsh clubs

Four Welsh clubs - Aberdare, Barry, Mid-Rhondda, Treherbert - were admitted into the Northern Rugby League in 1908, joining Merthyr Tydfil and Ebbw Vale who joined in 1907. The League agreed to provide a cup valued at £30 for the Welsh League and the Northern Union granted a seat in its committee to Wales, the representative to be nominated by the Welsh Clubs.

County championship

Lancashire were crowned County Champions beating Cumberland 15 –8 at Workington and Yorkshire 13-0 at Salford. Cumberland finished with the wooden spoon losing 30-0 to Yorkshire at Huddersfield.

No sale

At a Northern Rugby League meeting on 1 December it was reported that W. Bayliss, secretary of Bradford Northern, went to Hull KR with R. Mann and T. Surman and received £120 for their transfer, £25 of which was given to Surman and £20 to Mann in the presence of Mr. Ambler the Hull KR president. The Bradford Northern representative at the meeting denied that Bayliss was acting on their authority and said that he had been relived of his office. He had not been seen since. Mr Ambler said that the fee had been paid in gold and notes. The players had agreed terms of £2 for a win, 30 shillings for a draw and 17s 6d for a loss. After taking evidence from the players who both differed in their version of the terms offered, the committee came to the following decision: "After considering the circumstances the committee are compelled to believe that Hull KR had, through their secretary, knowledge that the players Surman and Mann, were receiving from Bayliss part of the transfer fee agreed to be paid by Hull KR to Bayliss, and were thus parties to a breach of League Rule 16. Under the circumstances the committee orders that Surman and Mann repay the amount they received to the Hull KR club prior to again playing football and amount of loss sustained from the absconding of Bayliss shall be divided between the two clubs, Bradford Northern to pay £37 10s to Hull KR prior to playing Surman and Mann with their team. Subject to this decision the players are to be retained on the Bradford Northern register, and this being the first case of its kind the explanation of the players that their shares of the transfer fee were coming from Bradford Northern and that they were unaware that their action constituted a breach of League Rule 16 to be accepted."

A meeting of the Bradford Northern members was held to discuss the matter and it was disclosed that the two players had first been offered to Leeds for £150 in gold and then to Wigan but both clubs had declined. Votes of confidence were passed on the committee and the two players and it was decided to open a public subscription list to defray the loss to the club.

Bits and pieces

*After a period of very bad weather in January and February the Northern Ruby League decided that if necessary a game could be played in four quarters instead of two halves.
*St Helens were knocked out of the Challenge Cup by amateur side Whitehaven Recreation who beat their professional opponents 13-8.
*Amateurs Wigan Highfield drew 3-3 at home to Bramley in the Challenge Cup, the Yorkshire men winning the replay 8-6.

*Two days before they appeared in the Challenge Cup final Hunslet were fined £10 for not fielding a full side in a league game.

*Hunslet's Albert Goldthorpe became the first player to kick 100 goals in a league season ending the 1907-08 season with 101 goals, Goldthorpe also topped the points scoring chart with 217 and Wigan's Jim Leytham was the season's top try scorer with 44.

*In May Bradford Northern announced they were to move to the Bowling Old Lane ground at a rent of £30. The move was made because the Greenfield ground in Dudley Hill was too far out of town.

*On 11 August the Northern Union gave permission to Hull, Rochdale Hornets and Warrington to charge admission at practice matches providing the proceeds were given to charity. This was later extended to a large number of clubs.

*On 3 November Wigan obtained a summons against a well-known local man for an attempt to bribe two Wigan players. After the court case the Northern Union congratulated the Wigan club on securing a conviction and decided to ban Edward Croston from all football grounds under the jurisdiction of the Northern Union.

*Leigh objected to the result of their second round Lancashire Cup at Wigan on the grounds that W. Johnson, a Wigan player, left the field to change his jersey without first obtaining the permission of the referee. The Lancashire County Union upheld the objection and said the referee had committed a great error of judgement in allowing Johnson to take further Part in the game. The tie was ordered to be replayed. Wigan who won the original game 11-5 also won the replay 17-3.

*The Northern Union suspended Dawson of Keighley sine die because of his bad sending off record.

*Alf Mann was suspended and transfer listed by Bradford Northern because he failed to turn up for a game and for using abusive language to members of the committee. A telegram was sent to Mr Platt (Northern Union secretary) informing him of the situation and this ruled Mann out of the England side to play Australia.

*St Helens objected to the result of their league game against Salford claiming the touch judge signalled a goal, which they claimed, was not a goal. The objection was dismissed.

*The Northern Union committee met on 28 December to consider a tour to Australia and New Zealand. They came out in favour but decided that it was impossible to reach a final decision until word was received from New Zealand regarding the arrangements for that country.

Eddie Waring

Huw Richards reviews Tony Hannan's biography of Eddie Waring, while **Peter Lush** looks at his print journalism with the original *Rugby League Review* in the 1940s and 1950s.

Being Eddie Waring
The Life and Times of a Sporting Icon
By Tony Hannan

Good biographies illuminate much more than the individual life they are chronicling. Tony Hannan does an exemplary job of telling us about Eddie Waring the man, the journalist and the broadcaster. But his is a book that tells you about much more — about rugby league, its culture and history, about the North and its sensitivities and about the place of broadcasting in our lives in the second half of the 20th century.

It fills a huge gap in league's understanding of itself. Eddie Waring was without doubt one of the most important figures in the game's history. He defined the image of the game when, for the first time, it became widely accessible to those outside the heartlands through the agency of television.

And that, of course, was the problem. The debate over Waring's virtues and vices as a commentator was conducted like any league controversy — with a ferocity that shows Tony Collins' memorable characterisation of the game as sport's equivalent of Yiddish works for more reasons than it never having been the sport of any ruling class. League fans have an appetite for debate that would stagger Talmudic scholars.

That debate centred on a persona beautifully characterised by sportswriter Arthur Hopcraft as "a North Country act, more aware of his comicality than his audience imagines". It had a strong regional dimension. He went down extremely well outside the heartlands, not least with this writer (who is cited at length on page 273 and while on declarations of interest should add that Mainstream published two of his books), where his humour and sense of proportion gave him and league considerable appeal compared to the self-regard of the other football codes.

Within the heartlands the question was, as Hannan rightly points out, one of the eternal preoccupations of minorities and the marginalised 'Are they laughing with us, or at us?' Neither he nor Tony Collins, neither a man to stint, has found anything in the BBC archives pointing to the anti-league conspiracy long proclaimed in the game's trade press. Nor was it Waring's fault that his vowel sounds and other mannerisms were so eagerly seized up by Graeme Garden, Mike Yarwood and others. At the same time there is a reasonable argument that a metropolitan, overwhelmingly middle-class corporation wasn't too aware of the sensitivities of people who are neither.

Hannan analyses both sides of the debate, and the man in the middle of it, sympathetically. But that is no more than the reader will expect by the time he reaches those chapters in this perceptive and well-researched biography. Not least of its virtues is that it reminds you that Waring would have been a significant figure, as both a club executive and the journalist who moved league journalism away from sober match reporting into the world of personality and player profiles, had he never gone near a microphone.

More than half of the book concerns his life before he became, in the words of one of his defenders in those 1970s controversies "Not a commentator, but The Commentator". It is a worthwhile journey, chronicled with care and an eye for anecdote – it would take a very hard heart not to enjoy the suggestion that Waring got his break as a league writer filling in unofficially for a reporter who used matches as an alibi for visiting his girlfriend or the account of Hannan visiting Waring's old school and meeting pupils so accustomed to an all-female teaching staff that they addressed their 'bald 43 year old' visitor as 'Miss'. That Hannan made that visit, recording some evocative passages from the school's logbook from Waring's time there, underlines his thoroughness. He illustrates Waring in terms not only of life and times, but of place, proving a fine sketch of Dewsbury's social, economic and sporting history. It is odd that he omits to mention one of its most memorable rugby days, since Wales's first ever win over England belongs as much to league as union by virtue of location, being played five years before the schism of 1895 and the winning try being scored by a Dewsbury player, Buller Stadden.

That though, is a minor quibble to set alongside the scrupulous chronicling of a career that showed that, far from being chosen in the slightly random way of some pioneering sports broadcasters, Waring had earned his place as BBC's voice of league with a long track-record in administration and journalism and his own persistence at pushing at a frequently-closed door, writing his first letter to the corporation in 1931. Hannan's research shows us both the corporation's early doubts about Waring and league's deep distrust of television.

The title *Being Eddie Waring* is fully justified. There was always, Hannan shows clearly, the strong element of performance that Hopcraft detected. Waring created a persona displayed both as impresario of the league junction-box in the bar of the Queen's Hotel, Leeds and in his broadcasting. There was little doubt of his star quality – perhaps the most jaw-dropping quote in the book is Eric Ashton's remark that 'if you became a friend of his, you became a bit of a someone. There was a bit of stardust on him'. It says much about league's enduring appeal that a player as great as Eric Ashton should not think of himself as having stardust, still more about Waring that he was felt capable of conferring it.

But the act was also accompanied by a fierce determination to protect his and his family's privacy, and a huge amount of hard work. There are echoes of Gary Hetherington's Herculean labours in the early days of Sheffield Eagles in the revelation that Waring was a typewriter salesman while building his early career in journalism. The numerous stories he broke were the product of his assiduous cultivation of contacts.

Hannan also shows that a man often criticised for reflecting league's past was in fact consistently forward-looking. He argued, at a time when it was very much a minority cause, for expansion outside the heartlands, particularly in London and was a warm supporter of the young radicals who launched *Open Rugby* as a fanzine in 1976.

Eddie Waring was not always fairly treated during his colourful and productive life – or afterwards. Hannan is quite right when he points to the injustice of naming Man of the Match trophies after Lance Todd and Harry Sunderland, but having nothing in memory of a still more important broadcaster. But more than 20 years after a death probably made merciful by the savage onset of Alzheimer's – then little understood, but a factor in his undoubted decline in his last years as commentator – he has the biography he richly deserves.

Published in 2008 by Mainstream Publishing at £14.99. ISBN: 9781845963002

Eddie Waring and *Rugby League Review*

Eddie Waring has been in the spotlight recently. To many rugby league followers, he is mainly known for his role as a television commentator on the game, and undoubtedly played a major role in establishing rugby league in this medium.

However, he was also a major print journalist, and in the late 1940s and early 1950s was a regular to *Rugby League Review*. This was a spiky little journal, at first monthly and then weekly. It started in September 1946, and lasted until around the end of 1953 or early 1954. The editor and driving force behind it was Stanley Chadwick. He was often critical of the Rugby Football League and its secretary Bill Fallowfield. The RFL refused to give them press credentials for matches, and then Fallowfield sued Chadwick for libel. The case was heard in August 1952, and went largely in favour of Fallowfield. In modern terms imagine Richard Lewis suing Martyn Sadler or Danny Lockwood for libel and the impact such a case would have on the game.

Eddie Waring often portrayed himself as an advocate for the fans. To give him credit, although Chadwick had strong views himself, he allowed Waring a platform despite them disagreeing on certain issues. Waring also wrote regularly for the *Sunday Pictorial* (which became the *Sunday Mirror*), but this article looks at his work for *Rugby League Review*. Some of his pieces were either looking at team selections for tours, or were profiles of different people in the game. But there were also some that looked at how the game could be developed, and these are particularly interesting.

In the 1930s, there had been various attempts to develop new teams outside the heartlands, none of which had lasted longer than a season or two. Despite this, and often being portrayed as the arch-typical northerner, Waring was always a supporter of trying to make rugby league a national game, and establish a base outside its traditional heartlands in the north of England.

London

In 1966 Waring wrote his *Book of Rugby League*, a collection of articles looking at different aspects of the game's history and development. As a 'Last Word' he says "One organisation doing much to expand Rugby League is the strong London movement who are encouraging amateur sides. They have some good ideas for staging the game in and around the Metropolis and although their problems are many I've no doubt they'll succeed." Although he rather exaggerated their strength – reality was a handful of people in London at this time – he had always been a supporter of taking the game to London. It is interesting that he was writing this almost 30 years after the collapse of Streatham & Mitcham RLFC, the last club in the capital in the 1930s, and 14 years before the birth of Fulham RLFC in 1980.

In October 1947, Waring used his column in the *Review* to ask whether there should be development in "London or the North?" He interviewed Ivor Halstead, the former manager of Streatham & Mitcham, who advocated building the game from the bottom up in the capital. Waring also asks whether there is potential for new teams in Doncaster and Blackpool, both of which joined the RFL in the early 1950s. He does not put forward his own views, but does say "Unlike the Editor of *Rugby League Review*, I believe in the Wembley Cup Final." He also suggests that Harry Sunderland would be a good person to organise the game in London.

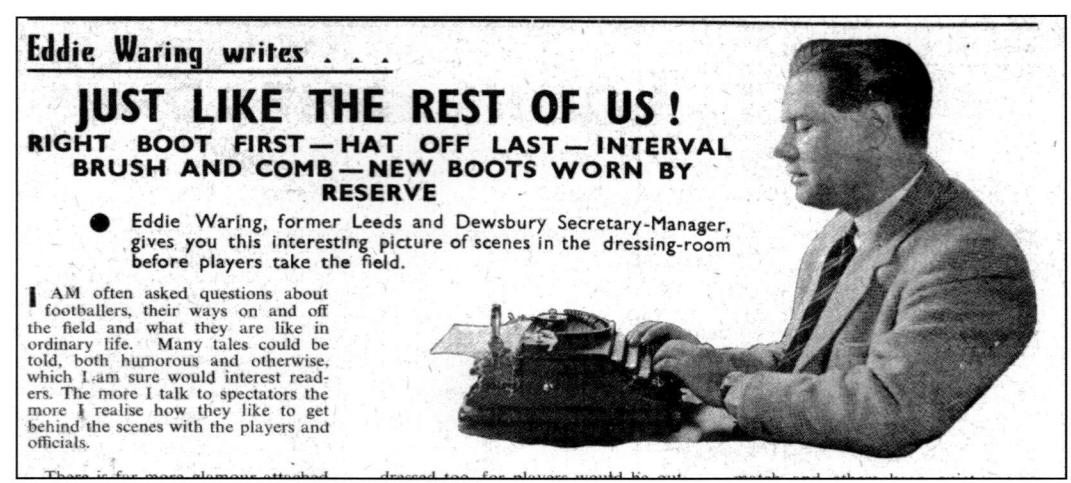

Waring's column in a 1949 Rugby League Review

Two months later, he looks at responses to his article. He says "Naturally the majority of letters favoured concentration in the north, but there was a general viewpoint which indicated the concern of the average follower who desired the game to extend itself." He also points out that he had over 100 orders for his recent book from outside the heartlands. What is interesting is that in 1947 Waring was holding this debate. As a foretaste of the Super League controversy almost 40 years later, he includes a letter from one writer in London who says that "teams like Featherstone Rovers would probably be well advised to move to larger towns where they would have better gates and thus avoid having to sell the players they have made." Another letter proposes "[working] south gradually with new clubs."

Wales

Another area that Waring looked at was the potential for the game in Wales. There was a strong Welsh team at this time, although he had concerns about how it was organised, at a club level, attempts to develop a structure or individual clubs had not lasted. In April 1948, he wrote about how disappointing the attendance at Swansea for the Wales versus France match was – estimated at about 6,500. He said there was a need for better publicity and "Preparations for these Welsh games are bad. Things are done in a haphazard way. Players are not assembled; they just roll up as if it were a club game; and the whole atmosphere is not of International standard but of a club game and a very ordinary one at that."

He advocated setting up an advisory committee for South Wales, but not one of men who had never been there and did not understand the country. He concluded: "The game has many friends in South Wales – men of standing who can help. One question should be asked. Do we want rugby league football in South Wales? **If the answer is 'Yes' then start properly and see that it is a success.**" (bold in original).

He returned to this theme in November 1948, encouraged by a better attendance – 15,000 for the latest match against France, despite little being spent on publicity. Again, he said there is potential for the game in Wales, but that "It is time a policy was decided upon and a statement made of the future the Rugby Football League plans to have in

South Wales." Once more, he supported a sub-committee specifically to build the game in Wales, and said it is important that winning international honours for Wales is taken seriously by the players.

A year on, some progress had been made, with the establishment of a Welsh League. He noted the enthusiasm of some of the people involved in Wales, but has concerns about the RFL: "But enthusiasm is not sufficient and I am not satisfied the detached way in which the game is being handled from the North..." He said that Wales should have a full-time organiser for the game – something that happened 40 years later. He concluded: "There is a small and gallant band of workers in the Welsh valleys. Guided properly they could do big things, but they urgently require help. Like the London business I still feel we're playing about in Wales and not getting down to the real job. **My advice is: give up 'kidding' at rugby league and get down to serious business. The game's the thing when it is run properly.**" (bold in original)

Another area ripe for development was Cumberland. Workington had joined the RFL in 1945, and in 1948 Whitehaven were also accepted into membership. Waring covered this, but mainly focussed on the exclusion of the press from the debate. However, in February 1951, he writes a very positive article about the development of the game there, showing the grassroots enthusiasm for it. He concluded: "What has been achieved in Cumberland can be done in Doncaster, in Blackpool, in Wales and even in London."

In October 1950, Waring put forward the idea of 'twinning' – looking at towns that had potential for development (albeit mainly in the north) and twinning them with an existing club. This idea has been used at different times, most recently to try to link a Rugby League Conference club with a professional one, with variable results. The towns Waring names as targets were Bolton, Sheffield, Blackpool, Doncaster, Carlisle, Liverpool (which already had Liverpool City RLFC) and Lancaster. Four of these later joined the professional game, and in the other three amateur clubs have since been established. He concluded that "Not until legislators become big enough shall we have a National game with National game rights. The right to be included in the 5.30pm BBC Sports Results. The right to have our match reports in every edition of a Sunday and daily newspaper. The right to talk about Rugby League in every town, and the right to challenge Soccer attendances."

Interestingly, two weeks later, Waring wrote a critical article about Liverpool Stanley. However, he was also constructive, outlining improvements he thought should be made, as he felt that the club, which was struggling with a poor ground, was not good enough to represent the sport in Liverpool.

Structures and resources

Waring often looked at how the game was run and the resources necessary to develop it. In February 1950, he pointed out that around half the professional clubs only had a part-time secretary or secretary-manager. He also wondered whether part-time training for players was enough, although also saying that "I always want a player to have a job apart from his football career." However, he felt that two hours training a week was not enough, and said that this "is where Soccer leaves us standing. Their preparation is far more methodical and effective than ours. I am not suggesting the rugby league code could afford all full-time professionals, but I do believe that part-time players are bringing part-time results." He also looks at the question of whether referees should be full-time. In January 1949 he had looked at a grading system for referees, based on ideas that a former referee had sent him.

In December 1950, Waring looked at the issues facing a committee that had been appointed to look at the game's administrative structure. He proposed having a chairman appointed for five years, rather than for one year through an annual election, so that they could see through changes and ideas. He proposed drastically reducing the size of the Rugby League Council to "eight just men and true". He said there should be one central authority to run all the competitions for senior clubs, with the League secretary having a full-time staff to do this. Again, he wanted a structure that would bring "national recognition and dignity." In May 1951, he was critical of the RFL's failures in the field of publicity, urging them to appoint a publicity officer, rather than someone to deal with publications. In January 1951 he had proposed using the Festival of Britain to take the game to new areas, saying that "Five hundred spectators at Sheffield, Blackpool, Coventry, Birmingham or Wembley would do more good than 20,000 at Belle Vue [in Manchester]."

In all these areas Waring was years ahead of his time. In October 1951, just as television (only BBC) arrived in the north, he was encouraging the game's authorities to have a positive attitude towards this new form of the media, and said that "At last we have the opportunity to go Big in a Big way through the channels of the television set... Rugby League football is ideally suited for television purposes." I wonder what he would have made of the coverage the game gets today – from the tone of the article I'm sure he would have approved.

There were many other areas that Waring covered in the magazine that space does not allow to be covered here. From the end of 1951, from my research, he did not write so frequently for the *Review*, although he usually covered the RFL Annual General Meeting. Whether this was because of other work commitments, or for another reason, is unclear. However, his ideas, at a time when many in the game had no concept of development or how to improve the game, are fascinating, and he was often borne out, as the strength of rugby league in London and Wales today shows.

Wayne English: Swinton's number one

Ian Jackson reflects on a modern day Swinton hero.

Loyalty to a single club is a scarce commodity in modern professional sport even in rugby league where teamwork is paramount. That is why a career spanning 10 years at Swinton Lions RLFC is evidence of the character of full-back Wayne English. As a Rochdale lad, Wayne has no actual connection to the Swinton area at any level. He was not born in Swinton and has never lived in the town. So the loyalty shown by him to a club that has had bouts of profound crisis during his playing career deserves wider recognition. Of course, the supporters and officials of the club know all about the loyalty of Wayne English and they are nearly always reassured to see his name on the team-sheet, since he has been a constant and consistent performer in the blue shirt of Swinton. On several occasions it would have been justifiable for Wayne to move-on, not least to improve himself as a player at a bigger club. To date, he has always decided to remain loyal to the Lions. There is little doubt that Wayne English is Swinton's number one and to mark this feat he has been awarded a testimonial.

The arrival of Wayne English into the world of professional rugby league was first recorded in the last ever *Rothman's Rugby League Yearbook*. The nineteenth and final edition in 1999 noted that Wayne signed as an 18 year old for Swinton Lions RLFC on 22 July 1998 from Kirkholt WMC & A, an amateur club from the Rochdale area. A big influence in this decision was John Prince, Swinton development manager at the time, who introduced Wayne to the club's Academy set-up. Wayne joined the Lions when the club was based at Gigg Lane in Bury and at a time when the players were possibly the best since moving from the spiritual home of Station Road in that fateful summer of 1992. Although Wayne's full debut was 18 months away, he signed for the Lions in the same year as former Great Britain international Paul Hulme from Warrington and the popular Kiwi international George Mann from Keighley. Already at the club were promising players Sean Casey from St Helens and Andy Craig from Wigan.

Wayne's initial season as a first team player is recorded in the fourth year of the *Rugby League Express Yearbook* in 2000-2001. In the 2000 season, he played a total of 12 games plus 3 as substitute scoring 5 tries. In the Swinton team that year were Andy Coley, Paul Smith and Ian Watson all of whom went onto play for Super League clubs plus Paul Barrow, Andy Craig and Jason Roach with recent Super League experience. Wayne made his try-scoring debut against Waterhead, an amateur club from the Oldham area, in the third round of the Challenge Cup on 1 February 2000. The renown rugby league journalist Dave Hadfield was on hand to record events for the *Independent* newspaper describing Wayne as "the 19-year-old full-back" who "claimed a try on his debut."

The Swinton legend Les Holiday was coach when Wayne signed for the club, but it was another former Great Britain forward who handed him his full debut. Mike Gregory was at the helm the night Wayne burst into the Swinton team. In his autobiography, *Biting back* published in 2006, Mike Gregory commented that he brought in some experienced players at that time including former St Helens trio Ian Pickavance, Jon Neil and Phil Veivers. "These were to complement a relatively young team with players like Wayne English, Shaun Furey and Mick Nanyn." In his book, Mike is also full of praise for

John Prince who was partially responsible for bringing Wayne to Swinton in the first place. Of course, Mike Gregory passed away sadly in November 2007.

To his credit, Wayne stayed at Swinton during the troubled 2002 season when the club was forced out of Gigg Lane and reduced to playing home games at Leigh and Chorley. He scored 5 tries from 13 appearances plus 4 as substitute. Wayne's loyalty was rewarded as the club found some relative stability at Moor Lane in Kersal, the home of Salford City FC. This move came after the successful formation of the Swinton Supporters' Trust which contributed to saving the club itself and was the first such Supporters' Trust to be formed in professional rugby league. In the 2003 season there was some relative success as the Lions reached the quarter-final of the Challenge Cup and were paired with Wigan at home. The tie was switched to the JJB Stadium, and Wayne was in the Lions side that was winning 6-0 after 20 minutes and were living the dream, albeit briefly. Wigan ran out comfortable winners in the end.

Wayne remained loyal as the Lions moved again to Park Lane home of Sedgley Park RUFC in Whitefield for the start of the 2004 season when he continued to excel as the club gained even greater stability under new coach Paul Kidd. The following season, Wayne was selected at full back in the *Rugby League World* All-Stars National League Two team for 2005. In the same team were three Swinton team-mates Marlon Billy, Lee Marsh and Phil Joseph. At last, the Lions were moving in the right direction and with Ian Watson back at the club as captain, alongside English, the Lions were competitive on the field, once more.

In 2006 the upward trend continued as the club reached the National League Two Grand Final at the Halliwell Jones Stadium in Warrington after a sterling cup run saw victories against Barrow, Celtic Crusaders and Featherstone Rovers in the play-offs. By common consent, Wayne played his best match for the Lions against Sheffield Eagles in the Grand Final even though Swinton fell at the final hurdle. *Rugby League World* in November 2006 was full of praise for Wayne who was given the man-of-the-match award for the Lions. Wayne was mentioned for his performance that "stood out above the rest" and described him as one who "epitomised the fight in the Lions" as he set up Swinton's second try for David Alstead following a clever break down the left wing. Further evidence of Wayne's playing ability also came in 2006 when he was named in the top 50 players in Britain outside of Super League by *Rugby League World*.

Throughout 2007 Wayne continued to play mainly at full back but also four times on the wing (twice on each flank) and in 2008 he suffered a bad jaw injury making a courageous tackle away at Workington Town. In addition, at the start of the tenth year he has been awarded his testimonial season. Over this period, Wayne has always been reliable, brave and steadfast for the Lions. So much so, that Wayne has played home games for Swinton at Bury, Chorley, Kersal, Leigh, Salford and Whitefield (not to mention the home tie in the Challenge Cup that was switched to Wigan). He has been coached by Les Holliday, Tony Barrow, Mike Gregory, Phil Veivers, Peter Roe and Paul Kidd while with the club.

It is fitting that Great Britain international Kenny Gowers also from Rochdale was the last Swinton full-back to receive a testimonial when he had the second of his two testimonials in 1973 having amassed a grand total of 2,105 points for the Lions in a 19 year period from 1954 to 1973. Wayne is the first Swinton player to be awarded a testimonial since Alex Melling received his well-deserved benefit in 1992. In this day and age, one thing is for sure, Wayne English has also certainly earned his testimonial.

Wayne English in action against Moscow in 2005 (Courtesy Ian Jackson)

Charging forward against London Skolars in 2008 (Courtesy Ian Jackson)

All local lads! The famous St Helens and Pilkington Recreation

Alex Service and **Denis Whittle** reflect on the only works team to play in professional rugby league.

Born out of a major industrial company's desire to develop sporting and social provision for their workforce, St Helens and later Pilkington Recreation have always been an important part of the sporting fabric of St Helens. Although links with the famous glass-making giants have diminished over the years, the famous red, amber and black jerseys signify a club still highly respected in the world of rugby league and BARLA in particular.

Their story actually encompasses three codes of football – rugby union, association football and rugby league. They provided the town of St Helens with it's first-ever rugby international, Jim Pyke, in the early rugby union days and became one of the most feared and respected teams in Lancashire. Although the call to the Northern Union was not heeded initially, the club did take part in the 1897 Challenge Cup competition.

The Pilkington workforce voted unanimously for a change to association football 12 months later and the Recs duly made their mark in the Lancashire Combination and Lancashire Cup, beating top reserve outfits from the likes of Liverpool and Manchester United. It was during the football years that their ground at City Road was developed with stands and changing facilities to rival many other enclosures in the North West. They also had a superstar goalie, Teddy Doig – the Peter Shilton of his day, who had played with distinction for Sunderland and Liverpool, together with a winger called Harry Welfare, who went on to break scoring records in Rio de Janeiro as a bustling centre forward for Fluminenses and Corinthians.

They returned to Northern Union rugby in 1914 and gradually built up a team of local lads who would be accepted into the re-formed professional league at the end of the First World War and the 'Babes' made an immediate impression, by drawing 0-0 against mighty Huddersfield at Fartown in the Challenge Cup, only to fall 7-4 at a packed City Road in the replay – a match still talked about even today. Led by their star scrum-half Johnny Greenall and with the famous back three of Smith, Fildes and Mulvanney, the Recs won the coveted Lancashire Cup before their rivals, the Saints, in 1923. Four years later, the team topped the league table and beat St Helens 27-0 in a controversial semi-final at City Road before a narrow 13-8 defeat came against a powerful Swinton side at Wilderspool, Warrington in the Championship Final.

The Recs also provided three players for the 1928 Australian British Lions tour – hooker Oliver Dolan, prop Frank Bowen and hard-tackling second-rower Albert Fildes as the Lions returned with the ashes. The Recs were a whisker away from the first-ever Wembley Challenge Cup Final in 1929 only to be denied by a contentious refereeing decision - and a 13-12 scoreline - in their replayed semi-final clash with Wigan at Leigh.

Although the Recs' fighting spirit was paramount throughout the second half of the 1930s, the famous team of the past decade had broken up and gates had plummeted – not that they had been good for many years and invariably, Pilkington Brothers pulled the plug at the end of the 1938-39 season. They simply could not afford to shore up the club's ailing finances any longer. It was to be another 10 years before the famous red, amber and black jerseys were seen again in combat, albeit in an amateur context, when the newly named Pilkington Recreation joined the local St Helens League. Despite many problems facing amateur rugby league in the 1950s, the Recs soldiered on and won the Lancashire Cup against Salford Juniors at Weaste in 1957. The club's first amateur international, Ron Leyland, came to prominence at this time, to be followed by second-rower 'Buck' Casey, full-back Bernard Jeffries and a young forward called Geoff Fletcher. The team also reached the Challenge Cup first round in 1961, but lost heavily at Hull KR.

Saturday 9 October 1971 is a day no-one at City Road will ever forget. Recs' captain Jackie Pimblett died as a result of injuries sustained when a scrum collapsed during a match with UGB. Yet it was the catalyst for a remarkable transformation in the club's fortunes as team-mates vowed to succeed in his memory. From the mid-1970s to the early 1980s the club won BARLA's National Cup competition on four occasions, cementing their place in the pantheon of great amateur teams. In the Challenge Cup and John Player Trophy, professional clubs were given the fright of their lives by the amateur underdogs. Great players such as John McCabe, Billy Simmons, Syd Wright, Kevin Whittle, Kenny Cross, John Forster and Joey Hull were virtually irreplaceable and although the club joined the inaugural National League in the mid- 1980s, a return to the North West Counties competition followed as financial pressures began to bite, with players finding it difficult to get time off work with the travelling involved.

For the past decade, the club's major strength is in the depth of teams from under-7 to open age and 2008 proved to be a most successful year on the field. Indeed, the under-12s won the Lancashire and North West Counties cups and toured France in June 2008 – the first overseas tour for any junior team in the club's history; the under-16s achieved promotion to the Premier Division and the under-17s reached the Lancashire Cup Final, but were beaten by Hindley. However, the under-18s produced a superb two trophy haul, including the club's first National Cup final success since the early 1980s, beating Wigan St Pats at Hunslet's South Leeds Stadium. Six players were also called up by Lancashire, full-back Danny Filson, half-backs Greg Smith and Danny Lynch, plus forwards Tom Connick, Mark Briody and Jonathon Peers.

Despite victory in the St Helens Cup in 1986, glory eluded the first team until 2008, when the club won the North West Counties Premiership trophy by beating Simms Cross of Widnes 18-12 at St Maries and finished runners-up in the North West Counties Premier Division. Under coach John Ledger, the side has a fine blend of youth and experience, including star full-back Mark Ashton, captain and loose-forward Steve Rawsthorne and young Ryan Rogers, a talented stand-off, who is attracting the attention of several professional clubs.

Unfortunately, there have been long-standing problems with City Road, their spiritual home, which has been up for sale for several years. The days of being a 'works team' as such have somewhat disappeared. The thought of Recs leaving the Windle district is unthinkable, yet the social club on the site was closed in 2007 and there are only minimal changing facilities remaining. Although City Road is used as a training base, teams are spread out across the town. The ideal situation would be a new headquarters with an adequate number of pitches to cater for the players who turn out for this most durable of clubs. Everything is still in the melting pot - a mixture of social, economic and political factors that needs to be resolved as soon as possible for the sake of a club which continues to play a vital role in the sporting life of our proud rugby league town.

All local lads – the story of St Helens Recs RLFC by Alex Service and Denis Whittle will be published by London League Publications Ltd in November 2008.

Top: The St Helens Recs' team with the Lancashire Cup at City Road after the 17-0 defeat of Swinton at Wigan in November 1923. Back, left to right: Tommy Smith, Bill Mulvanney, Albert Fildes, Dickie Ramsdale, Jack Hughes, Harry Grundy. Front: Joe McComas, Jim Pyke, Johnny Greenall (captain), Colonel Norman Pilkington (club president), Jimmy Owen, Fred Halton, Tommy Gormley, Tommy Dingsdale. (Photo: Courtesy Alex Service)

Bottom: Pilkington Recs' Jeff Gormley looks to the referee for confirmation after one of his two tries against Castleford in a man-of-the-match performance. The Recs lost 23-22 in this First Round Challenge Cup tie on 26 February 1978 - one of the finest matches in the club's history. (Photo: courtesy *St Helens Reporter*)

League and Union

It is now 13 years since that historic day in August 1995 when rugby union became an 'open' game and accepted professionalism. Many things have changed in the relationship between the two codes over the last 13 years. Players can switch codes without problems; indeed alarm bells are ringing in Australia with the defection of league players to French rugby union, although there has not been the huge exodus of league players that we once feared. And some who tried union have returned – Iestyn Harris, Henry Paul (who is about to become the first player to switch codes three times when he joins Leeds Tykes in September), Gareth Raynor and Chev Walker among others. Jason Robinson became a union star, but would they ever have discovered a black youngster from a poor background in Hunslet? Rugby league did. Andy Farrell has played for England in a rugby union world cup, and numerous coaches have gone from league to union. And league has played matches at all the major British union grounds.

And Shaun Edwards writes a weekly column for *The Guardian* about rugby union; the idea of which would have seemed surreal back in 1995. It's a very good read by the way.

Also, the influence of former league coaches, combined with union learning how to develop players professionally, has seen changes in the way union is played, compared to 1995. However, there are still major differences between the two codes of rugby.

These articles look at different aspects of the relationship between the two codes, and the state of both games today. What arguably is true is that supporters still mainly only follow one code of rugby. Rob Burrow has recently been doing film and music reviews for Radio 5live – also slightly surreal, especially early on a Saturday morning. When asked by the presenter if he would be watching the union Tri-nations match on television, he firmly replied that he wouldn't as he was a rugby league fan. Most league fans would agree!

Just because you're paranoid...

David Hinchliffe reflects on the relationship between League and Union.

There were various things that got me thinking in that particular week, but I'm still trying to work out my position. Thirteen years on from rugby union going professional, just how should rugby league people now view that sport? Has the hatchet been well and truly buried and have we more in common than divides us? Is it an important fellow traveller and ally in a battle with sport's lowest common denominator – association football? Are we partners in the struggle to project the immense attractions of the oval ball? Or are we rivals and competitors fighting over a limited market? Have the historical enmities between the two codes largely disappeared or are the gloves – in many respects – still off? More importantly, what does the relationship between league and union tell us about Britain in the 21st century?

On that Saturday afternoon something quite unusual had happened. I had sat down to watch the latter stages of a Six Nations Championship match on the television. I rarely watch rugby union because, with few exceptions, it usually bores me. I suppose I view the game very much from a league perspective and inevitably get frustrated and annoyed at the tactics adopted. But my father-in-law was staying with us at the time and he has the enviable ability to enjoy all sports. And, as a Welshman, he had more than a passing interest in the outcome of this particular game.

It was Scotland versus England at Murrayfield and reminded me of why I so often avoid rugby union. It was a drab, dour affair with the ball being kicked, often aimlessly, at every verse end. In the old days it would probably have had Bill McLaren in raptures but it had me asking the same old question. Why on earth would nearly 68,000 people pay good money to watch this stuff?

With less than two minutes of the match left, and England trailing by just a few points, their full-back gathered the ball just inside his own half. The scene was set for him to link with his threequarters creating an overlap for a try that, converted, would win the game. To my astonishment – but in a manner entirely consistent with what I had seen of the rest of the game – he hoofed it down the field into the hands of the Scottish defence who held onto the ball until the final whistle.

Maybe I had picked the wrong match. On the limited occasions I have watched union in recent times I always seem to. Maybe, as some of the union scribes would have it, the subtleties and technical aspects of their game are simply beyond us rugby league types. Maybe, as I would genuinely concede, I am viewing their sport from the perspective of someone steeped in very different tactical traditions which is not conducive to its proper appreciation. Or maybe, if you cut through the overwhelming hype of the union-obsessed London based media, I had, quite frankly, been watching a sporting product considerably inferior as a spectacle to the one I'm used to watching every week.

Media coverage

The following morning my Sunday newspaper had almost 10 full pages of rugby union coverage. In their 9 centimetres of rugby league coverage they hadn't even managed to list the fixtures on the correct days. Had I travelled to the south of France on the day they said my team were playing the Catalans I would have had a rather lengthy wasted journey. Their treatment of the sport was frankly contemptuous.

For some unknown reason I had managed, later that day, to find out when the Super League Programme was on BBC1. The constant shifting of its scheduled time means I usually miss it as, I suspect, do many other potential viewers. I have often wondered whether those people at the Beeb who evaluate the viewing figures for this programme take account of the fact that it takes little short of an act of genius to work out when (or if) it's actually on. Anyway, I caught this particular show and, of course, this year has marked the great breakthrough, with the BBC agreeing to the programme being nationally networked. But we might have known, and presenter Harry Gration's own thoughts on the issue were fairly apparent when he announced at the end of this programme that "for the nation's milkmen" the show would be repeated nationally the following morning "at 4.05am".

I didn't stay up to see it again but, pondering on the media's comparative treatment of the two codes of rugby, I was struck by something that journalist and broadcaster Martin Kelner wrote in his national newspaper column that morning. Having read Tony Hannon's excellent biography of Eddie Waring, Kelner speculated as to whether Waring had actually been part of an establishment conspiracy against rugby league.

His idea may have been in a light hearted vein but I can vividly recall being involved in serious debate with fellow league followers in the late 1970s on the subject of whether the BBC regarded our game as a legitimate and respected sport or some sort of comedy space filler, the broadcasting rights for which could be acquired pretty cheaply.

Regardless of Waring's undoubted lifelong commitment to rugby league, in the latter stages of his broadcasting career he undoubtedly became a national figure of fun and the image of the game he was associated with was, and I would argue still is, tarnished as a consequence. As Hannon notes in his detailed analysis of this period, unprecedented depths were reached during one particular live broadcast of a match from Headingley. A particularly troublesome stray dog had interrupted proceedings several times and the BBC broadcasting team determined that it would be a good idea to display, while it was on camera, the on-screen caption "K 9". For those of us who doubted that the Corporation genuinely regarded rugby league as a serious national sport this episode was cast iron proof that its projection of the code bordered on farce.

When I consider the question of the way in which league followers should view contemporary rugby union I find it hard to put to one side the very different ways in which our national public service broadcaster has treated these two sports. I have absolutely no doubts that the image of rugby league projected during that earlier period by the BBC still significantly influences attitudes towards the game some 30 years later. Let's not forget that many of our key decision-makers – in business and, more importantly, the national media itself – were in their formative years when, long before multi-channel television choices, the regular Saturday afternoon BBC fare of Eddie Waring, was watched by millions. In many instances, for a very large number of our middle-aged movers and shakers, that was then, and unfortunately still is, their sole perception of the sport of rugby league.

Against a background of minimal national press coverage of rugby league, union has during the intervening period emerged, largely unchallenged, as "rugby" in media-speak, and, in my experience, the view of many outside the league heartlands is that the game is some sort of mysterious hangover from a bygone era, a quaint somewhat baffling activity occurring on the fringes of our society. And with the greatest respect to the efforts made by rugby league's contemporary broadcasters, the game currently has insufficient genuine clout within its media and broadcasting presence to project the reality of a very entertaining and generally vibrant, modern sport.

And while I have conceded that my largely negative view of rugby union as a spectacle may well arise because I see the game through league eyes, it is very important to note that league's limited national media coverage is not infrequently projected through union eyes. I have no wish to denigrate in any way the rugby league credentials of either gentleman but it's no coincidence that BBC TV's main league commentary team of Ray French and Jonathan Davies have both played international rugby union. It's almost as though the BBC sees the need for such a qualification in explaining league to the civilised world.

But in the written media, at national level, league is even more blatantly projected through the eyes of scribes who are 100 per cent rugby union. I have genuinely lost count of the articles I have read on actual or potential converts from league to union which have a barely hidden agenda of denigrating the sport of rugby league, its skills, spectacle and spectator support.

There is an industry of national journalists – way beyond the likes of noted league bashers like Stephen Jones and Simon Barnes – who revel in the opportunity to rubbish players who cross to union. They assert a common theme that it is a sporting step too far. Union is simply beyond the capability of even the best of league.

I read the coverage of Andy Farrell's difficulties not with disbelief, but growing anger at what was entirely predictable. Here we had a rugby league prop forward who, in his late twenties, after the best part of a decade and a half at top level in the code, had found that his knees required a little bit of surgical attention. Before he had played even a single game of rugby union he found himself named in the England squad and expected to play at either half-back or threequarter.

When his long period of fitness problems was over, the league knockers in the national media had a field day and it went way beyond which position he should play in XV-a-side. Here was a top level league star – a legend some might say – who simply wasn't up to "rugby". We saw it as well to a lesser extent with other top switchers like Iestyn Harris and Chev Walker and more recently Lesley Vainikolo, another direct transfer to union from the knee clinic. But the bizarre notion that an ageing rugby league prop would immediately hack it as an international back made Farrell the fall guy for a journalistic tradition that needs little invitation to put the boot into anyone or anything remotely connected to XIII-a-side.

By all accounts Andy Farrell is a decent guy and he didn't deserve the treatment he received. But while the international athlete Dwayne Chambers, despite his past record, received a broadly sympathetic analysis of his efforts to try a new sport with Castleford Tigers RLFC, by and large Farrell gained no such understanding of the challenges faced in taking up a very different game. Chambers may have taken banned substances but Farrell came from rugby league.

Perhaps more worrying from a league perspective is the increasing trend in our national press of highlighting the prospects of up-and-coming rugby league talent changing codes and becoming future stars of the England Rugby Union team. I was particularly struck by a feature article I read on Kyle Eastmond, the young St. Helens player, which was written around the theme of whether he was "the next Jason Robinson". The entire basis of the piece – about a new league talent – was whether he would at some point turn his back on the code and 'progress' to rugby union. The scarcely disguised message to the outstanding league players of his generation was that their real future, in terms of fame and fortune, lies in changing codes.

Now the media's treatment of union does indeed mean that if they achieve success in XV-a-side they will gain a profile way beyond anything they might expect in league. The simple fact is that rugby union gets the treatment it receives in the establishment media – and especially the BBC – not just because it is played more widely nationally and internationally but because, unlike rugby league, it is an integral part of that establishment.

Class system

It is a remarkable testimony to the British class system in the 21st century that in many northern towns and cities where rugby league is a major, if not the main, spectator sport, the local grammar and private schools still stick valiantly to teaching their pupils rugby union. It is as though a 'proper' upbringing means studiously avoiding league. The 'Gentlemen and Players' distinctions in cricket disappeared while I was still a kid but that ethos is still apparently alive and well when it comes to how the handling codes are viewed by many in Britain today. It might be unfashionable – even impolite – to use the C word nowadays but to understand the continuing relationship between league and union and their relative treatment in the national media it is impossible to avoid a discussion of both the British establishment and social class. While a Six Nations Championship match would be unthinkable without the presence of a member of the Royal Family, the Royal Box at the Rugby League Challenge Cup Final is, year in, year out, a guaranteed Royalty-free zone. And while the New Year and birthday honours lists are usually peppered with union types, despite enormous behind the scenes efforts by rugby league, its representation in the OBEs and MBEs is, as often as not, painfully thin.

Sport in Britain, perhaps more than anywhere else in the world, reflects the continued existence of our unique class system. Nowhere is this more apparent than in the relationship between, and comparative treatment of, the two codes of rugby. The very existence of rugby league is a stark reminder to those who might deny it that we remain a socially divided country. And behind much of the treatment of rugby league in the establishment media is a largely unspoken, but genuine, belief that the game is something of an anachronism and a reminder of conflicts and divisions which are supposedly long behind us. Rugby league really ought to have gone the way of outside toilets and dolly tubs.

So it's a real challenge for our southern media types to fathom out why rugby league hasn't quietly gone away and died but, in the era of professional rugby union, is not only surviving, but doing rather nicely, thank you. Rather than doffing its flat cap and heading for the exit, rugby league continues to stick two fingers up and expose rugby union for its limitations and faults. The more objective of our media friends sometimes concede this, and some even admit that league constrains union from becoming more spectator-friendly. Does anyone honestly believe that – if it wasn't for the existence of league – professional union would not have reduced to XIII-a-side by now?

So is union really friend or foe in this day and age? While we could not and should not forgive and forget the steps taken by union in the past to kill off rugby league, my deliberations lead me to no overall conclusions. In many areas the two codes are working together in commendable ways, often to mutual benefit. Clubs share facilities and do development work together, to the benefit of local communities and both codes. Players at top level in both codes genuinely respect each other. And at a personal level, through my membership of the RFL's Benevolent Fund Committee, I see, for example, the obvious advantages of having a welfare officer who deals with players who have been seriously injured in both league and union.

I have to accept that my personal view of union isn't based on what I see on the field of play. If I'm honest, for all its faults, I would far rather watch rugby union than association football and cricket. My view of rugby union stems from my continuing belief that it represents in sporting terms those divisions in our society about which I feel profoundly uncomfortable. My view stems, as well, from a perception that union's representation in our national media shapes a picture of league in the collective mind-set which is frequently and almost consistently negative.

Some would say it's all in the mind. But who was it said "Just because you're paranoid it doesn't mean to say they're not out to get you"?

Rugby league at Rugby School: Rugby Raiders opening match against Wolverhampton Wizards

Left: Ben Gronow, who kicked off the first international at Twickenham before switching to rugby league. Right: Martin Offiah, who played union for Bedford while playing league for London Broncos, before deciding to concentrate on league.
(Photos: Ben Gronow courtesy Robert Gate, Rugby School and Martin Offiah – Peter Lush)

Wigan versus Bath

Rugby league writer **Michael O'Hare** and former Bath RFC chairman **Richard Mawditt** reflect on two seminal contests.

Beware! There's a whole new sporting urban myth rearing its head. Over the past couple of years, especially following the only modestly successful rugby union conversion of Andy Farrell and a few of his ageing contemporaries, it has been suggested – usually by rugby union journalists or chief sports writers in the national newspapers — that the famous cross-code matches of 1996 between Wigan and Bath somehow saw both codes and both clubs emerge from the contest as equals. The latest person to toe this particular line is Nicholas Hobbes in his new book *Stumped: The sports fan's book of answers* where he baldly quotes the facts, suggesting that Wigan winning the league match and Bath the union match tells us nothing. This attitude has become common currency.

Leaving aside the fact that 82-6 to Wigan in the league match and 44-19 to Bath in the union game giving an aggregate of 101-50 is in no stretch of the imagination parity; and leaving aside the fact that had the union scoring system applied to tries in the league match the aggregate score would have been 117-51, the mere fact that both teams won their respective games does not reflect in any way what happened in them.

Here are the bare bones of what went on during that month of May 1996. Invited to bury the hatchet of 100 years of rugby animosity after union finally went professional in 1996, the English champions of both codes agreed to play each other under the opposition's set of rules, while midway between the two matches Wigan were also invited to compete at union's annual Middlesex Sevens.

First up was the league clash on 8 May at Maine Road, Manchester which saw Wigan run in 16 tries (six of them from Martin Offiah) in what looked like a training romp. Only three days later Wigan beat four famous rugby union clubs – Richmond by 48-5, Harlequins by 36-24, Leicester by 35-12 and Lawrence Dallaglio's Wasps by 38-15 – to win Twickenham's Middlesex Sevens in front of a virtual full-house of union supporters. However, the treble did not come off. Two weeks later on 25 May at Twickenham, Bath and rugby union heaved a huge sigh of relief by winning on home turf 44-19, but they knew it had been a close-run thing. Wigan scored two long-range tries in the final quarter through Craig Murdock, described by the *Independent*'s union writer Steve Bale as "better than anything Twickenham had witnessed all season", and seemed set to add more as they came to grips with the code.

Despite defeat in the 15-a-side union fixture, for league fans there were some delicious moments to savour over those heady couple of weeks. The most gratifying? My personal favourite was sitting in the club house at Hemel Hempstead RLFC as somebody in the Twickenham stands kept us updated over Wigan's progress in the Sevens, and the thrill when we realised they were going to win. But for those there or watching on TV there was even more pleasure. How about the young bloke with flushed cheeks, dressed in a dazzlingly striped school blazer despite being in his twenties, desperately waving his arms at the referee during Wigan's victory in the Sevens as he attempted to persuade the official to disallow a Martin Offiah try? And there was the sound of that same crowd being reduced to booing Wigan's victory... and then walking out early when it became clear who would win the competition. Or how about Jeremy Guscott crying off the Maine

Road match and then spending the next decade telling everybody what a dreadful game rugby league is? Or perhaps Wigan twice coming from three tries down to win their Sevens games? Or what about the union supporters bursting into "Swing Low, Sweet Chariot" when Wigan were losing at Twickenham? It was a red rag to a bull and it visibly kicked off Wigan's revival – *schadenfreude* is too mild a word to describe it. But in the end I'd settle for Sky Television's Mike Stephenson continually screaming "One point for every year of bigotry," as Wigan ran riot at Maine Road.

But 12 years on, it seems that month in May has taken on a completely different complexion. Surely, both codes came out of it equally, runs today's version of events.

Well, that wasn't what rugby union writers were saying at the time. Steve Bale wrote in *The Independent* "Some of us will never again look at rugby union skills in the same light after what we have seen over the past week from Wigan… hundreds of small object lessons that together formed a definitive rugby seminar. For union, it is a time of humility." His colleague Peter Corrigan in *The Independent on Sunday* wrote that in the league match "Wigan had possession for only two minutes longer than Bath… which proves that it's not the amount of ball you get but what you do with it." Mike Langley, who was later to pick the 1996 Middlesex Sevens as the most significant sporting moment he ever saw, writing in *The Observer* said "A match that shook the world? I'll give you four. All played in a few hours on Saturday 11 May." Paul Hayward wrote in *The Daily Telegraph*: "From here, it looked like rugby league won the series hands down. It is impossible to escape the conclusion that Wigan excel in the kind of skills all rugby followers most value: running and handling. They made union look like a game for farmers, and dazzled throughout." And cross-code international player turned journalist Jonathan Davies, a man who should know, added "Bath will have learned the more valuable lessons from the two games". "Whether the die-hards like it or not," added John Mason in the *Telegraph*, Wigan "demonstrated a host of superior skills currently absent from the union game, those common to both sports." Former England union international Paul Ackford was even more blunt in *The Sunday Telegraph*, stating "Wigan are better because they are better rugby players. Full stop."

And such was the cultural significance of the matches following 100 years of sporting and class animosity that they even made the political pages of the national newspapers. Perhaps the most unequivocal assessment of the outcomes came from *The Independent*'s leader page. "Wigan's players are fitter, more flexible, more skilful, better-disciplined and cleverer than their union counterparts. They think harder and more analytically about each ingredient of their game. As a result, they produce thrilling, entertaining, running rugby. Wigan's win was the triumph of an approach to sport. The financial feeding frenzy that is accompanying the professionalisation of rugby union completely misses the point: that it is still a thoroughly dull game. If investors in rugby union think that they will make money from this kind of second-rate entertainment, they should think again. Rugby union has a lot of stock-taking to do." And Richard Williams in *The Guardian* wrote: "Quite simply, Wigan annihilated Bath. And if the absent Jeremy Guscott could be persuaded to show in the course of an entire season as much invention as Wigan's mesmerising Jason Robinson showed in this one match, then he would be a far more effective player." "We're miles ahead," crowed *League Express*, and well it might because these do not sound like people talking of honours even.

In fact only Stephen Jones, league's bête noir from the *Sunday Times*, offered a dissenting voice. Talking of the Twickenham match under union rules he was compelled to write "One had to condemn the lengths Bath went to in pulling their punches to prevent a massacre". But even his inability to attribute anything positive to rugby league was virtually a ringing endorsement. Sour grapes can taste like a wry Sauternes when drunk from the cup of Stephen Jones. And, more pertinently, his comments were refuted from the front line. Jon Callard who scored Bath's only try in the league encounter said "Wigan were awesome. They are bordering on being god-like figures. It was quite devastating really. It was an object lesson on how to play rugby regardless of the code. I would like Bath to do one league training session a week. If we did, we would be a far better side."

But 12 years is a long time and those staking claims for parity between Wigan and Bath are either truly in ignorance of what happened back in 1996 or are fully aware that memories can play tricks. If you tell people often enough they may believe it. Fortunately we have newspaper reports and video with which to refresh our memories. So were honours even back in 1996?

You would have to argue that they were not. As any practitioner of either code knows, in union there are many things that a league team does not do: rucking, mauling, scrummaging and jumping for line outs are obvious examples. Yet when a union team turns its hand to league it should be able to cope with all the skills. League is packed with tackling, running, passing, scoring and touch kicking, all things that are part of a rugby union match. Yet when asked to put these skills into practice the union team fell short... by 82-6. On the other hand, Wigan – playing a game studded with what union people call the technical complexities – managed to give a passable performance and, when they played the curtailed seven-a-side version of the game, they actually beat union players at their own sport.

League Express saw things along these lines at the time. Describing the series in its editorial of 27 May 1996 it stated: "Most people would probably accept the simple premise that in a game of rugby, the winning team should normally be the one with the most rugby talent. At Twickenham [in the XV-a-side match against Bath] Wigan were undoubtedly the team with the most talent, and yet they lost largely because they were starved of possession. In contrast, [in the league game] at Maine Road, Bath had almost half the possession. And that tells us an important story. Rugby league is a game that cannot be won by a team attempting to starve its opponents of possession. To win a game of league requires commitment and creativity. To win a game of union a team can attempt to keep possession and lure its opponents into conceding penalties. The more talented team may therefore lose." Clearly there was not only disparity between Wigan and Bath, but one of the codes looked preferable to the other too.

And in the aftermath of the matches it became clear that other factors had been at work. In the league match Shaun Edwards has since revealed that Wigan were under a "gentleman's agreement" not to score more than 100 points, something he apparently learned at half-time after insisting before kick-off that "a lot will come down to how strictly it is refereed. We are not in the business of feeling sorry for anybody. I'm sure that when we play rugby union we will get penalised if we get on the wrong side of the rules and it should be the same for them." Despite Edwards's earlier assertion made in ignorance, Wigan played more than 20 minutes of the second half of the league game with only 12 men. They also agreed to allow Bath unlimited interchanges and swapped key players such as Henry Paul and Andy Farrell for junior ones, playing many of their remaining stars out of position. So much for Stephen Jones complaining that Bath had to pull their punches in the union game.

But more obviously than Bath were in the league match, Wigan were competitive at

Twickenham in the return game. It has since been suggested that Bath agreed to uncontested scrummages (although the Bath pack's constant swamping of the Wigan forwards after Wigan had heeled successfully would make one question in what way the scrums were supposedly uncontested). Nonetheless, on a good day for Wigan the result would have been far closer. One of Bath's tries was, predictably, a penalty try, another the result of the most wicked bounce of a rugby ball you are ever likely to see, that utterly flummoxed Martin Offiah. Wigan had two tries disallowed for players held up over the line and another for a forward pass at the end of a wonderful sweeping movement that replays later showed to be valid (and how often do they ever call play back in union for a forward pass?) By the end of the game Wigan had come to terms with the challenge and were scoring tries at will. Indeed, the referee blew time two minutes early presumably to preserve the dignity of the union team (who, incidentally and perplexingly, were presented with a trophy at the end of the match).

On a lucky day Wigan would have won the union game, on an average day they would have lost by only 10 or 12 points. And let's not forget that Wigan won the Middlesex Sevens in between the two cross-code matches, playing union teams under union rules. The notion that the two teams and two codes came out of the 1996 matches as equals is mere historical revisionism as anybody who was there or has the games on video can testify.

If one wishes to unearth a modern-day endorsement of the effect the matches had on both codes of rugby, one need only watch both codes today. Line-outs, rolling mauls and rucks have not been adopted wholesale by rugby league, but one only has to watch union to see the recycled possession – à la unlimited-tackle rugby league – running, passing and defensive-line structures to see which code had most to learn.

At the end of the day, however, the matches provided one more outcome – perhaps the most important after the century-long battle that waged between the codes. And that outcome was rapprochement, best summed up by Simon Barnes in *The Times*. "Allen Ginsberg once declared that the world's problems would be solved the instant Khrushchev and Kennedy got naked together. At last the two rugby codes got together in naked competition and discovered, shock-horror, that tearing lumps off each other was bloody good fun."

Yes, Wigan were better in that month of May in 1996, and no amount of modern day newspeak can change that fact. But at least they got the chance to prove it. Maybe even more than the chance to show rugby league to an unsuspecting nation, the greatest result was achieved off the pitch when a century of animosity was put to one side and rugby league was finally given the chance, which it grabbed with both hands, to show why it never deserved to be the 20th century's sporting pariah.*

* Quite frankly the author thinks this is a load of rubbish. Wigan thrashing Bath at League and then winning the Middlesex Sevens was the finest possible outcome, not rapprochement, but in the interest of détente he's pretending it wasn't.

A Soliloquy on Equality
It's that game again! *Wigan versus Bath - or was it Bath versus Wigan?*

As someone who has never read a *Rugby League Review* and has only witnessed one single league match (an international at Wembley Stadium one evening in the 1960s) I write with absolutely no authority on the merits or otherwise of who came off best from the now historic occasion when the champions of your game (Wigan before they were Warriors I believe) met in the challenge match against my club Bath (and certainly before they were Bath Rugby plc – just plain old Bath).

However, it seems that they - that is the admirable writer Michael O'Hare and, if I comprehend his article correctly, his *bete noire* Nicholas Hobbes, who has scribed much on 'that' game in his recent book (*Stumped: The Sports fan's book of answers*) are at it again with the temerity to say that honours were not as equal as I remember them.

Yes, the aggregate score did favour Wigan somewhat, yes Wigan did score more tries; and yes Martin Offiah; Jason Robinson; Henry Paul; Andy Farrell *et al* did turn up whereas Bath's Jeremy Guscott could not make it on the night in Manchester (or indeed later in the month at Twickers) but Bath never made the excuse that they had a pretty busy weekend before the match up at Maine Road on the Wednesday following the Cup Final on the previous Saturday. The Bath players did not even start learning the rules (not that they remembered them) of League until a training induction on the morning following the Saturday celebrations of winning the Cup again (for the 10th time for those readers unfamiliar with Bath's achievements); not the best time to learn a new trade bearing in mind they had to go to their various jobs on the next three days before bussing it up to Manchester on the Wednesday evening!

What the Bath players unfortunately did not realise (clearly an oversight by the 'amateur' coaching staff) was that every time that Wigan scored a try it was Wigan who kicked off (most unfair and a stupid rule was the common view, or at least by those players who had a view!), so to be out of position from a restart was an understatement. I would like to add that the Bath players were expecting more scrums so that they could win a few balls but unfortunately the less than sporting Wigan players did not make any mistakes so Bath never got the ball.

However, going back to who came out best, the Bath committee would like it to be known that they felt that Wigan certainly can take all the credit for providing the best beer and pies; better car parking; and over the two games Henry Paul's shorts were certainly cleaner than any of the Bath players (although Jerry Guscott would have run him close if he had got the right dates in his diary for the games).

As for the game at Twickenham, Bath were far more sporty when it came to allowing uncontested scrums (or something close anyway) and to give the Wigan supporters something to cheer a couple of gaps appeared in the Bath defence, not seen for many a game, to give some practice to the Wigan attack as they had shown in the Middlesex Sevens, which Bath felt they should not contest that year to allow others a chance. Wigan took full advantage of this friendly gesture.

So, to come back to Michael O'Hare's article I am afraid, as you can see, that although I do not understand all of his words such as "rapprochement" and "schadenfreude" (is that like getting excited on Wigan's Pier on a Saturday night?) I do get the distinct impression that even after all these years there is something of an inferiority complex by some who still feel the result of these historical games was not, shall we say, equally balanced.

I can, however, give everyone who has reached this point of reading this short riposte, that as far as the players and the committees of both these distinguished and champion clubs, honours were precisely even with both clubs sharing revenues of around £250,000, which enabled the clubs to reward the players at the top of their game a well deserved bonus to reflect the tremendous pleasure they had given their supporters and themselves over the many years of rugby (in both codes) achievement for which there can surely be no dispute.

Richard Mawditt
Past chairman, Bath Rugby Football Club

Editor's Note

In inviting Richard Mawditt to write the above article, and giving him Michael's contribution to read before he wrote his piece, we unintentionally created an uneven playing field for the two writers.

Michael submitted his article early in 2008. In June 2008, Peter Lush attended the first South African Sports History Conference at Stellenbosch University, where Richard Mawditt was the guest speaker. We had not planned to have a response to Michael's article from a Bath viewpoint, but having spoken to Richard at the conference, it seemed too good an opportunity to miss, as we believe that a rugby league publication has not published this view before. We welcome Richard's contribution which was done at short notice for us.

However, on reflection we should have treated both writers equally, and are giving Michael a couple of paragraphs below add to his original article. Maybe we should then have given Richard further space, but we had to stop somewhere…

"I accept the argument that Bath had no time to train for the cross-code league game, but then again, because rugby league is derided so frequently by the likes of Jeremy Guscott and the *Sunday Times*'s Stephen Jones as being a very simple, stripped-down version of the more cerebral union code, I'm surprised Bath needed to. There is no key element of a game of rugby league that a union player should not be able to cope with – running, passing, tackling, kicking and scoring tries should not be difficult for a union player to master.

My article essentially records what other people (not myself) wrote at the time of the 1996 cross-code matches. It is not a revision of history (that has come since with the notion that the games ended in a de facto tie), it is a verbatim account of reports written back then, much of it by union journalists, and no amount of counter-revisionism can alter it. To that end, the charge of an inferiority complex seems notably unfair."

Michael O'Hare

Rothmans reports

It is also interesting to recall what the *Rothmans Rugby League Yearbook* said about the games. On the league match, Wigan "swept aside Bath to race in for 16 tries" and "It was 16 minutes before Bath retained possession through a set of five tackles and their defence was frequently in disarray as they struggled to master the more intense demands of rugby league"

On the union game, "Bath gained some revenge with an emphatic defeat of Wigan under rugby union rules... Although they did not quite match Wigan's complete domination of the first game, they monopolised possession and steamrollered their way to a 25-0 interval lead." The report said that "The two tries by Craig Murdock were rated among the best ever seen at the famous old stadium, the half back finishing off attacks begun in Wigan's own in-goal area and maintained with breathtaking speed and support play for the full length of the field." In the interests of fairness, it also says that "Bath's seven tries included one superb score when they moved quickly round the blind side of a scrum for Jon Sleightholme to sprint 50 metres to the corner."

However, Wigan "never got near to mastering the rucks and mauls or incomprehensible laws of the game." Clearly Wigan could not adapt to the different forward play in union: "Recording of the rucks was abandoned after Bath won the first 20 and Wigan did not handle the ball in their opponents half until the 18th minute. They were literally trampled into the ground and looked completely bewildered when Bath were awarded a penalty try in the 15th minute for a scrum infringement."

Peter Lush

Henry Paul, pictured at the 2006 end of season celebrations at Harlequins RL. He played in both the matches between Wigan and Bath for Wigan, and then joined Bath on a short-term contract before resuming his rugby league career with Wigan. (Photo: Peter Lush)

OK..., it is boring!

Glyn Robbins reflects on what has happened to rugby union.

For years I've had to defend rugby union (my game, as opposed to 'Our Game') against those who say 'it's boring'. Sadly, I now have to admit they're right. Union has become sterile: locked in a formulaic style of play that reflects its new commercialism. But it's not just the game itself, but the players and attitudes around it that make me yearn for the glory days of the past!

Rugby league has to take some of the blame. The influence of league players and coaches and particularly defensive strategies, has created the type of situation graphically illustrated in the 2008 Grand Slam game between Wales and France. At times, almost the entire Welsh team (brilliantly coached by Shaun Edwards) was strung out in a defensive line across the width of the pitch. The rather nonplussed French forwards clearly didn't know what to do and resorted to a combination of slow, ineffective short drives and aimless kicking. But where had I seen this before? Oh yes, in the World Cup Final and virtually all the games that England have played in the last 12 months.

It's a strange irony that the England team was loudly celebrated for its World Cup performance. Terms like 'gritty and determined" used to be euphemisms for the kind of 'stuff it up your jumper' rugby that turned people off. But now rugby union is a brand and the most important selling feature is winning. It used to be that only people who had played the game could appreciate the beauty of a 15 yard rolling maul! But the new type of passive television rugby union spectator only focuses on the final product. Who cares if you run the ball from one end of the field to the other, it's still only five points. The attritional, overly tactical, risk-averse game has become the norm in big international matches and with the excessive substitutions and leviathan size of the players, it is increasingly reminiscent of American football – but gridiron still fills huge stadiums so the marketing people are happy.

Although I've never admitted it publicly, league is less stifled by this form of hyper-organised defense because it's generally a more fluid game, with no line-outs and scrums that are barely worthy of the name, but these odd traditions have always been intrinsic features of union. Set-pieces were also part of democratizing the game - for players like me, who had very little skill with the ball, but were prepared to graft to win it for others. Now these institutions are under threat. The union scrum has followed league by allowing the ball to be fed into the second row's feet, while line-outs have become some sort of circus act.

The demise of the set-piece also reflects the loss of a certain kind of rugby union player. Not only is the character of union being lost, but also the characters. The likes of Colin Smart, Geoff Probyn, Gareth Chilcott and other specialist props, who's main function was to secure the scrum, won't be seen again. It's not that they weren't capable of being the all-round athletes demanded by the modern game, it just didn't fit with their lifestyle. I recall Dean Richards saying that when Clive Woodward gave all the England payers a rowing machine, he put his in the garage and the only person who used it was his wife. Richards was also known for having a quiet cup of tea before a game, just as others were getting into high-energy drinks and growling a lot. Such stories can become a bit romaticised, but that's the point. There was something interesting about these players. They had jobs, families and did other things, besides being exceptionally good at rugby. As Kipling didn't say, 'what do they know of rugby who only rugby know?' Sadly, the small-world view of current players is also demonstrated in their post-match interviews where the football school of cliché is in full session. But as with footballers, it isn't that these men are stupid or inarticulate, it's that they have been coached to speak as they've been coached to play – don't give anything away or do anything that isn't in the plan.

To watch a game of international rugby union from the 1970s or 1980s, it's almost impossible to believe it's the same game. Having been bored rigid by Wales versus France 2008, I went to Youtube and called up Scotland versus Wales from 1971. What a game. There are some big men on both teams and all of the players would have been just as capable of putting on two stone of muscle as today's generation, but they look weedy by comparison. OK, the line outs are a mess and some of the players are blowing hard, but the running, handling and vision are on a par with anything we see today and there's a spirit of adventure that died with the advent of professionalism.

I can accept that rugby union at the highest level has changed and in some ways, for the good. As a spectator, you don't experience the same highs as from some of the great games and players of the past, but you don't get the same lows either. The days when two sets of forwards could slog it out in the mud for 80 minutes have gone. But as a former-playing colleague of mine once said 'who cares if it's entertaining, the main thing is that the players enjoy it.' This has also become an old fashioned point of view. But what I find harder to accept is that the attitudes of professionalism at the top have permeated down to all levels of the game. When I last played, about five years ago, it was at what I think was literally the lowest level of first team rugby, but my club was still fixated with the importance of league games and even talked about 'resting' players for what they saw as less important fixtures. Some of the teams we played were highly organised (we weren't!), with several coaches, fancy drinking bottles, flashy track-suits and complicated moves that would have been very impressive if they'd been able to catch! It all made me feel very old. When I started playing seriously, there were no leagues – every game was as important (or otherwise) as the next. I remember when merit tables were first introduced: they were almost like a guilty secret and disapproved of in some quarters almost as much as being paid to play – the ultimate sin! Many smaller clubs have struggled to survive under the self-imposed pressure of the league system. Two that I used to play for have folded and many that used to run three or more teams now struggle to put out two.

Professionalism has done a lot of damage to rugby union, both in terms of the style of play but also the spirit of the game. My first love was football, but I now have virtually no interest in a sport that is dominated by commercialism at the expense of values. I worry that I will become equally alienated from union. Perhaps rugby league is fortunate. It got its professional convulsions over with long ago and has established itself in a niche market. That's not intended as a back-handed compliment. I don't think league will ever grow beyond its heartland and for the good of the game, I don't think it should.

Editor's note: As a rugby union follower, Glyn would not be aware that rugby league has grown considerably beyond its original 'heartlands' and shows every sign of continuing to do so.

'That's entertainment' says David Watkins

Rugby union should be studying rugby league's recent history. That's the claim made by Newport Gwent Dragons president David Watkins MBE.

And the 66-year-old should know what he is talking about because among a string of many records and honours he holds in both codes of rugby, he is still the only man to have captained both the British Lions Rugby Union team and the Great Britain Rugby League side.

Speaking frankly Watkins said: "Union would do well to see what happened in league during the 1950s and 1960s because that's the state of affairs we have in union at the moment. Back in the 1950s and 1960s rugby league was plagued by negative play when the best sides could dominate games by recruiting big players who could hold the ball for long periods and simply grind the opposition into the mud.

Take a look at rugby union today and what do you see? The top sides signing up the best players and able to hold the ball for long periods which stifles open play and crushes their opposition.

Don't misunderstand me, rugby union has come a long way in a very short space of time but when it comes to producing fast, flowing, fluid rugby in most of their games then rugby league is still out in front."

And Watkins added: "Because rugby league has successfully addressed the issue of having possession of the ball dominated so easily their players are brought up to develop their attacking, open play skills," says Watkins. "It's a far more colourful game while union still has problems behind the scrummage that we need to address. I watch league on the television and their games continue to deliver high quality of entertainment because it's not so easy for one team to dominate another in any of their games".

Watkins believes that union has shown that it can hit the heights and that was shown when Wales won the Six Nations Grand Slam this year. He said: "We've just got to allow our players to show what they can do by giving both sides in any game a fair share of the ball. As it is at the moment any club with a huge pack of forwards can completely shut out the opposition."

Watkins, who besides his rugby union position is an official patron of Wales Rugby League, said: "I think the rugby league should be applauded for their decision to stage 'Millennium Magic' [2008] in Wales. The sport never has it easy in Wales and this year they've had to contend with Wales winning the Grand Slam and the Triple Crown. But perhaps they can benefit from the fact that so many grass root Welsh rugby supporters have not been able to see as much top rugby this year. It's a fact of life that there is a section of the community who are attracted by success. They are the folk who want to be associated with a winning team and be seen at all the top events.

And then of course there is always the increasingly important corporate hospitality market. Both those factors make it harder for the ordinary rugby supporters to see the best action. It prices them out of the big, important matches.

By making ticket prices affordable and offering so many packages like all-day tickets or weekend tickets the Rugby League have made 'Millennium Magic' accessible to everybody."

This article is taken from an RFL press release prior to the 2008 Millennium Magic weekend, and we would like to thank the RFL for permission to use it.

Book review: *London's Oldest Rugby Clubs*
by Dick Tyson

The history of our clubs has so often been ignored and undervalued in the Super League era that it almost feels like a duty to keep linking rugby league's past to the current day.

The publication of a wonderful new book has further underlined that need. *London's Oldest Rugby Clubs* is a beautifully-produced illustrated history by Dick Tyson, a Saracens man, who has spent most of this millennium travelling around the capital's rugby union grounds unearthing a magical trove of trivia and treasure, collating it in a book as aesthetically pleasing as any sports book I have ever read.

You may wonder why such a book features in *Rugby League Review*. Well, not only is Tyson an Eddie Waring fan of old but his tome would be appreciated by any rugby fan and particularly those in the capital.

By examining the roots of the 100 oldest clubs, Tyson inadvertently covers the period up to 1895 when we were all in this together. A period of which, to my chagrin, many rugby league fans are ignorant or dismissive. *Rothmans Rugby League Yearbooks* of the 1980s stated foundation dates for a whole string of clubs as 1895 when in fact they had been going strong for 10, 20 or, in Hull FC's case, 30 years before the formation of the Northern Union.

Of course, no London rugby league club existed in the nineteenth century, but Tyson's wonderful array of artefacts come from a string of grounds which have hosted League. I have personally seen League played at Blackheath (founded 1858), Richmond (1861), Streatham-Croydon (1882), Saracens (1876), the University College School in Cricklewood (where I saw the Kiwis train a couple of years ago) and, of course, Harlequins at The Stoop.

Among the nuggets of trivia within the book, I have learned that, after changing their name from Hampstead FC, Harlequins spent their first season — 1869-70 — at Clissold Park in Stoke Newington. I wonder if the tree planted there in memory of my late sister-in-law (whose grandfather played for Saracens) would have been behind the sticks.

I also never knew that Martin Offiah's old club, Rosslyn Park, which has staged London amateur rugby league finals in the past, is named after a private garden in Hampstead, not the area on the South Circular where they now play, or that Saracens' home ground was once behind the Cherry Tree pub in Southgate Green, where I enjoy end of term drinks.

Tyson also tells the tale of Polytechnic FC and the Chiswick ground they shared with Fulham RLFC, several of whose players graduated from West London Institute, now part of Brunel University. Rugby was first played at Borough Road College, as it was then known, in 1891, when rugby was not league or union but just 'rugby football'.

London's Oldest Rugby Clubs highlights how extraordinarily high-brow were the founders of most of these teams: public schoolboys, doctors and majors abound. But this class barrier was not restricted to the capital. As rugby league historian Tony Collins has explained in his majestic works, 'the split' was driven by class, not geography: Hull FC were founded by graduates of Rugby School, Cheltenham College and St Peter's; Barrow by Lancaster Grammar School old boys. There are links in London with 'our clubs', too. For example, Halifax RLFC was the lovechild of Tom Scarborough from Mill Hill School, whose Old Boys rugby club was formed in 1879 and is still going today.

Despite their obvious upper and middle-class roots, just like the Northern Union clubs in the 19th century and our amateur clubs in the 20th, the vast majority of London's first rugby clubs were formed over liquid refreshments and spent their early years changing in pubs and playing on park pitches. Unlike their rugby league counterparts though, many were not community-entrenched but were social clubs for a particular group. They were nomads. Their only commitment was to the old boys, medics or military men of which their membership was comprised, therefore they could play anywhere in London: and the likes of Harlequins, Wasps and Saracens did – and still do.

Although most of our now traditional major rugby league clubs were already up and running by the 1890s – many drawing five-figure crowds, thus forcing the professionalism issue – there were so many rugby clubs in London there was no need for even the more adventurous capital-based clubs to leave the south-east in search of challenging fixtures. This resulted in little interaction between what became established league and union clubs prior to the 1895 split. The lack of transport also made long trips arduous and anyone bar the aristocracy required the Christmas or Easter holidays to have sufficient time to travel to another part of the country to play rugby.

Most famously, W.P. Carpmael's County and International Team did just that at Easter 1890, going on a Yorkshire tour so successful that when they returned to London he formally christened them the Barbarian Football Club. The Barbarians returned north on their inaugural official expedition at Christmas 1890 and again at Easter 1893 before the split ended such adventures.

It was far more likely that the gentlemen of London clubs would venture north than the working man take unpaid leave to head south to play. There were exceptions: the original Bradford club toured the south, playing at Cambridge University in 1884 and returning two years later, taking in games with Oxford and Marlborough Nomads at Blackheath along the way.

My overwhelming reaction to *London's Oldest Rugby Clubs* is that our game desperately needs to continue to record its history such a tome. We pay lip service to our past but treasure so little of it. We still have no yearbook with even current players' details. We have a BARLA handbook with no historical content whatsoever. League historians have to plunder second-hand book shops and surf the net. More work remains to be done, including on the early links between the clubs that joined the Northern Union and those that stayed with the Rugby Union.

Published in 2008 by JJG publishing at £20 (available for less on Amazon).
ISBN: 978-1899163861

Gavin Willacy

Rugby league in Cuba

Phil Melling reports on his work in trying to establish rugby league in Cuba.

Rugby league isn't played on the island of Cuba but there is good reason to believe that in the near future it might be. Jamaica is 90 miles away and over the past six years under the inspirational guidance of Paul Morris Jamaican rugby league has been a story of unparalleled success. Paul was a visionary and it was always his belief that Cuba, Jamaica and the Dominican Republic should form their own West Indies Federation and alongside the United States create an important centre of rugby league influence with World Cup status.

Paul Morris was a breath of fresh air in the development of rugby league and one of the great pioneering figures. His is a remarkable story. He came from the West Country and was related to the Parfitts, one of the biggest names in Bath rugby union. Paul was also from rugby union until he got hooked on rugby league, retiring to Jamaica where he saw what rugby league had to offer. Paul was always quick on the uptake. You never once needed to convince him that the idea of introducing rugby league to Cuba was worth pursuing. He shared my enthusiasm as well as offering a reassuring voice whenever I struggled to persuade people in rugby league development circles that a Cuban initiative was a viable one. That was always the hardest part, trying to explain to people in the UK that I wasn't just another of those passing gadflies with no idea about development needs. I had thought that 30 years of rugby league development work at all levels in South Wales might count for something, but it didn't. For a year at least, I don't think any of my ideas were taken that seriously. During that period Paul was one of the few people who listened with enthusiasm. I remember telling him about one telephone call in particular when I was asked by a league appointee why I was interested in Cuba and what my angle was and what was I looking for? It did cross my mind to talk about Hemingway and Santeria and British Academy and Leverhulme research fellowships and 10 years work on the island, but I thought better of it, knowing full well the reaction I would get. Paul wasn't interested in where I was coming from, nor was Geoff Lee or my old colleague Tony Collins or Dave Hadfield, all of whom were excited by the possibilities of what might happen if the Cubans got their teeth into our game.

Che Guevara

And there was every possibility of that happening. Che Guevara, the poster hero of the Cuban revolution, was a scrum-half from Argentina who had headed north out of Buenos Aires. He had never quite made it to Wigan and his dairies to my knowledge don't record his opinion of Brian Nordgren's speed off the mark or Jackie Broome's passing abilities. But none of this mattered. Rugby league was a story of class revolution in the industrial communities of the north of England and it was bound to appeal to the political and sporting sensibilities of the Cubans.

Over the years I had taken whatever I could get my hands on, including videos, footballs, books and magazines. I hadn't been able to take the rules of the game in Spanish because they didn't exist. I thought this a bit strange given the desire of rugby league to be taken seriously as an international sport. But there it was and there was nothing I could do about it and in any case there were compensations.

Before he died in the early summer of 2008 Paul Morris promised he would do whatever he could to support the development of rugby league in Cuba. He and his wife, Sue, had booked to fly out and meet me in Havana for a series of meetings with Cuban sports officials. In the event, Paul was unable to attend, but the meetings went ahead nonetheless at the sports institute of Manuel Fajado.

Sporting excellence

Manuel Fajado is a centre of sporting and educational excellence on the north side of Havana and the meetings there had been arranged by a colleague, Osmar Rodriguez, whose story is told by Dave Hadfield in the February 2008 edition of *Rugby League World*. I met with the Dean of the college and the proposals I made were received with enthusiasm. Bureaucracy can sometimes be an enormous hurdle in Cuba and a major impediment in holding up new initiatives. Patience is the key to success, especially so if political vetting has not taken place at the appropriate level. In this case there was room for genuine optimism that a linkage between Manuel Fajado and a similar institution in the United Kingdom might come into being to the benefit of rugby league. This is something we are now working on.

Rugby league is still well behind rugby union which is played throughout the island in the major cities and regions. The Cuban Rugby Union is an associate member of the International Board and falls under the aegis of the French Rugby Union. On my last visit I attended a training session of the local, open-age rugby union club in Havana. I also spoke with the French Rugby Union delegate who was on a working holiday in the capital. He was from Toulouse and a nice enough guy and very straight talking about the standards and styles of rugby union play on the island. According to him it was typically Latin, excitable, slightly disorganised and prone to indiscipline. The session I watched was ok but nothing to write home about and a lot of the players did not seem fit, a huge contrast to the students at Manuel Fajado who are all physical education specialists and very athletic.

Manuel Fajado is the leading tertiary institution for students in Havana who are selected for their sporting abilities. It lies at the top of a pyramid structure of sports colleges and is responsible for all new policy initiatives adopted by colleges throughout the country. At every sports college in Cuba students choose to specialise from a menu of different sports, in which Cuba is world famous – athletics, boxing, wrestling, baseball, etc. Sports that are included on the curriculum are taught to the community by graduate students who work as teachers at the primary and secondary levels. Centres of excellence therefore are able to determine not only the type of sport Cuban children are taught, they also maintain standards of excellence by offering sports science courses to those students who have demonstrated a high level of expertise whilst still at school. If rugby league were chosen as a curriculum sport, even at a minor level, there would be every likelihood that it would become dispersed throughout the island when students, on graduation, returned to their home communities taking their skills with them.

This is a particularly fortuitous time in Cuban history. We have entered the era of Raoul Castro. We are seeing the emergence of a new kind of openness in which sports institutions like Manuel Fajado are being asked to internationalise their agendas and make themselves more accessible to the outside world. The advantage of a link up across a range of sports, including rugby league, with a college of sporting excellence in the United Kingdom – Leeds Metropolitan comes to mind – brings with it enormous political and practical advantages. In Cuba, furthermore, there appears to be a genuine willingness to collaborate in a programme of joint sporting excellence with a UK institution. Rugby league could feature prominently in this and there is no reason why in the near future Jamaica could not have its closest neighbour playing rugby league. Leeds Metropolitan has already shown an interest in becoming a partner of Manuel Fajado. The benefits in prestige and publicity are self evident, as they would be to other colleges who might wish to collaborate and enter into consortium agreements.

Cuba remains a tough nut to crack. It operates under a communist system which means that a lot of people are unable to travel outside the country without special dispensation or financial support. It has already taken a long time to travel a short distance but in a country where sport is of huge importance in the revolutionary ethos rugby league might one day make its own distinctive contribution.

Get rid of the video referee

David Ballheimer examines the role of technology in match decision making.

I am well aware that my wish will not come to fruition because the broadcasters have invested too much time and money in the technology just to give up on it. But, before I go any further, I must stress that my stance has nothing to do video referees as such; it is the imperfection of the system currently employed in this, and most other sports. Once a video referee system – in any sport – is proved to be infallible, then bring it on.

As far as rugby league is concerned, I have are four areas of concern with the current system: the laws, the decisions, the timings and the officials. This is not intended to be a witch-hunt against individuals or teams, so while I will quote situations and some people, no names will be mentioned.

We'll start with the laws, because that is easiest one. Quite simply, rugby league is currently played with two sets of laws: one set of laws for games shown live or tape-delayed on television and those played without live camera feed. The former matches have video referees and no in-goal judges; the remainder have in-goal judges and no video technology. The upshot of this that the high-profile, championship-chasing clubs get more matches on television, ergo more games with the eye in the sky. Either every game has to have a video referee, or none should. The ludicrous situation that only Super League refs can be video refs is merely a way of ensuring that their full-time status is utilised more fully; recently retired referees are perfectly capable of doing the job too.

Next is the decision-making process, which is in three parts. I have watched a number of sports where video technology is routinely used to decide incidents (cricket, tennis, both codes of rugby, American football and ice hockey to name but six) and in none of them is the system foolproof. Quite simply, there are times when even a video camera cannot show for certain whether a ball was caught or touched or hit the ground, the line was broken or crossed, etc. Even when technology becomes so advanced that cameras have a 360 degree angle of sight with limitless height, some decisions still will be impossible to make with complete certainty, and that is because there will be players inadvertently getting in the way of the camera's line of sight.

The second part is, if anything, more important than the first. If the video referee cannot make a decision because the camera angles available to him are inconclusive, this official must not make a decision. There is nothing wrong for the eye in the sky to say, "Sorry, there is no conclusive evidence one way or the other. Ref's or Ump's call." At that point the decision must go back down to the officials on the field. The game is played by humans, and refereed by them too. If they make a mistake, so be it. Let's face it most players make more mistakes in a game than the match officials. If the referee awards a try because of benefit of doubt, that is acceptable; the video referee being asked to make a decision is always called upon because there is an element of doubt.

If a referee makes a mistake, it is excusable because he or she may not have been in the best position to make the call or got incorrect information from a touch judge or assistant. When – and there have been too many cases in the last 18 months – the video referee makes a wrong call it is utterly unforgivable. I will accept 100 wrong ref's calls before I will countenance a single error from the eye upstairs. He has no excuse, ever.

The last part of this argument starts with the acceptance that video evidence will not judge forward passes, no matter how blatant they might be. Why is this? We are told that the camera angles are not perfect for this decision. Why then are these same unreliable cameras used to determine the validity of a try? What is becoming clear as players get more and more used to the eye in the sky, is their ability to win decisions. The obstruction play is now so widespread and so open to different interpretations that one coach last season stated, "I no longer know what is a try and what isn't." Dummy runs and missed passes are part of the beauty of rugby but now players run out of the defensive line to initiate contact with a dummy runner, fall to the ground and, if a try is conceded, appeal to the referee to go to the video referee. In a number of cases over the last couple of seasons I have seen wily defenders save tries with this deception. This becomes even more confusing when different referees have different interpretations of the same rule and the call on the field would be different to the one in the box with the same evidence.

Next we turn to time and this is where we have to remember that sport is an entertainment. About a dozen years ago, I wrote a match report where I found the referee's repeated visits to the eye in the sky becoming tiresome. I also noted that the video referee had made at least one decision that could not have been made with the naked eye. Referees are pressured from above, when doing televised matches, to go to the video referee whenever there is a scintilla of doubt. Such is the speed of the game today, it means that practically every score now can be subject to scrutiny. Not only does this take away the spontaneity of a try and the celebration, it slows everything down. This means that what seems an obvious score now takes a minute or longer to be confirmed. Half a dozen referrals in a half will probably result in the period lasting the best part of 50 minutes, bringing ever closer the concept of an 80 minute game lasting two hours.

This can be rectified by a rule that no video referee referral will last more than 90 seconds; if the man upstairs can't make a decision in that time – except in the event of a technology mishap – the decision must, automatically, revert to the referee on the pitch. One decision last season was reached after two minutes and 45 seconds – and the consensus around the ground and on the pitch was decision, when it eventually came, was the wrong one!

I would also like, when decisions are being reviewed, that the video referee has a choice of camera angles and not only those provided by the broadcaster. The stadium screen should be blank while the decision is being reviewed because it is possible for the man upstairs to be influenced by the crowd reaction. In American football, the video referee has a choice of cameras, not only from the broadcaster but also from the stadium, and the match referee views all the available angles under a hood, where he communicates with his colleague. While fans get to watch the television angles, it is quite possible indisputable evidence is found from another camera. It occasionally adds to the tension, but incorrect decisions are still made and that is the bottom line.

Finally, we come to the officials themselves. Not the video referees, but the men on the ground. I have spoken with a number of them over the years and more than one has said that they have/had their own opinions on decisions sent to the video official and one reckoned that in half a dozen years, he would have got one call wrong. Put this into perspective: if this referee officiated in 15 matches per season with the video referee, and deferred on three decisions per game, it meant he would have got one scoring decision wrong out of 270. I'll take a 99.63 percent accuracy rate from any referee or umpire in any sport.

It appears that more and more decisions are being referred upstairs by the men in the middle and I think I know the reason. I believe that because they know that any close decisions will be referred to a video referee, subconsciously, they don't go at full speed to be in a perfect position to see the ball grounding. When I was training to be an umpire in another sport, it was repeated ad nauseam that hustling to get into position was absolutely vital. If you are in the right place – the thinking goes – it is easier to make the correct decision and players are less likely to dispute your call.

On the opening weekend of the 2006 Super League season, at the end of a blowout, I watched one of the senior referees trot behind the posts and thus be out of position as the ball was grounded. Had he run to the correct position, he would have seen the ball being grounded and a meaningless try would not have needed video referee approval, something which arrived within about 15 seconds of its referral.

As I wrote at the start of this piece, this is not Luddite thinking; it is a matter of wanting the system to be perfect and if we can't have a perfect system, I'd rather not have it at all.

The Co-operative National Leagues: The Future

Ray Warburton looks at the future for the professional game outside Super League.

At last the decision has been made and most peoples' favourites, Salford City Reds and Celtic Crusaders, have been selected to play in the Super League in 2009. It is a bit of a surprise that both Wakefield Trinity Wildcats and Castleford Tigers have both been given franchises for 2009 as they are geographically very close together, their new grounds are still several years away and it perpetuates the imbalance between the number of clubs from Lancashire and Yorkshire in the Super League. In 2008 Yorkshire had seven clubs in Super League to Lancashire's three; it would therefore have made more sense to select Widnes instead of either Castleford or Wakefield for Super League next season. This would have resulted in six Yorkshire clubs and five Lancashire clubs out of 14 in Super League.

The decision to abandon promotion and relegation in future will have a major effect on attendances in Super League as meaningless matches have little crowd appeal. In the last two seasons, especially towards the end of the season, a large number of the exciting matches were relegation battles; it is hard to believe that Sky are happy to be without these exciting games in the future. Perhaps a compromise could be that promotion and relegation be suspended for three seasons so that the more ambitious National League clubs could reach the required standards.

Now that the decision has finally been made it is very important that the National League clubs stop whinging, think positively and treat this situation as an opportunity not a disaster. For clubs to say that there is no future if they are not in Super League and 'go for broke' trying to get in would be disastrous for them, the National League and the game in general. They should have a positive and optimistic attitude and start planning for the future now.

This future should be a full-time National League 1 (or whatever it may be called), starting in 2010, consisting of a geographic cross-section of clubs which meet strict criteria with regards to finances, ground and many other off-field activities. The latter includes a commercial department which should actively promote and market the club throughout the year and the club should be an active and essential part of the community. The long term aim should be that in seven years they will be able to match Super League clubs in terms of playing standards, grounds and crowds; it is therefore important that only clubs who meet the demanding criteria are selected for this new league. This objective to reach Super League standards in seven years may be a little over-ambitious, but if you don't aim high you often get nowhere.

When forming this new full-time professional league there should be no limit to the number of clubs accepted as there will be play-offs at the end of the season, but because of the high standards demanded it is unlikely that there will be more than 12 clubs in the first season; a minimum of 10 clubs would be needed to make the league viable. Ideally, as stated earlier, there should be a geographical spread of clubs as this will make the new competition more attractive to the national media, in particular national television.

Standards

Before naming the possible new clubs which may comprise the new league, the strict standards expected should be stated in more detail:-
1) Each club should be able to get crowds of 3,000 to 3,500 on average in the first season. Exact crowds would of course depend on performance on the field. This is achievable in view of the improved facilities and the more professional marketing of the new league and the individual clubs.
2) A ground capacity of 7,000 would be initially acceptable, mainly under cover and with some standing areas if possible. There should also be the potential to increase capacity to at least 12,000, but preferably 15,000 in seven years. Many of the clubs joining the new league will already have a capacity of over 10,000 and the others will have no trouble reaching this standard within seven years. Standing areas are important as this gives rugby league its unique atmosphere; an atmosphere difficult to attain in all-seater stadia. Similarly, this unique atmosphere is lost in grounds with running tracks round the perimeter of the playing area, so hopefully most grounds will not have this feature. There should, of course, be adequate corporate facilities and they should also be able to meet the needs of press, radio and television.
3) All clubs must have appropriate staff in place to promote and market the club effectively; one person's main responsibility should be for the sale of season tickets as this brings money up front and fans are more likely to attend the games if they are season ticket holders. The club will also have these fans' names and addresses, including e-mail addresses, for marketing opportunities. The club should be an active part of the local community, forging links with schools, colleges and local amateur teams. The ground should, if possible, have community amenities such as a social club, fitness centre and teaching facilities. Basically this means that the club is an essential and desirable part of local life. A good example of a club who have done this, and continue to work hard, is Warrington, and this has been reflected in their crowds.
4) Each club should pay a fixed sum of several thousand pounds a year to the league so the latter can employ professional companies to deal with promotion, marketing and publicity; including negotiating television deals. Some clubs may be reluctant to contribute, but this will definitely be money well spent.
5) The new league will need a salary cap and £800,000 in the first year seems reasonable, rising to £2,000,000 after seven years.
6) The issue of overseas players needs to be addressed. The number of Australian and New Zealand players should be limited to two, or possibly three, per club. A number of players from developing countries (including France for up to three years), should also be allowed, say four per club. By doing this it would help develop the game in countries such as Ireland, Morocco, Samoa and others. This would also increase the pool of players available to National League One clubs.

My suggestions for the new National League 1 would be: Widnes Vikings, Whitehaven, Halifax, Leigh, Sheffield Eagles, Doncaster, Oldham, Featherstone Rovers and Barrow. Other possibilities are a Welsh side, another French team, a London team, Dewsbury or Batley and possibly a team from Dublin. Some of these clubs would need to do quite a lot of work on their grounds in order to meet the minimum standards, in particular those from Cumbria, but it is very important that this rugby league hotbed has two teams in this new league. Sheffield Eagles, as a big city club with potential, are in,

Keighley Cougars versus Celtic Crusaders, NL2 in 2006 (Photo: Peter Lush)

although their ground has a running track and no standing areas. Doncaster has a new ground and are ambitious in spite of recent problems.

Of the clubs who are not in the new league initially; Rochdale have a good ground but a small fan base and little potential, York have crowd potential but problems with their ground and not owning it is a big drawback for many reasons. Swinton, a famous old club, don't own a ground, presently play on a rugby union ground with only one stand and only have a small nucleus of fans. Considering Cougar mania of about 16 years ago, it is a shame Keighley Cougars cannot be included, but the biggest disappointment of all is Hunslet Hawks. Here is a famous old big city club, situated in a rugby league area, with several amateur clubs within a short distance yet look at the situation they are in at present. Let us hope that the people currently trying to save the club, and ultimately bring back some degree of success, get the support of local people and the backing of some people with money to make the job a bit easier.

The clubs suggested for this new league give rise to several local derbies, including Sheffield Eagles versus Doncaster, Whitehaven versus Barrow and Widnes versus Leigh. The addition of several clubs from outside the traditional areas hopefully means that the television companies, including those from Wales, France and possibly Ireland will be interested in covering matches in the new league. Although it may be expensive, it would be money well spent to get professional companies to negotiate television contracts and to promote and market this new league.

With regard to the promotion and marketing of the clubs; Super League clubs have shown, rather belatedly in many cases, that if you do the right things, crowds will increase, even though they are out of the national media spotlight. In the last 10 years several clubs have doubled their attendances, including Warrington Wolves, Hull FC and Huddersfield Giants; there is no reason why clubs in the new National League cannot do the same if they do the right things. Cougar mania was mentioned earlier and during this time Keighley Cougars increased their crowds from 400 to 4,000 in three years with no help from the national media. This shows what can be achieved if the right things are done, with a lot of hard work. Due to their work they put in local community, especially the schools, they managed to take nearly 1,000 school children in a fleet of coaches to a Wembley test match between Great Britain and Australia; quite an amazing feat.

To sum up: the National League 1 should become full time starting in 2010. It is very important that the clubs have a confident and positive attitude and they work together with all the other interested parties to bring this ambition to fruition. Even if promotion and relegation are resumed after three seasons, or the RFL's latest thinking on the subject are approved by the present members of Super League, the National League clubs should still aim to reach Super League standards within seven years. If this could be achieved, then after each League's Grand Final, the winners could play a 'Super Bowl' for want of a better term, to determine the ultimate champions. Unlike the Grand Finals and the Challenge Cup Final this Super Bowl could be played at a different venue every year so that the game would be promoted around the country and possibly in venues on the European mainland such as Barcelona.

Finally the message to all probable National League 1 clubs is be to positive, professional and put in the hard work as there is a vibrant full-time future for your league, it is in your own hands.

National League 2

There will be some professional clubs are never likely to be full-time and these clubs will form the basis of a new National League 2. A few clubs in this league may still aspire to become full-time but this would take a lot of effort and considerable amounts of money, especially as the fan base of the majority of the clubs is just a few hundred. Famous old clubs such as Swinton and Hunslet, both mentioned earlier, have lost generations of fans and it seems highly unlikely that they will ever compete at the top level of the game again.

The future of some clubs, for example Gateshead, may be to ground-share, in Gateshead's case with Newcastle Falcons rugby union club, which would give them a good ground and without the atmosphere-killing running track which spoils their present one. Other clubs which may be able to ground-share include York, Workington and London Skolars; in the latter's case this is very important as another viable professional club in London is urgently required.

A major criticism of most clubs presently in National League 2 is a total absence of promotion and marketing by the individual clubs; if it is happening then it is certainly not very successful. One club's sole marketing ploy was for the chairman to say "If you don't support us we will go bust." This was almost certainly true but unfortunately, in this modern age, a little more than this is required. It is quite appalling that at least six clubs presently in this league only have a nucleus of 300-400 supporters when many amateur clubs have crowds far bigger than this, without the advantage of being professional.

As this is a professional league each club should appoint a full-time commercial manger to promote and market the club: their many duties would include advertising, community work, selling season tickets, getting sponsors and increasing corporate involvement. Any club that thinks they cannot afford to employ such a person should realise they cannot afford not to. The aim of the National League 2 should be to get average crowds of 1,300 to 1,500 with those clubs at the top getting around 2,000. These figures are achievable if the clubs act professionally and put in the hard work. Clubs that can't get this level of support have no chance of becoming full-time in the future unless they are lucky enough to get a millionaire backer.

There is a future for a healthy part-time National League 2 and hopefully it can be expanded with some of the new clubs coming from outside the heartlands of the game. It is from these newer clubs that future full-time members of the higher leagues are likely to come rather than the old established clubs presently in this league. The league should be open to all clubs as long as they meet the necessary standards, both on and off the field, and two divisions could be formed if numbers warrant it. It would seem sensible if the two divisions were split geographically so that there would be more derby games and would cut down on travelling expenses. Finally as said earlier about National League 1 clubs, there is a future and it's in your own hands.

The rugby league press

Peter Lush considers the rugby league trade press, and **Gary Slater** looks at 'blogging' and rugby league on the internet.

What our papers say

There have been complaints for many years from rugby league supporters about the limited coverage of our sport in the national newspapers and media. Books have even been written about this. However, we very rarely look at our own media with a critical eye. Now that London League Publications Ltd is no longer a magazine publisher, and we are not a 'competitor' in this area of publishing, I think it is time for an article that looks at how the 'trade press' covers the game. This is a purely personal point of view, written by someone who reads a daily paper, *The Guardian*, which covers the game well with match reports and some news (although I would like more!), but does not read a local paper that covers my team. I also do not use the internet very much for news about rugby league, and must admit that I rarely look at 'blogs'. So the printed rugby league press is important for me as my main source of information about the game.

We are fortunate to have two weekly papers, offering diversity and choice. If *League Weekly* had not arisen from the ashes of the *Rugby Leaguer*, both the weekly *League Express*, and (at that time) only monthly paper, *Rugby League World*, would have been owned by the same company, which would not have been healthy for diversity and different opinions within the game.

Both papers come out on a Monday, with a lot of material on the weekend's matches. Both are well produced technically, with full colour. In my opinion, *League Express* probably has the edge on layout, but not by much. Both cover the news about the game well, as much as a weekly paper can. If the big event is on a Tuesday, as happened this week with the announcement of the new clubs joining Super League, a weekly paper will feel a bit dated. Rugby league is getting better at press releases and information, with the RFL providing a regular stream, backed up by the clubs.

Both papers use around two thirds of their space on match reports, and this is one of my criticisms of them. Surely it is safe to assume that most supporters also read a daily paper, and – certainly in the heartlands – a local one that covers their club. By all means cover Super League in detail, but do we need half page match reports on National League Two matches. Why not cover a key game each week in detail, and have smaller reports on the others? Do we need two or three pages of match reports on the Australian NRL in *League Express*? *League Weekly* usually restricts this to one page, which I feel is enough. And do we need almost a full page on a reserve team report? I could have done without a blow-by-blow account in *League Express* of Wigan 86 Harlequins 0. (Quins won the return match the next week by the way). And the coverage of the RL Conference is at times a little too detailed for the size and following of these clubs.

I recognise that the BARLA amateur game has wide support, and I think both papers have that about right. It also means I can find out how Sharlston Rovers are doing.

One of the key parts of both papers for me is their columnists, and in this area I think that League Weekly is well ahead. Both editors / owners, Martyn Sadler and Danny

Lockwood have their own columns in their respective papers, often comment on key games, and I wouldn't change that, although I don't always agree with them, that's fine. If anything, their columns could be a bit longer. Both papers also have columns from Australia, both are well written, although I find *League Express's* Malcolm Andrews more interesting. He does some good articles on the game's history as well.

In *League Weekly*, I don't always agree with Ray French either, but he provides a well informed column, often linking the game's history and current affairs well. Maurice Bamford's best material is when he writes about old times. The idea of a player writing a column is a good one, but I feel that Shaun Briscoe struggles to find good material every week. Maybe four players writing once a month would work better. I also enjoy Dave Parker's gossip column. And on the amateur game, Phil Hodgson is excellent, although he often concentrates on BARLA rather than the national picture.

League Express only has one other column apart from the editor and Malcolm Andrews, and that is a news / information / people focussed one by Mike Stephenson. It also has a news / events / gossip column at the back, more informative than Dave Parker's but not as lively! Their interviews with players each week are usually worth reading. Although League Publications could argue that they have opinion columns in *Rugby League World*, I think the weekly has to be considered on its own, and this, in my view, is a major weakness. Letting some other people have a say on current events in the game would make it a more interesting paper. Their League Talk column seems to have become more team photos from festivals rather than comment recently, which is a pity, in my view it could be more lively.

Both papers have editorials, which comment on current issues, but both could be longer and maybe take up more topics. The letters pages are usually lively, but sometimes degenerate into inter-club sniping rather than real debate.

Magazines

There are six national magazines which cover rugby league. *Rugby League World* is very well established as the successor to Harry Edgar's *Open Rugby* and is by far the most widely read. I was uncertain about new editor Richard de la Riviere's initial emphasis on list, 50 of this or that, which lead to articles with one paragraph pieces on the 50 greats or whatever. However, that seems to have gone now. Dave Hadfield and Andy Wilson are both among the game's leading writers, although I feel that Andy's talents could be better used than in doing a glorified match report which was his contribution to the current issue. And surely there is a better role for the excellent Phil Caplan than in doing player interviews which are sometimes a bit trivial.

The international coverage is good and there is a bit more history than over the last year. Mike Latham's series on innovations within the game was excellent, and hopefully a new role for him in the magazine can be found. However, the one part of the magazine that regularly annoys me is Garry Schofield's column. He was one of the great players of his generation, and one that I remember watching both in club matches and for Great Britain. However, in my opinion he is often negative about development of the game outside the 'heartlands' and in particular in London. In the August issue he has a dig at Quins for the 66-12 defeat against Castleford, but must have known the club had five players suspended and a long injury list, resulting in a severely weakened team playing against Castleford. I note that he didn't mention Quins' victory over Leeds a couple of weeks earlier. I do question his prominent role in a magazine that otherwise has a progressive attitude towards development.

For many years, this magazine could not decide if it was for the serious fan, or those who wanted lots of colour photos. The current editor seems to have got the balance about right.

A new kid on the block is *Code 13*. Aimed at a younger – under-35 – audience, it is printed in full colour, and has more material on London, where it is based, and other events outside the heartlands. Very little history is found here, with more emphasis on current events in the game. Well written and well produced, it has found a niche in the market, appealing to a slightly different audience than *Rugby League World*. On a personal note, it would be nice if they could sort out offering subscriptions – I had to join eBay to get a copy.

Occasionally as a monthly it can be out of date. The August edition did not have the make up of Super League from 2009, just a feature on teams contending for the franchises. Surely it would have been better to wait a couple of days to cover one of the biggest stories of the season.

I have an enormous amount of respect for Harry Edgar, who I regard as the founder of modern quality rugby league magazine writing. I did some research recently in *Open Rugby* from the late 1980s and early 1990s, which I regard as the magazine's best period, and the consistent quality was tremendous.

Harry has spent the last six years developing the quarterly *Rugby League Journal*, which nostalgically looks back at the history of the game. I have mixed feelings about this publication. On the one hand, it is currently the only one which specialises in the game's history, and that is to be welcomed and supported. There is consistently good material, great photos, book reviews, and a reasonable diversity of writers. I would certainly recommend it on that basis. However, as someone who is broadly, but not uncritically, supportive of the way rugby league has gone in recent times, I find the editorials and some other material pessimistic and even negative about the modern game. Not everything was great in the past, and the magazine doesn't say that. But a more balanced view would be welcome at times. But each to their own, and *Rugby League Journal* should be supported, both for its many good qualities and to ensure more diversity in the game's trade press.

Another magazine that probably many supporters don't see is *Running Rugby*. It is only for people working in the game or directly involved in it, rather than the supporters. Uniquely, it covers both codes with equal enthusiasm, and concentrates on the business of operating and running rugby clubs. Areas such as maintaining grounds, sponsorship, commercial development, catering and others are linked with interviews with leading people in the game. It is well produced, and free! I certainly find material here about the game that I do not find elsewhere.

A magazine produced by supporters is *TGG*, published by the Rugby League Supporters Association. A mix of opinion pieces, humour and the occasional book review, the magazine has had a few changes of editor over the past couple of years, and seems to come out only two or three times a year. An entertaining read when it appears, but some material can be out of date due to the irregular publication schedules. However, this has improved with the latest edition, and hopefully this will be maintained in future.

The official magazine of the RFL is the *Rugby League Bulletin*. It is produced by the Rugby League Services Department, and Tom Hoyle is the main contact for it. Well produced in full colour, it has a good selection of articles about various areas of the game, with a recent issue including a report on the Colleges Final, Touch Rugby and Masters matches. It reflects what the RFL is doing in its community work, and is well worth a read. Not controversial, but then I wouldn't expect an 'official' publication to be.

One important point about all the publications is their lack of regular book reviews at a time when more rugby league books are coming out than ever. I write this not just as a book publisher, but also as a historian committed to developing and preserving the history of the game. Arguably, books are the best way to do this, giving far more information than DVDs of old matches, or even interviews with old players, although these do have their place in the game's heritage. *League Express* recently had a couple of pages of book reviews, but these have been rare apart from at Christmas. *League Weekly* has over the past few months dropped its book quiz for space reasons. And *Code 13* says its readers are too young to be interested in history! *Rugby League Journal* is a good source of book reviews, but *Rugby League World* rarely features them.

The same is true with obituaries. Both weekly papers do them from time to time, particularly for famous players. *Rugby League Journal* also regularly provides them, but again they are not very often in *Rugby League World*.

So enjoy the trade press. Let's hope all the current publications continue, and more develop. Diversity of opinion is important to allow for full debate on all the issues that face rugby league.

Contact details:

League Publications: 01484-401895 or www.totalrl.com
League Weekly: 01924-454448 or www.league-weekly.com
Rugby League Journal: 01946-814249 or www.rugbyleaguejournal.net
Code 13: info@code13magazine.co.uk or Code 13, South Bank Technopark, 90, London Road, London SE1 6LN
TGG: www.rlsa.org.uk or RLSA memberships, 12, Greenock St, Armley, Leeds LS12 3JH
Running Rugby: markj@runningrugby.com or Running Rugby Ltd, 32-33, High St, Ascot, Berks SL5 7HG
Rugby League Bulletin: rugbyleagueservices@rfl.com or RFL Services, The Zone, St Andrews Road, Huddersfield, West Yorkshire, HD1 6PT

The future is bright, the future is the internet

Gary Slater looks at rugby league on the internet

For as long as I can remember, rugby league supporters have been complaining – with some justification – about the lack of coverage in the national press. Well, I have some news for you on that subject. The number of column inches devoted to rugby league is shrinking, not growing, and that situation is going to continue.

National newspapers are focusing their efforts on fewer and fewer sports, notably, of course, football and, primarily the Premier League. Rugby league is being squeezed out by football, rugby union, cricket, Formula One (the Lewis Hamilton factor), tennis, golf, horse racing, athletics (or rather the Olympic Games) and boxing. One of the biggest "rugby league" stories of 2007 – at least in terms of coverage – was Dwain Chambers joining Castleford Tigers and that wasn't even a genuine rugby league story. It was a human interest about a disgraced sprinter trying to make a living.

We can argue from now until the next World Cup about whether rugby league is being treated fairly, about increases in attendances and viewing figures, about the game's proud history and its role in binding communities together, but it won't make any difference. Rugby league is going to command less space in our national daily papers.

Let's accept that fact – grudgingly, of course – and move on. Move on, in fact, to the internet. There is a whole worldwide web out there and there is lots of rugby league to be found, to be read, to be watched and to be commented upon. Every day – and often many times a day – I log on to the BBC Sport website (http://news.bbc.co.uk/sport/) to check what is happening in the Greatest Game. And every day there are new stories to be considered and digested.

The service is first class, although there is always room for improvement, and you can be sure of one thing. Every time you click on to the rugby league home page on the BBC Sport website that click is being counted. Just as newspapers measure their circulation and broadcasters worry about their viewing figures, websites count their 'hits' and the more hits they achieve the better.

Every time you read a rugby league story on the net you are making it more likely that more rugby league stories will appear on the site. The BBC site has a report from every Super League match, complete with quotes from both coaches along with the teams and scorers. The report is not extensive but is more than sufficient to give a flavour of the contest.

The site also provides results, fixtures, tables and live scores, that is running scores from matches in progress, so that you are able to follow your favourites in action from a different country or even a different continent. All of the above you would probably expect, but there are also other features such as audio interviews with leading figures from the game and, perhaps best of all, a regular column by Jon Wilkin, the St Helens and Great Britain forward.

Many player columnists, in print and on line, can be dull, dull, dull. Not Wilkin. How about this from a column in May: "I keep dreaming about my teeth falling out while doing everyday stuff like eating and brushing my teeth."

Another feature of the internet, of course, is that you are encouraged to comment – "join the debate" as we say in the trade – and ask questions about what you have seen and heard. So one reader from Algeria, yes Algeria, told Wilkin that his recurring dreams were very Freudian and that subconsciously he was fearing the approach of old age. Heaven's above, he's only 25. The reader also suggested that he saw a psychoanalyst!

This is not, perhaps, the sort of discussion you would expect on a rugby league website but who cares? It certainly brought an element of fun into the proceedings. Another point about this is that Wilkin will undoubtedly be paid for his time and effort and there is nothing wrong with that. We probably don't want rugby league players to be paid so much that they lose touch with their roots and with reality, like some footballers, but we are a long way away from that point. In conclusion, then, if you have not visited the BBC Sport website and checked on the rugby league home page you are missing out.

Sky Sports, too, supply an excellent rugby league service at http://www.skysports.com/ to back up their superb television coverage. You can even watch their magazine show *Boots 'n' All* again on your home computer if you missed it first time.

The Sky Sports site covers most of the same ground – news, match reports, fixtures and tables – but where it has an edge is with their expert columnists, Mike 'Stevo' Stephenson and Phil Clarke. Both write regular pieces or "blogs". Blogs is short for web logs, or diaries, but is just an internet word for article.

Stevo was particularly poignant with his tribute to David Topliss, who was a fellow member of Great Britain's World Cup-winning squad in 1972. In an article headlined "Farewell My Friend", Stevo wrote: "To see Toppo in full flight was amazing; he appeared to glide across the turf with style and speed and could score tries from near-impossible situations."

If Stevo is "the face of rugby league", then Clarke must be the thinking man's rugby league pundit and argued persuasively that the Rugby Football League were right to enter England and not Great Britain in the World Cup: "I have not met many people who, when asked abroad on holiday where they come from, proudly answer 'Great Britain' – they usually say England, Scotland, Ireland or Wales," wrote the former Great Britain captain and manager.

Not to be outdone, the Rugby Football League and the engage Super League have also beefed up their websites at www.therfl.co.uk and www.superleague.co.uk. There was also a special website for the Millennium Magic weekend, www.millenniummagic.co.uk/ complete with music, *A Kind of Magic* by Queen.

Sites like these are incredibly important to show that the sport is vibrant and forward-thinking. They are also extremely useful for finding out what is happening and for buying tickets and merchandise, like the new England kit.

The RFL site includes a "Rugby League Club Locator" so that wherever you live in the country, simply by typing in your address or post code, you can find out your nearest amateur and professional clubs. As you would expect, the site also has an interesting section on the history of the game and on the Hall of Fame, although that was not quite as up-to-date as you would expect.

Ellery Hanley, Douglas Clark and Martin Hodgson were inducted into the Hall of Fame in 2005, but when I checked two years later there were no biographies of the players, just a message saying "more details to appear here shortly". Oh dear.

The jewel in the crown on the Super League site is the free video highlights of games which were made available, free of charge, in June. Each Monday up to 15 minutes of video from all the weekend's games is uploaded to the website for supporters to enjoy.

Record numbers, more than 100,000 people, watched the highlights in the first three weeks and those figures are likely to keep on growing as word gets around and as supporters become increasingly computer-literate.

Another interesting feature of the site is the statistics. Supporters can judge how their team and their players match up against the rest of the competition.

Newspapers, too, are becoming increasingly aware of the need for an interesting service on their websites to pull in more readers and, of course, more hits. And, put very simply, the more hits, the more advertisers have to pay to appear on the site.

Chris Irvine, of *The Times*, and Andy Wilson, of *The Guardian*, are leading the way with their thought-provoking blogs. Andy Wilson's news and comments can be found at www.guardian.co.uk/sport/rugbyleague while Chris Irvine's ideas, including a list of the 50 greatest Super League players, are at www.timesonline.co.uk/tol/sport/rugby_league

Chris's blog has been so successful and generated so many responses that they are being turned into a book *Down and Dirty – A Rugby League Blogging Year*.

Every Super League club also has their own website and, by and large, the bigger the club, the better the site. So the Leeds Rhinos side (www.leedsrugby.com) takes some beating. But if you have not checked your own club's site then it is about time you did! The more supporters use the sites regularly, the better they are likely to become.

The internet, of course, is a vast and ever-expanding universe full of information. Once you begin searching for your favourite teams or favourite players, there is no telling what you will find. It might not all be entirely accurate, you should try to check information against another source, but it will entertain and inform.

For example, if you search for Cliff Watson (the former St Helens and Great Britain forward) and rugby league you will stumble across a site luxuriating in the title "Era of the Biff, The Greatest Era of the Greatest Games of all" at www.eraofthebiff.com/p-30.html

With a total disregard for political correctness, the site boasts: "Pom, Aussie, Kiwi and Frog – it's all here."

Here, indeed, you can find some fascinating archive photographs and the following words of wisdom from Watson: "There is only one way to beat the Australians. You have got to get in there and thump them. If you let them run at you, they'll annihilate you. It's always been the same; if you belt them, they don't like it."

The free online encyclopedia, Wikipedia, also has hundreds of league entries. If you search for Alex Murphy and Wikipedia, for example, you will find an interesting profile of perhaps the world's greatest scrum-half at http://en.wikipedia.org/wiki/Alex_Murphy As it says in the article: "You either like him or loathe him, but you certainly can't ignore him!"

The same can be said of rugby league on the internet. You might prefer to have all your rugby league news neatly packaged in a national daily newspaper but, increasingly, the place to look is the internet. Get clicking.

The Rugby Football League Benevolent Fund

Tim Adams and Stephen Ball outline the work being done to support seriously injured players.

The Rugby Football League is very proud of its origins and its projection as a family game. Its heritage can be traced through adversity and a caring compassionate well-being of generosity. While there were relatively few incidents of seriously injured rugby league players, a couple of serious injuries back in 2005 highlighted the need for the game to make extra provision in caring for its own. As a consequence, the Rugby League Benevolent Fund, a registered charity, was established in early 2005 in order to raise funds to support players whose lives are affected by serious injuries suffered playing rugby league.

The fund has grown dramatically since its conception three years ago. Sourcing funds had to be established and the Presidents Ball was re-established back in 2005, specifically for the purpose of the fund. The inaugural year's finances were given a further boost when profits from Ray French's book were kindly donated to the fund.

Once established, the funds have risen exponentially to approximately £230,000 in 2007, with further growth forecast for 2008. A social network has been established for those players who have been seriously injured and many social events have been procured on the rugby league calendar for and on behalf of the Rugby Football League Benevolent Fund.

The rapid growth of funding for the fund could not have been achieved without the generosity and support of literally thousands of supporters. This is highlighted through their £1 contribution levied on the tickets for the Challenge Cup Final and the Super League Final.

Leeds Metropolitan University, which organises an annual challenge, is always supported by students, rugby league supporters and by RFL staff. In addition RFL staff undertake sponsored individual initiatives on behalf of the fund.

The Steve Prescott Foundation has kindly made the fund one of their beneficiaries. Steve was a senior player who is best remembered for playing for St Helens and Hull. Despite being diagnosed with a rare form of cancer, Steve and his supporters regularly organise events with the proceeds being split equally between Christies Cancer Charity and the RFL Benevolent Fund.

A number of clubs, both professional and amateur continue to make donations from a variety of activities. Individual donations, which are often gift aided, has also seen a sharp increase.

Further sources of funds have also been established in 2008. Engage Mutual, the sponsors of Super League, are donating £100 from every televised Sky game through their man-of-the-match award. We understand that all future fines levied by the RFL disciplinary committee are going to be donated to the Benevolent Fund. Keep up the bad work boys!

While our fundraising is often very social and fun, the RFL Benevolent Fund never loses its perspective and focus in providing support for seriously injured rugby league players. Its variety of ways is broad, and it can be best summarised as to provide rehabilitation beyond that offered by the NHS or the state, for recently injured players or by improving the quality of life when, unfortunately rehabilitation is no longer an option. The RFL Benevolent Fund is a lifelong commitment to players' care and welfare.

In its first three years, the Benevolent Fund has assisted 24 individuals and has paid or committed to pay over £250,000.

A good example of the funds rehabilitation assistance is the help offered to Pete Stephenson. Pete was badly injured playing for amateur club Hull Dockers in August 2005 and was immediately hospitalised at Pinderfields Spinal Unit at Wakefield. Quick to respond, the fund met the travelling and overnight expenses of his partner on her frequent visits to Pete during his lengthy stay in hospital.

Pete was originally told that he would probably be confined to a wheelchair for the rest of his life. Through hard work and exceptional determination, he was able to prove the diagnosis wrong.

Since leaving hospital, he has been receiving extensive physiotherapy, paid for by the Benevolent Fund. The fund has also been able to assist in modifications to his home to make easy access available for him. Happily, at the Carnegie Challenge Cup Final in August 2007, Pete was able to walk onto the Wembley pitch at half-time to collect a cheque from Leeds Metropolitan University on our behalf.

"The support of the Benevolent Fund was essential as I could focus on planning my recovery without the financial concerns of how I could pay for my physio and rehab. The Benevolent Fund was able to offer me a degree of financial strength and guidance in what was a difficult period of my life", added Pete.

For those former players confined to a wheelchair, life can be very difficult, particularly for those unable to work. Disability benefits only meet the basis day-to-day living costs. Home improvements, which many local authorities will not fund, are for many, unaffordable, even if absolutely necessary. The Benevolent Fund has been able to assist significant home improvements on several occasions, including a personally designed wet room for John Burke, who was badly injured in 1981 playing for Workington Town.

John commented: "The new wet room allowed me time and access to a basic facility that most people take for granted. The installation of the wet room dramatically improved the quality of my life".

The Benevolent Fund has been able to assist in providing white goods and furniture to replace very old, even antiquated items, which would otherwise be unaffordable.

Certain NHS authorities will only provide basic wheelchairs or part financed specialised ones. The fund recognises the need to make the basic provision of a comfortable wheelchair a priority. Consequently, we have provided custom built wheelchairs on five occasions and also paid for significant alterations in one other case.

Of course provision of material goods is not the only way we can give added value to help in people's lives. Fees for education courses have been provided, including university tuition fees for a three year law degree.

Leisure pursuits have also been covered for through the provision of computers and televisions with Sky Sports annual rental being paid in order for that important weekly diet of live rugby league.

A social calendar has been established for our entire wheelchair bound beneficiaries. An annual trip to Wembley for the Challenge Cup Final is arranged, which is very popular. Two nights in a hotel, lunch at the stadium, followed by the match itself. A chance to visit London on Saturday night follows for all of them, including their helpers; such an occasion is widely regarded as a wonderful opportunity for everyone to meet up.

Paul Kilbride, a.k.a 'Killer', was injured whilst playing for the Leeds club, Milford in 1995 and enjoys the social network the Benevolent Fund provides. "Going to special functions and mixing with the rest of the lads has provided us with great experiences and enabled us to enhance our friendships with a whole range of people", commented Paul.

The Super League Grand Final, with its dinner beforehand, is also on the agenda and in October 2008 'Killer', Pete Stephenson and Jimmy Gittins, their helpers and a physiotherapist to assist, are off to Australia to see the World Cup. No doubt the three week trip will be a once in a lifetime experience.

Jimmy Gittins, who was seriously injured playing for Sharlston Rovers in 2002 said: "This is a fantastic and unique opportunity to be part of something special in rugby league, I am really looking forward to the whole experience. I can't wait!"

A vital facet of the Benevolent Fund is the provision of counselling through the funds welfare officer, Dave Phillips. Dave is in regular touch with everyone and assists with applications made to the charity. He co-ordinates the social calendar and most importantly, provides the caring face of the fund. He is the first to meet the players after they get injured and provides a constant connection between injured players and the fund. The role of a welfare officer is seen as paramount to the continued efficiency of the Benevolent Fund.

The charity is in the advanced stage of establishing its own website. This will be regularly updated to provide the latest news on fundraising activities and assistance given. Application forms for assistance and Gift Aid forms for those who wish to make donations will also be provided.

The media and in particular Sky Television, have helped raised our profile and extend our positive influence. It is hoped our social network will allow us to build further upon our success.

There is no doubt that the work done by the RFL Benevolent Fund is a response to the big family of rugby league. Its clubs, players, sponsors and supporters have been instrumental in its success. It is an acknowledgement of a game that cares and supports its most vulnerable members. The RFL Benevolent Fund is here to stay and commits itself to a lifelong establishment of care and welfare for those in the rugby league who may need it the most.

Donations can be made to the RFL Benevolent Fund by sending them to the RFL at Red Hall. Additional funds are generated for the fund if donors use the Gift Aid facility. More information is on the RFL website.

Rugby league worldwide

Garry Clarke looks at the development of the game internationally.

Later this year 10 countries will come together in Australia for a month long carnival of Rugby League, all trying to win the Rugby League World Cup.

The five main test playing nations of **Australia, England, France, New Zealand** and **Papua New Guinea** were granted automatic entry to the final stages, while the other five contestants who will join them down under in October and November had to qualify via a worldwide qualifying tournament.

The Rugby League World Cup Qualifying tournament, which kicked off on 28 April 2006 in Hoek Van Holland and ended in Featherstone on 14 November 2007, spanned the globe comprising 23 games at 19 venues as far apart as Aston, Dublin, London, Rotterdam, Sydney and Tbilisi. Altogether 16 countries from all the corners of the globe entered the qualifying tournament aiming to rub shoulders with the big boys in Australia.

First to book their places in Australia were **Tonga,** who won the Pacific Group, and **Fiji,** who were group runners up. Qualifying from Europe were **Scotland**, winners of European Group One, and European Group Two winners **Ireland**. The tenth and final place in the 2008 Rugby League World Cup was secured by **Samoa,** who qualified by winning the Repecharge play off series beating **Lebanon** in the final. The two other countries, which competed in this play off series, were **Wales** and the Atlantic Group winners **United States of America.**

The countries which failed to make it through their initial qualifying groups were from the Pacific Group the **Cook Islands**, from the Atlantic Group **Japan**, and from the two European Groups **Georgia, Holland, Russia** and **Serbia.** While both **South Africa** and the **West Indies** entered the Atlantic group but withdrew without playing a game in the tournament.

So 21 countries have been, or will be, involved in the 2008 Rugby League World Cup, a far cry from the inaugural world cup in 1954 which was competed for by just four nations. However, these 21 countries, while the leading rugby league playing countries, represent less than half of the world's rugby league nations. For during the two year period qualifying games were being played for the 2008 Rugby League World Cup, rugby league, at varying levels, was played in, or by team representing, a further 22 countries. Bring the total number of countries in which Rugby League was played between April 2006 and November 2007 to 43.

The majority of the 22 non World Cup countries can be found in three areas of the globe, Europe with 14, the Pacific Islands with five and the Americas with three.

The 14 other European countries, who are full or associate members of the Rugby League European Federation are **Austria, Czech Republic**, **Estonia, Germany, Greece, Italy, Latvia, Malta, Norway, Portugal, Spain, Sweden** and **Ukraine,** plus from North Africa **Morocco,** are also members of the European Federation.

On the other side of the Atlantic, rugby league is also played in **Argentina, Canada** and **Jamaica.** The five other Pacific Islands, which play rugby league, are **American Samoa, New Caledonia, Niue, Tokelau** and **Tuvalu.**

Forty three countries all around the world playing rugby league as the popularity of The Greatest Game spreads across the globe, which will be the next country to run with the ball and join the rugby league family?

Rugby league and South Africa

Peter Lush outlines the history of rugby league and South Africa, while **Hendrik Snyders** recalls Green Vigo's career and looks at the experiences of black and coloured players who went overseas to play rugby league.

It is notable that when selecting a rugby league side from the game's history for different countries, a Wales XIII would be one of the strongest, despite the game having often struggled to maintain a club structure there. The same could be said of South Africa – a very respectable team could be selected, particularly in the backs, but the game has only recently celebrated 21 seasons in the country, spread over three periods.

In 1911 the Northern Union was approached about a "coloured tour" from South Africa, which they turned down. This was a missed opportunity for the NU, and it is interesting to speculate about rugby league's possible development in South Africa if the tour had taken place and the game had become established in the coloured and African communities.

In 1901, Arthur Larard joined Huddersfield, having played two games for the South African rugby union team. But he had been born in Hull, and was probably returning home, possibly because of the Boer War, so did not really count as a South African convert to the Northern Union. However, in the 1920s and 1930s, a small number of South African union players had joined rugby league clubs in England, including six at Wigan in the mid-1920s, but the game had no base in South Africa.

In 1953, Ludwig Japhet contacted the RFL about staging rugby league in South Africa. This resulted in the first attempt to develop the game in South Africa, a tour by Great Britain and France in 1957 of three matches. The tour was controversial in British rugby league, especially as the famous black Wigan and Great Britain winger Billy Boston was clearly not welcome in South Africa. British rugby league seemed to have forgotten its strong record of participation by black players, and any political factors about playing in South Africa do not appear to have been considered, although to be fair to the RFL, there was no organised sports boycott at this time.

The tour was not a great success, as the teams treated the games as exhibition matches. One offshoot of the tour was that the potential of South African rugby union players became apparent for British rugby league clubs. Tom van Vollenhoven was signed by St Helens, and became one of the greatest wingers to play in Great Britain. Others followed, some, particularly backs, were successful with top clubs in Great Britain and Australia, others returning home – "too old and too cold" in the case of forward Ivor Dorrington. Players who made an impact include Jan Prinsloo, Wilf Rosenberg, Alan Skene, Oupa Coetzer, Colin Greenwood, Fred Griffiths, Trevor Lake and Len Killeen, and the black and coloured players covered in Hendrik Snyders' article below.

Why the RFL wanted to try to build in a rugby union stronghold is unclear. Ludwig Japhet died soon after the tour, and nothing more was heard from South Africa until 1961. Then the RFL was contacted by businessmen who wanted to start a professional rugby league competition in South Africa.

But the RFL then found it was dealing with two leagues, which started in 1962: the National Rugby League and Rugby League of South Africa. Tours by Wakefield Trinity and the British Lions followed. The RFL tried to broker a merger between the two, which eventually happened. Both Wakefield and the Lions won their matches easily.

Tom van Vollenhoven, Jan Prinsloo and Duggie Greenall training.

The press coverage was usually by rugby union writers, who were hostile to the code. And the South African RU placed every obstacle they could in the way of the development of rugby league. However, newspaper reports did say that the loss of players to rugby league did hit South African Rugby Union.

In July and August 1963, South Africa toured Australia and New Zealand. Not surprisingly, they were well beaten twice by Australia, but managed a 4-3 win in New Zealand on a 'very muddy pitch'. Reports say that again the South African forwards lacked experience to compete at this level. However, the competition in South Africa had attracted some prominent union players, including Dawie Ackerman, Martin Pelser, Natie Rens, Hennie van Zyl, Mannetjie Gericke and Chris Bezuidenhout.

But the competition in South Africa had collapsed by 1964, with what little research has been done saying that the defeats in Australia undermined the competition at home. A report of the tour says that "An official Australian decree stipulated there was to be no reference to politics during the visit". But one must ask why the RFL were trying to build links with South Africa in this post-Sharpeville period, when other sports were starting to move away from having links with the apartheid regime.

By the late 1980s, the barriers between the two codes in Great Britain and elsewhere were starting to come down. This coincided with huge political change in South Africa, with Mandela's release from prison in 1990. Also, by now the RFL and rugby league's international board had a far more expansionist outlook at this time.

In 1988, two British ex-patriots, Dave Southern and Tony Barker, started to build the game. A newspaper advert they placed attracted 60 people to an inaugural meeting. Friendly matches were played in Johannesburg in 1990 and 1991. This led to the launch of the South African Rugby Football League on 26 August 1991, with former Wigan rugby league winger and junior Springbok Trevor Lake as its president.

One of the problems that has faced rugby league when entering a new area or country has been how to establish the game. In England and Wales this meant either: start with youth and schools, or establish a professional club to spark interest in the game. In fact, both are necessary – young players need a professional club to aspire to play for, and young people – or even older ones – watching the game also want to play.

In South Africa, this debate developed in a different, but similar, way. Dave Southern believed that the way forward for the game was to build in the townships, aiming at African youngsters with a thirst for sport. Union had no base there, and politically this was the future. But this was a long-term strategy, without necessarily a senior competition and the glamour of international matches to come immediately.

Other people in the fledgling SARL looked towards white rugby union players for recruits, putting an emphasis on starting a club competition, which they did in 1992, and playing international matches. On 13 November 1992, South Africa played Russia (the Commonwealth of Independent States), losing 30-26 and 22-19. The previous month, it was reported that the SARFU had banned any player that played rugby league, breaking the international 'free gangway' agreement for amateur players.

In 1993, the SARL had a bitter split, with Trevor Lake and Dave Southern leaving to continue developing mini league in the townships. Their work attracted a lot of attention and support in Great Britain, with former Great Britain captain Phil Clarke writing in 1995 that his experience in Soweto and Alexandra was "the biggest challenge of my life" and "an experience that will linger forever in my mind." Supporters in Great Britain had collected shirts and equipment for the project. It continued until Southern left South Africa in 1999. The project had received support from the British and Dutch governments, and sponsorship from Ericsson.

In 1997, a multi-racial South African under-16 team played a London team at Wembley as a warm up to the Great Britain versus Australia match.

At a senior level, in 1993, the SARL hosted a tour by the BARLA, and with more publicity for the game through coverage of Australian Rugby League on television, the game looked to have a bright future. However, the road ahead was not a smooth one.

The South Africans were put into the 1995 World Cup. Coached by former Great Britain player Tony Fisher, they were clearly out of their depth, and would have fared better in the emerging nations tournament run parallel to the main competition.

In the 1980s and 1990s, a few South Africans played league in Great Britain, including Rob Louw, Ray Mordt, Nick du Toit, Mark Johnson, Jamie Bloem and Andre Stoop. Today, London Skolars have Rupert Jonker, Richard Louw and Mario du Toit their squad.

Since 1995, the game's progress in the country has been uneven. The game's leadership has at times been attracted to 'quick fixes' through seeking big business sponsorship, including for a short period the involvement of former Rugby Union stalwart Louis Luyt at one time, who with his political and rugby union history, which included involving Nelson Mandela as a reluctant witness in court case was hardly someone who would be a pole of attraction for the majority in South Africa.

Entry into the 2000 RL World Cup did not bring the financial rewards hoped for, and since then they have made few excursions onto the international stage, mainly due to the cost of playing overseas. However, a club competition is well established, and in June 2007 the British amateur team once again toured South Africa. There is some development work being done in the townships and schools, but not on the scale it was in the early 1990s. The current SARL leadership under the direction of chairman Dave van Reenen have a very positive attitude towards development among the African community, and have worked out development plans for the game at every level, including tours to the country, which are an important development tool. A presence has been re-established in the Western Cape, which should prove fruitful in the future.

Dave Southern's work in the townships showed huge potential for rugby league, given union's relatively weak base in the African community. In 2001, in an interview, Tas Batieri, head of rugby league's global development programme, claimed 60,000 players in South Africa, mainly from the Mini-League work. The same article said there were 40,000 players in Great Britain. Even allowing for some exaggeration, it is interesting to speculate what could have happened if the SARL had concentrated its energies in youth development in the townships at this time. The youngsters who played league in the early 1990s would now be in their 20s and 30s, giving the game a strong base among the majority community in South Africa.

Hopefully the game can now build on the base it has, develop among the majority community in South Africa, and fulfil the potential it showed in the early 1990s.

Peter Lush

Peter Lush and Hendrik Snyders are working, with the SARL, on a comprehensive history of South African Rugby League, hopefully to be published in 2010. This article is adapted from a paper by Peter Lush presented to the first conference on Sports History in South Africa at Stellenbosch University in July 2008, and, as with the other two in this feature, uses some terms from the apartheid era. This is almost inevitable in South African history and does not imply acceptance of categorisation of people in this way.

Green without Gold: The Green Vigo story

Hendrik Snyders looks at the career of one of South Africa's greatest rugby league players.

In 1971, during the first ever rugby union tour of the United Kingdom by a black South African team, a young and extremely talented centre took the first steps towards rugby fame and recognition on a bigger stage. Sadly, this player like most of his generation never got the opportunity to represent his country on any of rugby union's holiest grounds such as Twickenham. He also never received the recognition due to him outside his own community for his exploits on the rugby field.

When the South African Rugby Union in 2001 decided to give recognition to past players that represented their segregated national rugby bodies but never had the opportunity to represent their country in official test matches through the Yesterday's Heroes Programme[1], a small, but significant, group of players never bothered to claim their symbolic Springbok colours. Apparently, the South African Rugby Union also erred by expecting of these players to apply for their official colours. Some former players rejected this requirement as an insult. Others also refused to receive something that they continue to associate with apartheid.

One of these players is Green Gregory Vigo, who represented the Proteas, the national team for 'coloured' players of the former South African Rugby Football Federation (SARFF) during the short British tour mentioned above, and against the visiting England side in Cape Town in 1972. Following a notable career of representative rugby with the Swartland Union and Proteas, as a result of apartheid and lack of further opportunity at home, Green Vigo switched from rugby union to rugby league in 1973 after being spotted by a rugby league scout from Wigan. He made a name for himself at Wigan, then with Swinton and Oldham in Great Britain.

Rugby union

Green started his rugby career in the coastal village of Saldanha in the 1960s at Tigers Rugby Club, an affiliate of the Swartland RU which was affiliated to the SARFF. It is believed that the young and talented Green and another friend had a run-in with the law, but thanks to the timely intervention of the club leadership, especially Abe Williams (later Springbok manager of the 1981 tour of New Zealand) the energies of the two young men were channelled into rugby.[2] This was their saving grace. Within a short period of time, Green in particular proved to be an exceptionally talented player who was soon selected to represent Swartland in the SARFF Gold and Silver Cup competitions.

This was, however, a time of great division in rugby with separate unions for whites and blacks in addition to other divisions and structures based on ideological and racial grounds.[3] It was also a period that saw an increase in the volume of protest against apartheid South Africa. Despite these tensions and divisions, Green continues to excel and by 1970 was selected as a member of the national team for coloured rugby, the Proteas. On this level he played a significant number of internal tests against the then South African Rugby Association (SARA), which represented the African players, (by then known as the Leopards). These tests were bitterly fought affairs, but served as an important arena for players like Green to hone their skills and display their talents. After a string of successful performances on club and sub union level, Green was selected for higher honours and was included in the 1971 team to tour England and the Netherlands. Although he did not score a try in any of the six matches, he was a valued member of the touring team which won two matches, drew one and lost three. This tour was particularly difficult as a result of increased anti-apartheid protests. The game against Hertfordshire in particular, was seriously disrupted by on-field protests and demonstrations which undoubtedly impacted on the team's performance. Despite this, the tourists completed their tour with a final game against the Netherlands national team which the Proteas won 28–23 at Hilversum.[4]

Following their first overseas venture, 1972 and the incoming England tour brought new opportunities and further divisions for black rugby. In response to the demonstrations and political problems associated with South African sport, the RFU indicated prior to the tour its willingness to play against black teams. To prepare for this, the administrators from the various ethnic structures met to discuss a proposal for the selection of one unified black team consisting of Green's Union, the SARFF and the South African Rugby Union (SARU) for the big occasion. From the start, divisions between the two rival bodies dominated discussions.

The delegates from SARU argued that the timing of the tour was not only inappropriate but that participation in the tour match in itself would amount to selling out and would further be tantamount to active participation in their own oppression. It was further argued that such matches also contributed to the avoidance of serious discussions about the establishment of a non-racial society and sport. Given people's experiences of the damaging effects of the implementation of apartheid, including forced removals and segregation, divisions also occurred within the SARFF over the tour's appropriateness and timing.

Despite SARU's objections, the leadership of the SARFF and SARA (Leopards) decided to proceed with the match. This action intensified the divisions between and within the various black rugby bodies and led to further splits within their various ranks. Against this background, Green Vigo had his second outing against a fully representative international side in Cape Town before a crowd of 10,000 spectators. The opposition, led by John Spencer, included players such as Fran Cotton, Mike Burton and Chris Ralston, all of whom were later members of the all-conquering 1974 British Lions team. This historic match, an ill-tempered affair, provided black players with their first quality opposition and a yardstick to measure themselves against. Although England emerged victorious by 11–6, Green Vigo and Errol Tobias in particular, were singled out and praised by the rugby media as the most outstanding players on the day.[5] This acknowledgement and the meaning of this event were however overshadowed by the fact that the match was hit by a boycott by players and spectators as well as placard demonstrations outside the venue.

Following the England tour and the dissatisfaction with the decision to proceed with the Protea game, the SARFF experienced a split when a significant number of its clubs and unions decided to join the SARU. This significantly weakened the SARFF. Renewed attempts in 1973 to bring about the establishment of a united rugby controlling board, once again failed, leaving talented rugby players like Green Vigo, who found themselves outside the establishment, with very little hope of ever representing their country. Vigo therefore decided in 1973 to accept Wigan's offer to play professional rugby league. There was no rugby league in South Africa at this time.

Rugby league

Despite its historic nature, the 1971 Protea tour of Great Britain played no role in the recruitment of Green Vigo. The match that brought him to the attention of Wigan was the 1972 match against England. When approached to make the cross-over, he initially declined the offer and advised them to return a year later, in the hope of getting rid of the scout. This was not to be and the offer was renewed in 1973 [6] as Wigan embarked on a process to revive itself through the recruitment of "personality-plus players" (players that are both talented but who are also personalities).[7] Vigo described in news reports as "colourful" and a proven rugby talent clearly fitted this description. Despite advice to the contrary, Vigo at the age of 23, accepted a five year semi-professional contract comprising of R60 (around £30 then) for an away match and R45-00 (£22) for a home match[8] plus an undisclosed and confidential[9] initial signing-on fee. Given the nature of the confidentiality clause in his contract, it is believed that the sign-on fee represented a new record for a player by the club. Given his background as a young fisherman and the limited educational and career opportunities for black people in apartheid South Africa, made the Wigan offer extremely attractive. Apparently he also left with the blessing of the South African Rugby Federation although some felt that the player should have stayed at least until the 1974 British Lions tour in order to increase his monetary value.[10] Green also hoped that he would be allowed to play local rugby upon his return.[11]

The British newspapers hailed Green as a second Billy Boston. This was very flattering to a player that still had to make his mark in the league game. These early hopes were also frightening and caused some newspaper reporters to caution their counterparts against creating unreasonable expectations.[12] In addition, his new career during the 1970s coincided with the coaching term of Vince Karalius. This dedicated trainer and coach changed Green Vigo from being a union player into a complete rugby league player. Green regarded Karalius as the most important influence on his playing career in the hard world of rugby league.

Settling in

After his arrival in Wigan as a semi-professional, his new club still had to sort out his work permit[13] in addition to provide appropriate accommodation. Having departed South Africa in summer, the club also assisted the player with acquiring the appropriate clothing fit for the cold English climate. In addition Vigo as an Afrikaans speaker from a rural background, had to settle down to life in a total new world with its bewildering range of English language accents that frequently varies and at times also confuse. To ease his integration, he was set up with an elderly couple, Mr and Mrs Halliday, who according to Vigo treated him "like their own child". Staying within such an intimate set up, helped to get a grip on the intricacies of the English language. This was supplemented, according to contemporary newspaper reports, with extra English classes. While he waited for his work permit to be sorted out, he was utilised as club groundsman at a rate of R52 a week, far above the rate for similar work in South Africa.[14] But not everything went well and some reports also suggested neglect and poor orientation of the player by the club to the extent that often he was left to his own devices and struggled to find his home.[15]

The process of finalising the paper work, however did not prevent Wigan from immediately put to full use Green's "rippling mass of compact muscle" that seemed to have been "hewn from solid Cape oak"[16] in order to scare Featherstone, Dewsbury and Leigh at the TBA Sevens Tournament played on 11 August 1973 at Central Park. Five tries later and after a "five star display of classy centre work", Green Vigo became "Super Green" for the Wigan fans after Colin Clarke, who captained the side, collected the TBA Sevens Trophy.[17] In the aftermath of this tournament, the media headlines significantly read "Saldanha Tiger Roars" with a by-line that simply stated "Vigo, Gray shows class".[18] From the reading of the post match report, the journalist, appeared quite stunned by what he has observed on the field of play and he liberally used phrases such as "rugby renaissance", "some real class in the art of rugby", "dream debuts", "made two spectacular tries", "scored five beautiful tries himself," "being a magnificent effort" and "left the opposition standing."

Entering the league battlefield

After making a dream debut in the TBA Sevens, it was finally time to enter the real battlefield of rugby league with all its new rules, tactical plays and cultural practices. Green scored his first try against Whitehaven on 25 August 1973 in a 17-12 defeat. He scored again in a Lancashire Cup semi-final at Workington, won 20-4 by Wigan, and against Oldham in an 18-0 triumph in the league. Green's good form from South African rugby union continued and consistency became his early trademark, earning him further nicknames and status that also signalled his transformation from being the Tiger of Saldanha to becoming the "Wizard of Wigan"[19] and the "Saldanha Iron Horse".[20] Against Hull Kingston Rovers on 27 October, he scored a hat-trick of tries in a comprehensive 38-3 victory, firmly announcing his arrival and potential influence on the league scene.

His presence and potency on the field soon made him a target for opposing players, with them using all sorts of tricks to intimidate and prevent Green from scoring. Not able to counter his blistering pace and physical approach to the game, out of desperation the opposition forwards resort to tripping him in order to thwart his attack on the opposition try line. One of them was caught in the act of tripping him and the offender was sent off. During his full first professional game, he lost some teeth after a stiff-arm tackle.[21]

Underlining his continuing good form while still adapting to the XIII man game, Green did more than enough to maintain his place in the first team and played in 20 matches in the season, scoring 10 tries. He ended as the second highest scorer for Wigan, scoring a try every other game. He was included in the team that played the Lancashire Cup Final against Salford on 13 October 1973. Wigan won 19-9. Although Green did not score, the victory was satisfactory enough given that Salford went on to win the league. Green had enough reasons to feel that indeed the move abroad was worth while. Wigan ended the season in 11th place in the First Division, 20 points below the league champions.

Despite this good start, the first three seasons of his new playing career was unspectacular without setting the rugby league world alight. He was a consistent performer and quickly established himself as a pillar of strength for Wigan and a force to be reckoned with. As a rookie, there were still certain basic skills to learn before the lethal weapon that was Green Vigo, could be fully unleashed. His second season, 1974-75, was more consistent and his try tally improved. He played 27 out of 36 games and scored 12 tries. In comparison with the top try scorer of the season, Stuart Wright with 14 tries from 36 games, Green, in fewer games, scored 12. He was also one of only five players who played more than 25 games. It was obvious that despite his relative inexperience of rugby league, in only his second season, Vigo has succeeded in becoming a key player on the rugby league scene. An improvement in Wigan's form was shown with a much improved performance by the club who succeeded in moving up to second place in the league table, 11 points behind the new champions St Helens.

Green played most of the games the next season, one characterised by dominance by their arch rivals, St Helens, who annexed the Challenge Cup, Premiership Trophy and the BBC Floodlit Trophy. For a third year in a row, Vigo maintained his consistency in scoring tries, ending at number three for the season behind team mates Stuart Wright and Bill Francis who has scored 19 and 12 tries respectively. It was clear that without Green's presence, Wigan's chances of scoring tries and being competitive would have been much more limited. The club dropped from second to fifth spot in the league, a mere six points behind champions Salford.

The high point of his time at Wigan came in the 1976-77 season. On 21 August 1976, Green entered Wigan's history books by scoring seven tries in a match against St Helens in a Lancashire Cup match at Central Park. Despite the fact that Saints had internal problems, a player-management pay dispute, this was detract from Green's achievement. This ensured a place for him in the annals of Wigan rugby league history alongside heroes such as Billy Boston, Johnny Ring and Gordon Ratcliff. Prior to this impressive performance, Green had on occasions scored two or three tries against a variety of opponents. His seven tries were not a mere flash in the pan. His try record withstood a good number of onslaughts over a number of seasons and was only smashed in 1992 by Martin Offiah and Shaun Edwards and Martin Offiah who both scored 10 tries in a match. Offiah achieved this in May, Edwards following it four months later in September. His record lasted 16 years.

The rest of the season was equally impressive with Green now a regular scorer. He finished the 1976-77 season with 18 tries in 34 matches, and was Wigan's top try scorer. Unfortunately, his club could not match this impressive result and ended in the seventh position, 12 points behind the league champions, Featherstone Rovers.

He entered the next season with a vengeance, starting off on 21 August 1977 with a try against Oldham in a 42-5 first round Lancashire Cup win. In the matches that followed, Green devastated opponents with a minimum of two tries per game and even three on two other occasions. These were scored both home and away. Once again he ended as Wigan's top try scorer with 27 tries in 37 games. It was also during this season that he scored his only goal for Wigan. Like on a previous occasion, on the 28 September 1977 at Warrington, he had the pleasure of scoring one of the tries in the Lancashire Cup semi-final against Warrington that provided his club with a shot at the county trophy. They unfortunately lost the final against Workington 13-16. Green had to be content with a runners-up medal. Wigan once again were in among the also-rans and ended the 1977-78 season in fifth position, 15 points behind champions Widnes.

The 1978-79 season however proved to be a very disappointing. Disaster struck when Vigo broke his arm. He struggled hard to regain match fitness. The struggle to regain his place in the first team and among the club's best was particularly fierce. His battle however failed to bring results. The team ended sixth, 13 points behind champions Hull Kingston Rovers.

The 1979-80 season also started with the absence of Green who was still struggling to recuperate and to regain fitness. During his absence the club's bad run continued with regular losses, the odd win and a few draws. Despite the presence of new try scorers such as Jimmy Hornby, Wigan's sandglass was running empty. Green returned to play only four matches but could not make the same impact as before. At the end of the season, the club finished 13th was in the relegation zone, a distant 25 points behind champions Bradford Northern. A drop to the second division together with Hunslet, York and Blackpool Borough was the result. This had serious implications for overseas players like Green.

The relegation brought added pressures, given the fact that the club had to balance its books and had to seriously consider the way forward given its legal commitments to both sponsors and players. Maintaining players on the books in particular proved to be very difficult. Tough decisions had to be made. It was unavoidable: for the first and only time in their history, Wigan were relegated. Green was transferred to Swinton for £15,000, this offer beating Widnes's bid of £14,000. Curiously, he had never scored against Swinton in his seven years at Wigan. During his stay at Wigan, he played 166+2 matches and scored 86 tries and one goal for a total of 260 points.

The bare statistics and records do not do justice to Green's impact at Wigan, at a time when the club was in decline. Colin Clarke recalls him as a "class winger and a great entertainer". Wigan forward Bill Ashurst recalls Green's hat-trick at Leeds which helped his opposing winger, international John Atkinson, decide that he should retire from the game![22] In fact, according to Leeds historians Phil Caplan and Peter Smith, it was only a brief retirement: "[Atkinson] announced a brief retirement after being tormented by Wigan's Green Vigo in a televised John Player Trophy tie at Headingley."[23]

In his first season at Swinton, he scored a try against Wigan in a high profile Boxing Day clash at Station Road. At Swinton he was top try scorer in both his seasons with the club, with 14 in 1980-81 and 1981-82. However, he was not only a try scorer. Stephen M. Wild recalls in 1981-82: "Against York it was Green Vigo who had done the damage as Swinton raced into a 25-0 half-time lead. In one incident he found himself as the last line of defence and faced two opponents who had broken through alongside each other and looked certain to score. However, Vigo had other ideas and to make absolutely sure that he got the ball he literally threw both men virtually over the advertising boards in one almighty tackle." [24]

After two seasons at Swinton, it was time for a third move and on to new challenges. Green then joined Oldham in the 1982-83 season. During his three year stay with the club, he continues to pile up the points. In 1982, he left to join *Oldham RLFC* on a three year contract where he played a further 63 matches and scored 20 tries, scoring 73 points,[25] concluding a career that lasted more than a decade.

Representative rugby

During the 1970s, the Other Nationalities side was revived to try to add some interest to the waning county championship. Green made his debut at Hull against Yorkshire on 18 September 1974, a 22-15 defeat and then scored the next week on 25 September 1974, in a 19-12 defeat against Cumbria at Whitehaven. He played at centre, his winger being fellow South African David Barends. In 1975-76 he played three games, scoring against Cumbria. After that season, the team was disbanded. Green was eligible to play for Great Britain, and fellow South African David Barends played for Great Britain in 1979 on the Lions tour to Australia. Green had injury problems at this time, but it is interesting to speculate whether Green would have got that place – Barends himself acknowledges Green's natural talent.

After rugby

After a 12 year rugby league playing career, Green Vigo retired from the game and by choice, completely disappeared from the rugby league scene. His withdrawal was so complete that some newspapers prematurely reported his death. He however continues to live in the north of England far from the adulation of the supporters on the terraces and the gaze of the rugby league media. In comparison to other high profile former league players that capitalised on their league experience by becoming either coaches or managers, Vigo took a different route, making a clean break with the sport. He also readily admits that he never planned an entry into coaching nor does he think that he would have made a good coach.[26] Now, he spends more time with family and friends, and at times contemplates what was and could have been. In his home town, his example has not been forgotten and his sacrifices continue to serve as a source of pride and motivation for youngsters. During his most recent visit in June 2008, he gave permission to the newly established West Coast Raiders Rugby League Province to attach his name to their provincial club competition. The organisation in turn has forwarded his name for recognition to the South African Rugby League and their Pioneers Programme.

Photo of Green Vigo courtesy Robert Gate

References:

Books
Booley, A; (1998), *Forgotten Heroes: History of Black Rugby 1882 - 1992,* Cape Town, Manie Booley Publications
Dobson, P; (1989), *Rugby in South Africa: A history, 1861 - 1988*, Cape Town, The South African Rugby Board
Swanton, D; (1999) *The Central Park Years*, Wigan Warriors RLFC

Internet:
Vince Karalius at http:en.wikipedia.org/wiki/Vince_Karalius
Virtual Rugby League Hall of Fame: Vince Karalius at www.rlhalloffame.org.uk/Karalius.htm
www.wiganwarriors.com/SquadMember.asp?teamid=5&id=243
wigan.rlfans.com/fusion_pages/index.php?pagr_id=393
www.rugbyleagueheritageproject.com

Oral Testimony / Personal Communication
Green Vigo to Frank Daniels, 1 February 2007
Green Vigo to Hendrik Snyders, 1 February 2007

---

[1] H. Snyders, (2008), *Between the Springbok and Ikhamanga*
[2] A. Williams – Personal Communication
[3] A. Booley, (1998), *Forgotten Heroes*
[4] P. Dobson, (1989), *Rugby in South Africa*
[5] P. Dobson, (1989), *Rugby in South Africa*
[6] F. Kemp,(1973), "*Green Vigo, die Superster*"/ ("*Green Vigo, the Superstar*") in *Rapport Ekstra*
[7] Jeff Goodwin, (1973), "…..*Hunt*"
[8] P. Dobson,(1989), *Rugby in South Africa*
[9] F. Kemp,(1973) "*Green Vigo, die Superster*"/ ("*Green Vigo, the Superstar*"), in *Rapport Ekstra*
[10] George Gerber, (1973), "*Dis onwaar dat ons Vigo wou keer*" – sê mnr. Loriston"- *Rapport Ekstra*
[11] Rapport Ekstra (1974) "*Green Vigo wil weer vir S.A. speel*", in *Rapport Ekstra*, 20 Januarie
[12] Arnold Whycliff,(1973), "*Give Vigo a Chance*"- The Wigan Observer, Friday, August 17
[13] J. Humphreys (1973), "*Green for go as Vigo ends on-off saga!*", in *Daily Mirror*, July 24; p. 23
[14] F. Kemp,(1973), "*Green Vigo, Die Superster*"/ (*Green Vigo , the Super Star*") in *Rapport Ekstra*
[15] Colin Clarke in T. Collins & P. Melling (eds.), (2004), *The Glory of their Times*, Vertical Editions
[16] "*The Wigan Wizard*"
[17] "*Saldanha Tiger Roars*"
[18] "*Saldanha Tiger Roars*"
[19] "*The Wigan Wizard*"
[20] George & Marie Gerber, (1978),"*Green Vigo Is Nog Blitsig*" in *Die Burger Ekstra*
[21] "*Good marksman needed by Wigan*",
[22] *The Glory of their Times*, p.111, Mike Rylance chapter on David Barends. (Vertical Editions 2004)
[23] *100 Greats – Leeds Rugby League Football Club* by Phil Caplan & Peter Smith (Tempus 2001), p.11
[24] *The Lions of Swinton* by Stephen M. Wild (1999 – self published) p.494
[25] Personal Communication, Michael Turner (Oldham Rugby League Heritage Trust) – Hendrik Snyders; 13 December 2006
[26] Green Vigo, Personal Communication, 28 June 2008

Between the Springbok and Ikhamanga
The untold story of South Africa's black rugby exiles [1]

Hendrik Snyders looks at the lives of those from the coloured and African communities who left South Africa to play rugby league.

Introduction

Between the late 1950s and mid-1970s a number of very talented black and white rugby union players left South Africa in search of fame and fortune in the ranks of rugby league in Britain and Australia. Whereas white players who switched codes and moved overseas or played in South Africa in the early 1960s, like Tom van Vollenhoven, Colin Greenwood, Fred Griffiths, Dawie Ackermann, Martin Pelser and Wilf Rosenberg were internationally known, the case was different for the Goolam Abed, Andile (Duncan) Pikoli, Enslin Dlambulo, Vernon Petersen, David Barends, Louis Neumann and Green Vigo. All of these players were national representatives (Springboks, Leopards or Proteas) within South Africa's then racially defined rugby union structures. White players enjoyed full national honours and were able to compete regularly against the world's best at Twickenham, Eden Park and other famous union stadiums, but their black counterparts were denied similar opportunities.

In addition, their national rugby bodies were refused admission into to the ranks of the International Rugby Board (IRB). Despite their obvious talent, not all the players mentioned had the same measure of success in rugby league or were able to secure a successful life and career after their playing days were over. Their struggles, sacrifices, failures and successes are rarely acknowledged in the rugby mainstream and are further complicated by a lack of formal records. Although some individuals had their achievements acknowledged under the new South African Rugby Union's (SARU) Yesterday's Heroes Programme [2], the receipt of the national Order of Ikhamanga (Bronze) and induction into the South African Sports Hall of Fame [3] respectively, the greater majority is largely forgotten and unknown. Between their achievement of Springbok colours from their various ethnic associations and the receipt of the Order of Ikhamanga, lies a history of struggle and great sacrifice, obscured by the passing of time. This article aims to record the untold story of South Africa's African and coloured rugby exiles and to place it in the mainstream of South African history.

Writing black rugby history

Despite the pioneering work of professional historians such as Andre Odendaal (1995)[4] and John Nauright (1999)[5], as well as the contributions of rugby historian Paul Dobson (1989)[6] and others such as Manie Booley (1998),[7] the notion that black South Africans lack an established rugby legacy has continued into the post-apartheid rugby age. Whether this is as a result of a lack of interest in the academic history of the sport amongst rugby fans, or because of the superficial nature of popular rugby magazines such as *Rugby World South Africa* [8] or *Fifteen,* [9] is debatable. This situation has contributed to the continued denial of the black contribution to the building and expansion of the South African rugby and national identity[10] in an era where sport has become "an important signifier of national identity."[11] Given the well established link that has been observed between rugby and manliness in diverse societies and in academic discourse, this exclusion may even be interpreted as the continued denial of the manliness of these players. Against this background, Eastern Cape columnist and African rugby writer, Jimmy Matyu, as well as *uMkontho we Sizwe*[12] veteran, Basil Kivedo, used public platforms such as a newspaper column[13] and an arts festival[14] respectively, to highlight the achievements of some of the legends of black rugby. Critics such as Vuyisa Qunta, also accused the rugby establishment, broadcast media and the SA Rugby Legends Association, of not only ignoring the landmark publication by SA Rugby, titled *112 Years of Springbok Rugby; 1891 – 2003: Tests and Heroes*[15] but also of deliberately attempting to airbrush the black legacy out of rugby history.[16]

To aggravate matters, the biography of Chester Williams[17] by former journalist Mark Keohane, to this day remains the only publication that celebrates the career of a great black South African rugby player. Equally disappointing is Williams' own admission of his limited knowledge of the same rugby tradition he emerged and benefited from.[18] In contrast, a growing number of biographies and autobiographies, covering prominent white rugby union personalities with immediately recognisable forenames (with significant advertising value)[19] were published over the last decade.

The development of the study of South African rugby league in general and black players in particular, is far worse. In South Africa, beyond the existence of some cursory references to league in some rugby union publications, no official history or substantive body of local knowledge of the two topics exists. This is not altogether surprising if one considers that Hennie Gerber, one of the biographers of the late Dr Danie Craven, erroneously argued that most of those who left to pursue a professional career were nobodies and not famous.[20] The evidence shows that this type of statement is not only untrue but indicative of the general lack of knowledge amongst mainstream Afrikaans sportswriters about black sporting achievement in the heydays of apartheid and their slavish adoption of the establishment's view on rugby league. Allie, in a much harsher argument, argued that in the past, white sportswriters consistently displayed a sentiment that "'black' and 'top class' were words that didn't go together".[21] The preliminary study by Peter Lush (2008)[22] as well as the short biography of David Barends by Mike Rylance,[23] and interview with Barends in *Our Game* issue 14, therefore represent pioneering contributions towards the total reconstruction of South Africa's rugby identity.

Rylance's work on David Barends is also the first to unearth the hidden history of any of South Africa's black rugby league players.[24] To do justice to the full rugby legacy, writing a full history of all South Africa's rugby exiles, irrespective of colour and despite the problem of records, however, remains the ultimate challenge.[25] This was not helped by the fact that league, at the behest of local rugby union administrators, was officially repressed.[26] Matters seemed to have improved substantially under the current rugby union and league establishments. Both bodies recently announced concrete action to rectify the situation and to give equal acknowledgement to all local rugby traditions. South African rugby union, through its *Transformation Charter,* has formally committed itself to the official recording and recognition of the black rugby legacy in order to "...establish a deep internalised appreciation of the rich history and tradition of black rugby among all South Africans"[27] while South African Rugby League has started to collect the details of both clubs and players for inclusion in an Honorary Roll.[28] There is therefore a realistic hope that the attempt to fully document all the legacies that constitute the South African rugby identity, will succeed.

Politics and scouts – The making of a South African rugby league player

Rugby league was officially introduced in South Africa in the 1950s as a result of the efforts of Johannesburg businessman Ludwig Japhet who succeeded, after long negotiations with the Rugby Football League and despite public resistance in the United Kingdom,[29] in bringing the 1957 Rugby League World Cup national sides of England and France to Benoni, East London and Durban for a series of exhibition games. Despite the obvious historical significance of these games, it does not mean that these events represented the first exposure of the local rugby fraternity to the code. On the contrary, local players and administrators were not only well aware of its existence but also of the rewards on offer. Recent research by Peter Lush also indicated that as far back as 1911, the *Northern Union* received a request for a 'coloured' tour. This was however turned down and is today lamented as a lost opportunity and one that could have aided the code in finding a niche in the South African black communities.[30]

Key amongst the missionaries of the code were the league scouts who were also instrumental in recruiting white Springboks such as Attie van Heerden and Tank van Rooyen among others to play for British clubs in the 1920s. They did not only made a successful transition to the new code, but in due course also became club stalwarts[31] and given their previous union success, were able to further advance the rugby league cause – much to the dismay of union's administrators. As a result, the South African white rugby establishment adopted the same mindset of their overseas counterparts by declaring league scouts as the enemy, publicly portraying them as evil beings[32] and moral corruptors.[33] However, for those that were from the outset denied the opportunity to represent their country, the league scout was neither an evil being, reptile, "parasitical or viral agent", "wraith-like figure" or a "shadow presence"[34] but a chance for economic and sporting opportunities.

Based on the available evidence, Mr Japhet's initiative never attempted to involve or include black administrators and players. Nor was there any effort to capitalise on the existence of a near century long rugby tradition within the black community. The matches were thus unashamedly steeped in the ideology of racial separation and apartheid that dominated life in South Africa then. This special event in the end, also recorded rugby league's first contribution to apartheid by creating its own scandal when Billy Boston, one of Great Britain's most talented and able (black) players, refused to comply with apartheid South Africa's conditions for visiting such as separate travel and accommodation arrangements. His principals however decided to steer clear from politics and excluded him from the touring team[35] and proceeded with spreading the gospel of the XIII man code locally. Being black in a white team in segregated and apartheid-dominated South Africa during the 1950s, Boston learned, was all wrong.

Despite their exclusion from the rugby union mainstream, black rugby administrators continued to provide representative rugby for their charges in the form of inter-racial 'tests' between Africans and Coloureds. These tests over time acquired a special status within the black community and became important arena for the making of men.[36] These annual contests also served as a showcase for the available talent and an opportunity to display an equal measure of "commitment to muscle, and to arduous activity,"[37] while in typical working class – fashion, utilizing innovative play ("trickery"), intimidation and aggressive competition to ensure victory.[38] Against this background, preparations for Japhet's exhibition matches proceeded apace. It also roughly coincided with an equal amount of preparations for the fifth ethnic test between the South African coloured

Rugby Union XV (or the coloured Springboks) and South African Bantu (or African) Rugby XV set down for 5 October 1957 in Port Elizabeth through their respective inter-provincial Rhodes and Partons Cup competitions. This match as well as the previous four encounters and all subsequent contests, [39] as indicated were the racial alternative for full international competition. It was during these tests and from this background, that players such as Goolam Abed, Andile (Duncan) Pikoli, Enslin Dlambulo, and Winty Pandle, established their claims to greatness en route to carving their own niche in rugby league abroad.

Ever since his selection as a Springbok for the South African Bantu Rugby Board (SABRB) on 7 October 1950, Winty Pandle regularly made rugby headlines. After the first test, the post match report recorded that Pandle "grubbered into the goal area and chased after the ball, at which stage he was tackle" that resulted in a penalty try which helped to ensure a 14-3 victory for the Africans. Over the course of five tests between 1950 and 1952, the nuggety, but fast[40] Pandle set the standard for attacking wing play in the black rugby fraternity despite having to play under atrocious conditions, which often included having to dodge interfering spectators on township fields while scoring tries.[41] With his reputation cemented as one of the most dangerous backs in black rugby, there was however nowhere else to go in South Africa.

In order to provide incentives for further excellence for their players, the two non-white rugby boards engaged in talks to bring about the formation of a single body with a view to international touring. Unsurprisingly, the first destination on their tour wish-list was New Zealand to play the Maoris, the black alternative for the "old enemy" and the "one that count". To realise this dream, no time was wasted and no time was lost in starting a fundraising drive.[42] The idea was short-lived and a possible tour to Fiji, the victors in the series against Australia in 1953 was then investigated, seemingly as an opportunity to prove the ability of the local black rugby establishment to hold their own against the best. With this in mind, a combined non-racial African / Coloured Federation team that included players such as Pandle, was selected. The dream to formally represent their country against the same opposition that defeated their white compatriots, however, never materialised given the persistent opposition as well as "misgivings"[43] from the white South African Rugby Board (SARB).[44] In addition, the prevailing unstable political situation and increasing levels of political discontent[45] convinced the authorities to deny some black players travelling documents. Despite these setbacks and their obvious disappointment, the chosen players bounced back and continue to blossom and excel, albeit on their ethnic stage.

Unaware of the keen competition on the other side of the railway tracks, but greatly encouraged by the attempt by the locals to establish the code, the leadership of British rugby league and their charges, but minus Boston, continued with their tour. For their actions and compliance with South Africa's racial laws, they were severely criticized by sections of the British rugby league media.[46] In addition to this, the white South African Rugby Board, custodians of rugby union, went out of their way to oppose the exhibition of the rival code.

The events surrounding the Japhet initiative clearly showed Craven's willingness, even to the extent of compromising his principles, to use whatever means he had at his disposal to fight rugby league. Unable to prevent the exhibition matches, the SARB under his presidency, took active steps to repress the further growth of the new code amongst white players. To discourage their players from joining rugby league, affiliated clubs were encouraged to bar such players from their facilities. In addition, former union players were denied any further contact with the code while Springboks who have crossed the divide, were requested to return their national colours, an action labelled by the renowned rugby journalist, A. C. Parker (1970), as pure pettiness.[47]

Given the mainstream rugby establishment view, and its allegiance to the dictates of the IRB, the decision by both white and black players to go professional therefore represents their first step towards self-exile.

Despite its failure to make major inroads, the exhibition tour did enough to convince a few more white players to join the professional ranks. On 26 October 1957, a mere three weeks after Goolam Abed and Enslin Dlambulo made their respective debuts in the second inter-racial test, the legendary Springbok, Tom van Vollenhoven joined St Helens RLFC for a signing on fee of £4,000; the Saints having outbid Wigan.[48] In comparison, nothing changed for those black players who had just finished their second test on their less resourced facility in the township. At least the coloured Springboks walked away with full bragging rights for a year after their 18-11 victory in a match regarded by some as probably the highlight of Goolam Abed's South African career.[49]

In April 1958, as a result of tactical and personality differences, unity in the ranks of the SACRB was shattered by a breakaway of 14 unions and 10,000 players to form Western Province League. The new union in time became the driving force behind the founding of another 'coloured' national body called the S. A. Rugby Football Federation[50] and thereby added new difficulties to an already complex rugby situation. Despite the administrative squabbles within black rugby at large, new talent continue to emerge while recently capped players like Abed and Dlambulo, continue to make their mark.

The 1960s were a particularly bad time for all South Africans, including rugby players. The first major national shock of the new decade was the killing of 69 black protestors at Sharpeville on 21 March 1960 after a protest march against the country's notorious and restrictive pass laws. Following shortly thereafter on 8 April was the banning of the main black political organisations, including the African National Congress (ANC) and the Pan Africanist Congress (PAC), the declaration of a nation-wide state of emergency in more than 100 magisterial districts and increased repression of the opponents of racial segregation and apartheid (including black rugby players and administrators) as well as the declaration of the White Republic on 31 May 1961.

These events and the subsequent restrictions placed on freedom of movement, further limited the already sparse opportunities for talented Black individuals and left them with increased frustration. In the wake of these events and a lack of progress on rugby unity, leaving the country in search of self development became the only option. Encouraged and assisted by league scouts, local journalists[51] and ironically by the recommendations of white South African players such as Ivor Dorrington[52] and former Springbok Louis Babrow, various players were persuaded to depart for overseas.

From the South to the North – exits and new beginnings

Among the first to leave on the eve of receiving his fourth national cap in 1961 was Goolam Abed, accompanied by Louis Neumann[53] of Thistles Rugby Football Club, Western Province and the City & Suburban Rugby Union in a deal facilitated by Babrow and Jim Windsor, a Yorkshire bookmaker. As unknowns in the white media, but armed with the recommendation of a former white Springbok, both players were offered a guaranteed paid return trip and a stint as amateurs but with no guarantee of a professional contract[54] with Leeds RLFC. In contrast, their white counterparts based on their reputations (and possibly even race) were able to secure such contracts even before leaving South Africa.[55] Playing as amateurs meant that the rookies still had to prove their worth before being considered for a professional contract.

Ever since his debut match against Hunslet, Abed, a back, struggled to make his mark in a very competitive code. Neumann, on the other hand, had far less problems as a forward and was able to make his mark right from the outset. Ironically, within the Leeds set up both players find themselves as equals to their white compatriot and former Springbok centre Wilf Rosenberg. After a bumpy start as a trialist and with the assistance of Rosenberg,[56] Abed sufficiently impressed the scouts and was offered a five year contract worth £1,000 per year as a centre and wing by Bradford Northern (now the Bradford Bulls).[57] During his three year stint at the club, he played in 46 matches, scoring five tries and 55 goals.[58] This was followed by a further two seasons with Batley RLFC where he played 36 matches, scoring four tries and 44 goals, before his eventual retirement as a result of an injured shoulder.[59]

After his successful Leeds debut, Neumann fully established himself in the code and was able to secure a contract with the Australian club, *Eastern Suburbs* (later the *Sydney Roosters*) where he stayed for four seasons (1967 to 1971). During this time, he made 81 first class appearances for the club. In addition, he earned further accolades by becoming their player-coach during a difficult 1969 season, a mere two years after moving to Australia and added another 22 matches as coach, albeit with mixed successes, to his league record.[60] Having made his name with one of Australia's foremost clubs,[61] he obtained a new contract with Orange RLFC in New South Wales.[62]

After making his breakthrough in the new code and based on his own experiences, Abed had the opportunity to open the way for one of his rugby peers. When asked to identify a player of equal talent and ability for recruitment, he nominated his former opponent in the rugby tests between coloured and African, Enslin Dlambulo.[63] Dlambulo, an agile and athletic loose-forward[64] took the opportunity offered with both hands to suitably impress the talent scouts and joined Abed in 1962 at Bradford Northern.

At Bradford they were soon joined by another compatriot from black rugby, Vernon Petersen, an SACRB Springbok of the 1964 test against the SA Rugby Federation. In addition, the African Springboks Andile (Duncan) Pikoli and Winty Pandle joined Barrow RLFC in 1962-63 to add a further blow to black rugby in pursuit of their dreams but, like their predecessors, left "without any official recognition of their time wearing the national jersey" [65] or without having had the opportunity to "uphold the honour of the mother country and to symbolize national definition in the world".[66]

As at Leeds, Abed, Petersen and Dlambulo found themselves in the same team as one of their white compatriots, Rudy Hasse. During this time, which is also regarded in the club's history as its most difficult period, Dlambulo played 26 matches in which he scored three tries.[67] In addition, he also played for the 'A' team. It was at Bradford that white, coloured and black South African rugby players played for the same team for the first time in either rugby code.

This start was however soon complicated when, on 10 December 1963, the club went out of business. Fortunately for the newly-contracted players, it reformed in August 1964, in time for the 1964-65 season. During this difficult time both Dlambulo and Abed, with limited options at their disposal, remained with the club until the end of the 1964-65 season. This decision proved to be correct as it allowed them to repay their debt to the club and to get fully acquainted with the code. As a result Dlambulo was able to obtain a two-year contract with Keighley, where he stayed until his retirement in 1968.[68]

Ironically Rugby League South Africa, formed after a merger between the rival National Rugby League and Rugby League South Africa in 1963, and supposedly the custodians of the league code in South Africa, was in a very poor state.[69] Following the country's laws and customs of the time, they did not offer black players a local alternative to rugby union. In the end league racial exclusivity, disorganisation and internal squabbles in the ranks of black rugby associations together with rugby and political apartheid and hostility to league on the side of the IRB-recognised SARB, left talented black players with no other alternative than to seek a future abroad to progress their rugby careers. To further aggravate matters, unity talks between the various racially based rugby controlling bodies (SARFF, SARB, SARU and the SAARB) once again failed. By 1965, racial exclusivity on the social and rugby field was further strengthened by the declaration of the Prime Minister Verwoerd that the All Blacks would not be allowed entry if they decided to select Maoris for their touring side to South Africa.

By the start of the 1970s and with no significant change in sight, the second generation of talented black rugby players also prepare to leave. The first of this new wave to depart in December 1970 was David Barends, a SARU coloured Springbok and another talented player from the Roslyns club. Once again the efforts of Jim Windsor, assisted by Ivor Dorrington, resulted in the successful conclusion of a contract between Barends and Wakefield Trinity based on an initial signing-on fee of £1,000.[70] After scoring two tries on his debut, his place in the league ranks was assured that allowed him to settle down and spent three seasons with the club during which time he refined his game. He then moved to York where he spent four productive years and left with an enhanced reputation when he signed with Bradford Northern in 1977. During the Bradford years from 1977-78 to 1982-3, he made 202 appearances and scored 70 tries to establish him as one of their best players of that time.[71] Although not a British citizen at the time, by 1979 having fulfilled the required residency period and learnt his rugby league in Great Britain, his efforts and talent were finally acknowledged when he was selected to represent Great Britain on tour to Australia, playing two test matches.

Despite the on-going successes of South Africans in league and the worsening political situation at home, nothing much changed in the administration of the local union game. In 1973, rugby unity talks failed again and motivated more players to leave. Green Vigo, star of both the 1971 Protea (coloured) tour to the UK and the Protea versus England match the same year at the Athlone Stadium, became the most high profile black player of his era to join rugby league despite advice to the contrary.[72] Having proved his worth against some of the best of Great Britain, Wigan offered him a five year contract. His career is covered more fully elsewhere in *Rugby League Review*.

League and life abroad

In addition to having to learn rugby league, the rugby exiles had the additional challenges of getting use to playing with and against whites as equals as well having to adapt to living in a free and open society. Contrary to any preconceived ideas that they might have had, racism in its various guises has been part of rugby league ever since Lucius Banks of *Hunslet*, the first black player, joined the code in 1912. This is not fully surprising given the fact that the sport had "...Otherise[d] people of colour,"[73] leading to a situation where they, according to former league star, Roy Francis, automatically became 'personalities'.[74] Given the frequency of their selection as centres and wingers, the popular perception (and stereotypical view) of black players as 'dangerous' because of their speed and aggressiveness was omnipresent. Melling & Collins (2004) and others indicated that most black rugby league players, irrespective of nationality, had to endure incidences of racial taunting,[75] positional segregation,[76] physical manhandling as well as open spectator hostility [77] prior, during and even after matches. Participating in a semi-professional set-up also meant that black players had to be prepared for professional jealousy - "here is another one after your job". [78]

On the other hand, it should also be recognised that rugby league had far more black participants than football or rugby union at senior levels, and these players were often heroes in their local communities.

The South African rugby exiles, already burdened by their own racial experiences, then entered into an arena that was far from perfect. Several of them over the course of their playing career, were indeed subjected to disparaging and hurtful comments by their opponents about their colour and nationality.[79] They also encountered and were exposed to strangers making denigrating racial remarks off the field.[80] Although none reported a similar experience, it would also come as no surprise if they had, like others before them, on occasion suffered insults to wife and family.[81] Despite these difficulties, Abed remarked: "I left South Africa because I was restricted there and could not develop further. Although there was racial prejudice on the part of spectators at the time, in Britain I tasted freedom and far less restrictions than in South Africa. It was difficult at times when players on other teams made comments about colour and nationality. But I usually ended up having a drink with them and becoming firm friends"[82]

This statement clearly indicated the high level of resolve that existed in their ranks and not to allow these obstacles to cloud their vision. Furthermore, given the fact that some of them were playing for some of the most successful and trendsetting clubs in the game in the UK, these experiences to a certain extent were to be expected. The full extent of these experiences however remains to be fully researched.

In addition to coping with the demands of the game, successful integration into their new communities and adapting to the British climate became their other main challenges. Coming from the sunny southern hemisphere, daily exposure to rain and soft pitches was not to everybody's liking and made life extremely difficult.[83] The first player to quit as a result of his inability to adapt to the climatic conditions was Vernon Petersen. Even during his very short stay, he still succeeded in making his breakthrough by playing for Bradford Northern in six first team matches.[84] The fact that he was able to hold its own against competition from more experienced rivals stands out. His compatriots however decided not to quit but to stick it out in pursuit of their dreams.

Based the experience of so many other foreign players, English language proficiency,[85] adequate educational qualifications,[86] a proper support structure as well as an appropriate level of self-discipline [87] were identified as key factors to successful integration into their new communities. As could be expected, the players first and foremost had to overcome the psychological damage and feelings of inferiority inflicted upon them by apartheid.[88]

Competing successfully against and playing with former white Springboks as their rugby league equals, in this context has far greater significance. The fact that most were able to hold their own surely helped matters along. Matters on the social side were more complicated. From the available evidence, all the players, with the exception of Pandle and Vigo, had at least the benefit of a high-school education. The latter two only had a basic primary education and prior playing rugby league, both were at the bottom of the traditional career pyramid as a casual worker and fisherman, respectively. Rugby league was born out of the concerns of working people and with its close identification with that class, these educational deficiencies were never grounds for exclusion. On the contrary, possessing the necessary ball skill and talents carried much more weight.

Players like Abed, Petersen and Dlambulo at Bradford and Pikoli and Pandle at Barrow, were fortunate enough to begin their league careers at the same club. Being acquainted, they were able to share the stress and strains of relocation. In the case of the Bradford contingent, in time they also had the benefit of the company of a group of black South African cricketers (including Suleiman ('Dik') Abed, Goolam's brother) who were playing professional cricket in the UK.[89] Being former team mates of Goolam, they were able to meet on a regular basis and became a network of mutual support for each other.[90] In this situation, even the value of the presence of their white fellow country men such as Rudi Hasse and Wilf Rosenberg, cannot be discounted. There is also evidence of the existence of a warm and friendly relationship between the Bradford-[91] and Leeds - based South African rugby exiles. This allowed them not only with an opportunity to establish a 'family' away from home and to counter the inevitable home sickness during the course of their enforced exile, but also to maintain a support network for new arrivals.

Neumann who remained with Leeds and eventually left to further his career in Australia, as well as Vigo at Wigan, did not have the good fortune of sharing the overseas experience with fellow compatriots. From the evidence of one of his former team mates, it appeared as if Wigan lacked a formal player integration programme. According to Colin Clarke: "he was brought over from the outback in South Africa, dropped in the middle of Wigan and just left there. At the time there was no procedure to integrate him into society. He didn't even know how to get back to his lodgings after training. He was a class winger and a great entertainer, but he couldn't come to grips with the culture. [92]" They however provided the player with all the necessities for settling down such as the appropriate clothing for the British climate, lodgings with an elderly and caring couple, Mr and Mrs Halliday who, according to the player, treated him as an own child as well as arranging extra English lessons.[93]

Furthermore his segregated past and rural background seemed to have aggravated instead of assisting matters and combined to get the player off to a very problematic start. Without suggesting that his own personal flaws be excused, it also appeared as if these early experiences fundamentally influenced Vigo's subsequent career. Due to a lack of evidence, it is not possible to look at Neumann's experience down under.

The second player to quit his first club after the first two seasons in league, 1961 to 1963, with Barrow was Andile (Duncan) Pikoli. He subsequently played for perennial strugglers Liverpool City. His time at Barrow is known as the 'yo-yo' years that followed the 'golden years' which ended in 1957,[94] meant that their arrival and stay coincided with Barrow's demotion to the second division of the league. This placed them in a very difficult situation. Given their situation at home, they had no other option than to persevere and to remain with the club until their contracts ran out. At the end of this term Pandle returned home. Pikoli on the other hand, being much more outspoken and a political activist with links to the then banned African National Congress (ANC); did not place all his hopes on a rugby league career. As a committed and proud South African, it was his hope to play an active role in freeing his homeland from apartheid. This stance and open support for the banned political movements led to the refusal of the apartheid government to issue him with a new passport and signalled his formal political exile. Unable to return home, he enrolled for an arts degree in social work at Middlesex

Polytechnic. Upon graduation, he set up home in Surrey and embarked on his chosen career with the City of Westminster. When he became eligible for British citizenship, he refused on political grounds to apply.[95]

The issue of British citizenship after a prolonged stay represented for most of these players a very important watershed. Renouncing South African citizenship in favour of a British one, went way beyond merely satisfying economic and sporting ambitions and presented them with a new dilemma. By accepting new citizenship, they would in fact formalise their own exile, meaning their presence in the UK would cease to be a temporary sojourn. Already their successes on the playing field afforded them with new opportunities and a chance to enjoy life without segregationist barriers. What complicated matters further was the fact that over time, all five remaining the players, being single men, established romantic relationships and eventually married British women. This perfectly normal event however had serious political and social implications for the players concerned. Having married outside of their ethnic group was in direct conflict with South Africa's ban on mixed or inter-racial marriages and therefore represented an act of defiance. It therefore meant that none of them would be able to return home with their spouses. Any attempt to do so could only led to imprisonment and humiliation. This message was vividly brought home to all and sundry when after his marriage and acceptance of British citizenship, Goolam Abed was rewarded with a passport cut into pieces, signifying formal exile from his motherland.[96]

Despite these difficulties, the rugby exiles persevered and succeeded in establishing themselves as stalwarts for their respective teams. Being sufficiently competitive, enabled them to attract more lucrative contracts from other clubs and allowed them to build stable careers. It is clear that the rugby exiles did not only succeeded in mastering the code but were able to compete as equals with their British and international counterparts. Although only David Barends succeeded in obtaining national honours for Great Britain, all of them left an indelible mark on the clubs and communities in which they eventually settled. They, like their Australian counterparts, helped to shape and define the culture of rugby league.[97]

The after years

With their best rugby years behind them, the exiles retired to pursue new careers and interests. Crucial to this phase were the possession of special vocational or social skills (especially sporting skills) and the extent of their social integration into their respective communities to help them to cope with life beyond rugby league.

Having experience the folding of his first club at a very tender stage of his rugby league career Abed realised the necessity to diversify his interests and to use the full range of his capabilities. Being an accomplished cricketer in his own right, he developed a parallel cricketing career during the summer. Retirement from rugby in 1967-68 therefore signalled the beginning of a professional cricket career with Rochdale Cricket Club in the Central Lancashire League. Based on a successful spell at his first club, he secured further spells, both as a professional and amateur with Castleton Moor, Balshaw (Bolton Cricket Association) and Nelson cricket clubs. In addition to this, as a qualified printer engraver he established and developed a printing and engraving business in Rochdale. He also successfully combined his professional career with a variety of community roles on and off the field. Through this, he earned the respect of all and was honoured by his community as the "cricketer who broke down the racial barriers."[98]

Two of the South African stars who played in Great Britain: Louis Neumann (left) and Goolam Abed.
(Photos: Courtesy Robert Gate)

Like his friend and fellow player, Goolam Abed, Dlambulo also left Bradford Northern in 1964 and started a new career with Keighley. While playing rugby on a semi-professional basis, he took up employment with the multinational company, Magnet and remained there until he retired. Being a dedicated sportsman, he also played squash and took up practicing martial arts after his playing days were over. After qualifying as a black belt karate instructor, he expanded his community involvement by presenting martial arts classes and was active in the Association of Former Keighley Players.[99]

Life after rugby league, took a somewhat different turn for political activist and radical, Andile (Duncan) Pikoli. After his venture into league, he embarked on a career as a social worker. Career success was however no guarantee for marital bliss and Pikoli, the committed ANC veteran and cadre,[100] eventually divorced his English wife, never to remarry. On the economic front, things also did not work out as planned. At the time of his death in August 2004 at the age of 70, he was a lonely and impoverished man, estranged from his South African family. Sadly, they had to rely on the sympathy and assistance of strangers for his cremation in London and internment in South Africa.[101]

Winty Pandle like Vernon Petersen, as previously indicated, had a short stint with rugby league. Although he had all the required personality traits (loud, jovial and exuberant character and good dancer),[102] his career progress was severely constrained by his lack of a high school education. Being armed with only a basic primary education, securing a good life outside of rugby league became so much harder. Very little is also known about his life after he returned home. He passed away in 2003 without ever achieving the recognition he deserved.

After a 13 year playing career in rugby league, Green Vigo finally retired from the game in 1985 and continues to live in the north of England. By choice, he completely disappeared from the rugby league scene.[103]

In comparison, David Barends who had shared the league stage with him, went on to represent his adopted country in the international rugby league arena. Barends did not only won his fair share of honours in the game, but continues to work for the National Probation Service in South Yorkshire. He serves on the Community and Standards Committee of the South Yorkshire Police Authority's Policing and Racial Equality *Independent Advisory Group* that deals with Black and ethnic minorities.[104] He married an English woman in the early 1970s, and recalls being the first black person to move into Hemsworth, where he still lives. He has regularly visited his family in the Western

Cape, and since 1994, and the establishment of democracy at home, has been able to take his wife with him.

Conclusion

Based on the available evidence, the triple exiles, in terms of race, rugby code and citizenship and to a lesser extent even politics, were no less men than their white counterparts. As skilful and competent rugby players, their overseas venture proved beyond a doubt that they indeed possessed the required talent and ability and would not only have contributed equally towards the enrichment of South Africa's national rugby identity, but would also have brought honour to the national jersey. With rugby fields declared as arenas of war, and victory over the enemy as essential instruments of building national pride, the proven ability of the players established them as a counter hegemonic force and therefore an anathema to the supporters of apartheid. While in the current epoch in South Africa, others may reflect on the past in order to escape present realities or to legitimise their positions, this small fragment of the history of black rugby is both aimed at reclaiming the past in order to broaden the "knowable past" [105] and contributing to the efforts to record the fullness of South Africa's national rugby identity.

This is an edited version of a paper presented to the Sports History Conference at the University of Stellenbosch 30 June to 1 July 2008

---

[1] The Springbok has been the national symbol and highest honour of South African Rugby for all of the various former ethnic associations (as well as the current unified body, S. A. Rugby) for more than 100 years. Its history was captured in a specially commissioned publication edited by Dennis Cruywagen, titled: *The Badge: A Centenary of the Springbok Emblem*, (2006, Cape Town, S. A. Rugby).

Ikhamanga refers to the *National Order of Ikhamanga* awarded by the President of the Republic of South Africa to individuals who have made significant contribution in the field of arts, culture, literature, music, journalism and sport. This award is made in three categories namely gold (exceptional achievement), silver (excellent achievement) and bronze (outstanding achievement). For a fuller understanding of the insignia and illustrations thereof, see Chapter 5 of the publication *Highest Honour: South African National Orders*, (2004), Pretoria, Chancery of Orders, The Presidency; p.47

The term 'black' is used here to refer to all those rugby players who would have been classified as 'non-white' under apartheid.

The title is derived from the statements by Goolam Abed in an interview with the *Rochdale Observer* on 5 December 2003 after he received the Order of Ikhamanga. On that occasion he stated: "The new awards, as far as sport was concerned, went to those who were good enough to have played for the Springboks but for the apartheid system. These people had to go into exile to try and get to the top in their sports."

[2] Under this programme, players capped by the various Black ethnic rugby bodies were awarded with official Springbok colours based upon motivations from interested parties. This nomination process has proved to be wholly unsatisfactory and in fact caused a lot of unhappiness amongst the players concerned. The programme however remains open for nominations.

[3] R. Hartman,(2007), "*34 Named for SA's Sports Hall of Fame*", 6 December, available from www.themercury.co.za accessed 19/4/2008

[4] A. Odendaal,(1995), *'The thing that is not round': The untold history of black rugby in South Africa*", in A. Grundlingh; A. Odendaal; & B. Spies (eds), *Beyond the Tryline: Rugby and South African Society*, Johannesburg, Ravan Press

[5] J. Nauright, (1999), "*Rugby, Carnival, Masculinity and Identities in 'Coloured' Cape Town*", in T. J.L. Chandler & J. Nauright (eds.),(1999); *Making the Rugby World: Race, Gender, Commerce*; London, Frank Cass

[6] P. Dobson,(1989), *Rugby in South Africa: A History, 1861 – 1988*, (Cape Town)

[7] A. Booley, (1998), *Forgotten Heroes: A History of Black Rugby, 1882 – 1992*, (Cape Town, Manie Booley Publications)

[8] *Rugby World South Africa* is published monthly by *In-site Media (Pty) Ltd* under license from IPC Media Ltd in London and is under the editorship of Andy Colquhoun, newly appointed SARU Director of Communication. As a magazine, they concentrate more on the player's voice (if still alive) and less on the detailed history. Personal Communication: A. Colquhoun – H. Snyders, 13 August 2007

[9] *Fifteen* is the official SA Rugby Magazine under the editorship of Simon Borchardt, published by *Highbury Safika Media (Pty) Ltd* and is provided to all subscribed members of the Springbok Supporters Club.

[10] The process of building and rebuilding South Africa's national rugby identity is work-in-progress given the exclusion of the Black contribution and the impact of the isolation years of the 1980' in preventing the finalization of this process. See also A. Grundlingh,(2008), "*Rands for Rugby: Ramifications of the Professionalisation of South African Rugby, 1995 – 2007*", Paper delivered at the International Conference on the History of Sport and Sport Studies in Southern Africa, Stellenbosch, South Africa, 30 June – 1 July 2008; p. 3

[11] J. Harris (2006), "*(Re)Presenting Wales: National Identity and Celebrity in the Post modern Rugby World*", in *North American Journal of Welsh Studies*, vol. 6, no. 2, Summer; p. 1

[12] The military wing of the African National Congress prior to the establishment of democracy in 1994.

[13] J. Matyu, (2006), "*PE, Uitenhage townships strongholds of rugby*"; http://www.theherald.co.za/colarc/town/mj28062006.htm, (19/4/2008); J. Matyu, (2007), "*Exploits of sportsman supreme Eric Majola mustn't be forgotten*"; http://www.theherald.co.za/colrac/town/mj31102007.htm, (19/4/2008)

[14] B. Kivedo, (2007), "*Wie is die Bruin Gemeenskap?*"/ ("*Who is the Coloured Community*"), http://www.outlitnet.co.za/seminaar/kknkkivedo.asp, (26/07/2007)

[15] S. A. Rugby, (2003), *112 Years of Springbok Rugby; 1891 – 2003: Tests and Heroes;* Cape Town, Highbury Monarch

[16] V. Qunta, (2007), "*Airbrushed out of rugby history*", in *Mail & Guardian*, 25 April

[17] M. Keohane, (2002); *Chester: A Biography of Courage,* Cape Town, Don Nelson

[18] M. Keohane, (2002); *Chester: A Biography of Courage,* p. 159

[19] Book Review: In Black and White – The Jake White Story; www.rugby365.com, (27/4/2008)

[20] H. Gerber, (1982), *Craven*, Cape Town, Tafelberg; p. 190

[21] M. Allie,(2000), *More than a Game: History of the Western Province Cricket Board, 1959 – 1991*, Cape Town, W. P. Cricket Association; p. 49

[22] P. Lush, 2008, "*Rugby League and South Africa: A Preliminary Study*", Paper delivered to the International Conference on the History of Sport and Sport Studies in Southern Africa, Stellenbosch, South Africa, 30 June – 1 July 2008

[23] M. Rylance, 2004, "*David Barends*", in T. Collins & P. Melling, (eds.), (2004), *The Glory of their Times: Crossing the Colour Line in Rugby League,* (Skipton, Vertical Editions)

[24] The author is working on a short biographical essay on former Wigan player, Green Vigo.

[25] "*Tribute to South African League*", an article by B. Haslam, "*League in South Africa*" that was published in Open Rugby <http://www.angelfire.com/nd/rleague/sa.html>; (3/1/2008); "*South African Rugby League: History*",<http://www.sarugbyleague.co.za/history.html>; (2/5/2007)

[26] Previously Rugby League had to deal with a system that labelled and classified even video footage of a league final, as objectionable and undesirable material. National Archives (NA), Cape Town Archives Repository (KAB) 2/220: R84/3/69: *Objectionable Films and Videos: 1983 - Rugby League Grand Final*

[27] W. Basson, (2006), South African Rugby Union's Broad-based Transformation Process and Charter, Unpublished Policy and Strategy Document, Newlands, S. A. Rugby Union, June; p. 46

[28] "*South African Rugby League to Honour all their Pioneers*", 2008, http://www.sarugbyleague.co.za; (18/02/2008). In a recent circular to its provinces, dated 9 June 2008, S. A. Rugby League announced a partnership with Peter Lush to document the full history of the code locally.

[29] T. Collins & P. Melling, (eds.), (2004), *The Glory of their Times: Crossing the Colour Line in Rugby League*, p. 13

[30] P. Lush, 2008, "*Rugby League and South Africa: A Preliminary Study*", Paper delivered to the International Conference on the History of Sport and Sport Studies in Southern Africa, Stellenbosch, South Africa, 30 June – 1 July 2008

[31] D. Swanton, 1993, *The Central Park Years*, p. 91

[32] P. Dobson, 1994, *Doc: The Life of Danie Craven*, p. 149

[33] P. Melling, (1996), "*Definitions for Definers, not the Defined*": A Study of the mind-set of the two rugby codes", www.rl1908.com; (31/12/2007)

[34] P. Melling, (1996), "*Definitions for Definers, not the Defined*": A Study of the mind-set of the two rugby codes", www.rl1908.com; (31/12/2007)

[35] D. Kuzio, "*Racism in Rugby League*", http://www.wires.u-net.com/racismrl.htm; (13/02/2008); P. Melling, 2004, "*Billy Boston*" in T. Collins & P. Melling, (eds.), (2004), *The Glory of their Times: Crossing the Colour Line in Rugby League,* p. 58

[36] J. Nauright, (1999), " *Rugby, Carnival, Masculinity and Identities in 'Coloured' Cape Town*"; p. 28

[37] T. Chandler & J. Nauright (eds.), (1996),"*Introduction: Rugby, Manhood and Identity*", in *Making Men: Rugby and Masculine Identity*, London, Frank Cass & Co.; p. 6

[38] J. W. Martens,(1996), "Rugby, Class, Amateurism and Manliness; p. 38

[39] In the period 1950 – 1967, 11 tests were played. The *South African Rugby Annual* (2004) provides useful statistics with regards to the number of tests played by each of these players. It is however incomplete and must be read together with the publications of Booley (1998) and Dobson (1989).

[40] S. A. Rugby, (2003), *112 Years of Springbok Rugby; 1891 – 2003: Tests and Heroes*; p. 69

[41] J. Matyu, (2006),"*PE, Uitenhage townships strongholds of rugby*"

[42] P. Dobson, (1989), *History of South African Rugby*, p. 204

[43] A. Odendaal, (1995), "*The thing that is not round*"; p. 44

[44] P. Dobson, (1989), *History of South African Rugby*, p. 175

[45] A. Odendaal, (1995), "*The thing that is not round*"; p. 52

[46] T. Collins & P. Melling, (eds.), (2004), *The Glory of their Times: Crossing the Colour Line in Rugby League,* (Skipton, Vertical Editions)

[47] A. C. Parker,(1970), *The Springboks, 1891 – 1970*, London & Johannesburg (Cassell); p.237

[48] *Tom van Vollenhoven: Rugby League History*, http://rugbyleaguehistory.co.uk/?page_id=24; (31/12/2007); S. A. Rugby, (2003), *112 Years of Springbok Rugby; 1891 – 2003: Tests and Heroes*; p. 88

[49] SA Rugby,(2003), *112 Years of Springbok Rugby*; p. 98

[50] P. Dobson, (1989), *The History of South African Rugby, 1888 – 1988*

[51] V. Qunta, (2007), "*Unsung Heroes of S. A. Sport*", in *Your Sport*, 2nd Quarter; p. 10

[52] M. Rylance,(2004), "*David Barends*" in T. Collins & P. Melling, (eds.), (2004), *The Glory of their Times: Crossing the Colour Line in Rugby League,* (Skipton, Vertical Editions)

[53] Some sources including Allie (2000) based on interviews with Goolam Abed, spells his surname as Neumann and in one instance, namely the paper of Kivedo presented at the Klein Karoo National Arts Festivals, he is also referred to as Peter Newman.

[54] SARU,(2003), *112 Years of Springbok Rugby*, p. 98

[55] *Rochdale Observer*, (2003), "Going back to his roots", http://www.rochdaleobserver.co.uk/sport/s/33/33530_going_back_to_his_roots.html; (27/6/2007)

[56] M. Allie, (2000), *More than a Game*; p. 49

[57] SARU,(2003), *112 Years of Springbok Rugby*; p. 98

[58] Personal Communication, John Downes (Heritage Development Officer: Bradford Bulls Foundation) – Hendrik Snyders; 7/8/2007

[59] Personal Communication, Laurie Grailey (Batley Bull Dogs Club Historian) – Hendrik Snyders; 3/8/2007

[60] Personal Communication, Amy Herisson, Marketing and Membership Coordinator, Sydney Roosters – N. Goos; 27/3/2008

[61] Eastern Suburbs is one of Australia's State of Origin clubs being part of the small group of clubs that established the code down under. Becoming their player coach within a short time after his conversion to league, therefore speaks volumes of his talent and ability.

[62] Personal Communication, N. Goos – H. Snyders, 28/3/2008; see also V. Qunta, (2007), "*Unsung Heroes of SA Sport*; in *Your Sport*, 2nd Quarter; p. 10. An effort to establish the whereabouts of Newman, whose surname was changed to Neumann, thus far proved unsuccessful but continues with the assistance from contacts in Australia.

[63] Dispatch Online, (2004), "*England-based rugby veteran earns his Springbok Colours*", http://www.dispatch.co.za/2004/08/25/Sport/html ; (26/07/2007); Craven Herald, (2004), "*Rugby Union-hero honoured after 40 Years*", http://archive.cravenherald.co.uk/2004/9/17/971968html ; (26/07/2007); Dispatch Online, (2003), "*Rugby Veteran finally given his Bok Colours*", http://www.dispatch.co.za/2003/01/15/Sport/AGIVEN/HTM; (26/07/2007)

[64] SARU CEO, Mveleli Ncula as cited in "*Veteran earns Bok Colours*", http://www.news24.com/News24v2/components/Generic/News24v4; (19/4/2008)

[65] *Rochdale Observer*, (2003), "*Going back to his roots*", http://www.rochdaleobserver.co.uk/sport/s/33/33530_going_back_to_his_roots.html ; (27/6/2007)

[66] J. Harris,(2006), "*(Re)Presenting Wales..*"; p. 5

[67] Personal Communication, John Downes (Heritage Development Officer: Bradford Bulls Foundation) – Hendrik Snyders; 7/8/2007

[68] The author is in communication with the Keighley Ex Players Association with a view to obtain Dlambulo's career statistics
[69] "*South African Rugby League: History*", http://www.sarugbyleague.co.za/history.html ; (2/5/2007)
[70] M. Rylance, 2004, "*David Barends*", pp. 108 - 109
[71] Personal Communication, John Downes (Heritage Development Officer: Bradford Bulls Foundation) – Hendrik Snyders; 7/8/2007
[72] According to an article by George Gerber in the South African newspaper, Rapport, Vigo left with the blessing of his union, the South African Rugby Federation whose president thought that the player should have stayed at least until the scheduled match against the 1974 British Lions in order to increase his monetary value. See G. Gerber, (1973), "Dis onwaar dat ons Vigo wou keer" ("Its untrue that we wanted to stop Vigo"), Rapport Extra
[73] B. Hokowhitu, (2003), "*Race Tactics: The Racialised Athletic Body*", in *Junctures*, vol. 1, December
[74] T. Gibbons,(2004), "*Roy Francis*", in P. Melling & T. Collins,(2004), *The Glory of Their Times*; p. 41
[75] C. Hallinan, T. Bruce & J. Bennie, (2004*)*, "*Freak Goals and Magical Moments: Commonsense Understandings about Indigenous Footballers*", Conference Paper presented to the Australian Sociological Association, http://www.tasa.org.au/conferencepapers04/html , regard racial taunting by players and spectators as a clear demonstration of otherness and perceived difference.
[76] P. Melling & T. Collins,(2004), *The Glory of Their Times*; p. 13
[77] M. Turner, (2004), "*Alex Givvons*", in P. Melling & T. Collins,(2004), *The Glory of Their Times*; p.19
[78] D. Hadfield,(2004),"*Bak Diabira*", in P. Melling & T. Collins,(2004), *The Glory of Their Times*; p.119
[79] D. Appleton, (2003), "*Goolam's long wait finally over*", http://www.rochdaleobserver.co.uk/news/s/332/332624_goolams_long_wait_finally_over.html ; (19/4/2008)
[80] M. Rylance,(2004), "*David Barends*"; p. 114
[81] D. Hadfield,(2004),"*Bak Diabira*", p. 122
[82] D. Appleton, (2003), "*Goolam's long wait finally over*", http://www.rochdaleobserver.co.uk/news/s/332/332624_goolams_long_wait_finally_over.html ; (19/4/2008)
[83] M. Allie, (2000*)*, *More than a Game*; p. 50
[84] Personal Communication, Laurie Grailey, (Club Historian Bradford Bulls) – Hendrik Snyders
[85] H. Edgar, (2004), "*Joe Levula*", in P. Melling & T. Collins,(2004), *The Glory of Their Times*; p. 87
[86] C. Thomas, (2004), "*Cec Thomas*" in P. Melling & T. Collins,(2004), *The Glory of Their Times*; p. 210
[87] M. Rylance,(2004), "*David Barends*"; p. 112
[88] M. Allie, (2000), *More than a Game*; p. 49
[89] *Going back to his roots*", 29/08/2003; http://www.manchestereveningnews.co.uk/sport/s/333/333530_going_back_to_his_roots.html ; (19/4/2008)
[90] M. Allie, (2000), *More than a Game*; p. 50
[91] Personal Communication: Sharon Keanly (Daughter of Rudi Hasse) – Hendrik Snyders; 13/08/2007
[92] M. Rylance,(2004), "*David Barends*"; p. 111
[93] F. Kemp,(1973), "Green Vigo the Super Star"
[94] "*History of Barrow Rugby*", http://www.barrowrlfc.com/barrow_rugby_clubinfo.asp?ID=CLU1 ; (19/4/08)
[95] J. Matyu, (2004), "'*60's rugby star Pikoli dies alone in England*', <http://www.theherald.co.za/herald/2004/04/16/ncws/n23_16042004.htm>;(19/04/2008)
[96] "*Going back to his roots*", 29/08/2003 http://www.manchestereveningnews.co.uk/sport/s/333/333530_going_back_to_his_roots.html ; (19/4/2008)
[97] T. Collins, (2000), "*From Bondi to Batley: Australians in English Rugby League*", www.rl1908.com ; (31/12/2007)
[98] D. Appleton, (2001), "*Cricketer who broke down the racial barriers*", http://www.rochdaleobserver.co.uk/news/s/29/29664_cricketer_who_broke_down_the_barriers.htm ; (26/7/2007)
[99] Personal Communication, David Kirkley; Keighley Ex Players Association – Hendrik Snyders
[100] J. Matyu, (2004), " '*60's rugby star Pikoli dies alone in England*', available from http:/www.theherald.co.za/herald/2004/04/16/ncws/n23_16042004.htm ;(19/04/2008)
[101] J. Matyu, (2004),"*PE pro rugby player dies at 70*'
[102] SARU,(2003), *112 Years of Springbok Rugby*; p. 74
[103] Interview with Green Vigo, Saturday,28 June 2008, Protea Hotel, Saldanha, South Africa
[104] South Yorkshire Police Authority, (2003), *Community Affairs and Standards Committee: Joint Report of the Clerk and Treasurer and the Chief Constable: Consultation with "Hard to Reach" Communities: Black and Ethnic Communities*; 19 December
[105] J. Nauright, (1999), "*Sustaining Masculine Hegemony: Rugby and the Nostalgia of Masculinity*"; p. 235

Book Reviews

Rugby League Lions
100 Years of Test Matches
By Robert Gate

This book is a very difficult one to review because not only does it do what it says it does on the back cover, but it does it extremely well. Which is just as well, because over the last few years rugby league in this country has hardly covered itself with glory in the way it has handled some major centenaries. The centenary of the game's foundation in 1995, though ruined by the launch of Super League, at least produced Geoffrey Moorhouse's official history. The centenary of the Challenge Cup in 1997 was treated as a low key affair and the centenaries of the formation of the league and the Championship Final merited practically no official attention at all. This is sad because a centenary presents a perfect stage for reliving history, reactivating traditions and reinvigorating a game.

Once it became clear that the RFL was not intending to include an official history of the British team as part of its celebration of the centenary of test rugby Robert Gate was incensed. Fortunately for us, instead of sitting at home Robert decided to do something about it. Despite major obstacles such as a lack of sponsorship Robert sat down and compiled this superb history. And then he found a publisher willing to help.

From the moment you open this book you get a sense of Robert's passion for test rugby and its importance for the health of the game in this country. In this new book Robert has not only brought the history of the prestigious Ashes clashes up to date, but also has documented the test matches against France and New Zealand that have never perhaps been truly appreciated. This is no mean feat as over the century Great Britain have played over 300 test matches and Robert has coped wonderfully with the limited space available to provide a synopsis of each one. In addition the book is well illustrated with many photographs of players and teams.

Getting selected to take the field in one of those teams was one of the highest honours a player could achieve. It is unfortunate that while the book's appendices give a list of British captains, the leading cap winners, individual and team scoring feats that space could not be found to include a register of all those who have been privileged to make a test appearance in a British shirt.

As you work your way through this book you are reminded of all those days following the fortunes of Great Britain – and back come the feelings of pride, relief, disappointment and despair that were there when the final hooter sounded. Reading this book you realise there have been very many highs and not so many lows over the century. Although I knew how the book was going to end I couldn't help wishing that it might end with a resounding series victory over the Australians that would see the Ashes brought back to Britain.

Unfortunately that could not be and instead it has to end with the November 2007 series victory over the Kiwis. With the Kiwi camp in disarray, a lacklustre series marked a rather muted centenary. It was no way to celebrate a major milestone in the life of a great team. It should have been an event that enabled the fans to relive the achievements of the past and look forward to those to come. That was not easy when, with an amazing sense of timing and occasion, the decision had already been made that

Great Britain would cease to be our leading national team. In future British Rugby League will be represented independently by each of the four home nations.

Although we are told the Great Britain team might re-emerge in the future I cannot see that happening for some considerable time, if ever. And if it did could it ever be the same? So for now we have to assume that Great Britain will never figure on the rugby league landscape again. If that is the case then Robert's book will serve as a fine record and tribute to a great and long term standard bearer, both at home and abroad, for the qualities of the British game.

Published in 2008 by Vertical Editions at £21.99. ISBN: 9781904091257

Graham Williams

The patience of a Saint
St Helens Rugby League 1978 to 1996
By Mike Critchley

This excellent publication should be on every St Helens fan's bookshelf. It is of interest to supporters of a certain vintage because they were there, but the book should also be read by younger fans who might otherwise think that we older spectators have known nothing but success at the home of rugby league.

However, the book is far from simply a chronological account of Saints matches over an 18 year period. Particularly interesting is the way in which Mike Critchley has interwoven comments on the fashions of the time, together with political and social comments. The reader is able to relive what was happening at the time in St Helens, a good example of which would be the appalling demolition of the magnificent Helena House in the town centre. Snippets concerning his home life also add interest.

Obviously the nature of the book dictates it is a 'warts and all' account, and Mike is not afraid to retell some horror stories, such as Wembley 1989, which most fans would feel are definitely best left in the archives. However, despite some embarrassments we had to endure, the book provides a treasure chest of memories for those of us who, come what may, have always enjoyed their time at Knowsley Road and the camaraderie engendered among familiar faces at the matches.

His starting point is the 1978 Wembley Final, featuring Derek Noonan's unfortunate party piece because, as he says on the back cover, "1978 was a bad year to start supporting Saints." Mentioned a little later is the 1979 Challenge Cup semi-final against Wakefield Trinity which stays firmly in my mind as one of the biggest Saintly disasters I have attended, because it was after this that the decline really set in.

When I read the book, the memories came flooding back. The matches were played principally in winter and mainly before (even) lower crowds than those of today. They were games from a different era, and yet in some ways it seems as if they were played yesterday. All fans will have their own favourite vivid memories, but mine include Hull's visit for a Challenge Cup tie in 1981 when the visiting fans in their replica jerseys seemingly took over the ground and we had to move to the sanctuary of the Paddock, and the return cup tie at Hull in 1990 when one of the Hull hard man spectators came among us to keep us company. Although many would probably make this claim, it was me he stood next to! Saints won both matches - it wasn't all doom and gloom.

I made a list of the games which meant most to me, and obviously it was those where the results were good, such as the epic John Player Trophy win over Leeds in 1988, the 1986 slaughter of hapless Carlisle and the unforgettable 1992 rout of Wigan; if I close my eyes I can still see Sonny Nickle's try scoring run towards our corner of the ground. That was some Christmas present! Not on my list were Wembley 1987, when we should have won the Challenge Cup for the first time in 11 years, and a seemingly endless string of disappointments at the hands of our friends from Wigan including the 1990 Challenge Cup semi at Old Trafford when, after Les Quirk's wonder try, we were definitely robbed of a replay, and the 1996 Regal Trophy Final against Wigan, although that in itself was arguably a turning point. It now began to look likely that, after years of disappointment, we would soon be able to challenge Wigan's supremacy.

If I had the difficult task of choosing a favourite chapter, I think I would pick 1984-85 when the phenomenal Mal Meninga came and the trophy drought ended with two spectacular wins against Wigan and Hull KR. This was a season when three of my other personal favourites starred. Hard as nails local hero Chris Arkwright gave everything to the cause whenever he played, and he was often accompanied by that marvellous tough Cumbrian forward Peter Gorley whose biography I was privileged to write. The team was superbly led by Harry Pinner who remains the best loose forward I have seen in 42 years of watching the game.

To conclude, I can do no better than repeat what I said at the start - quite simply, this book needs to be on every Saints fan's bookshelf but, as with other quality rugby league books, other supporters who take an interest in our game's wonderful past will also find it an absorbing read.

Published in 2007 by London League Publications Ltd at £12.95. ISBN: 1903659328

Peter Cropper

Stevo – Looking Back
By Mike Stephenson

These days, if you've clocked up a reasonable total of television appearances it seems that a useful, and possibly lucrative, sideline is to write a book. And if Graham Norton, Posh Spice, Jade Goody, John Simpson and Katie Price can do it, so can Super League's very own Stevo.

I don't have Sky at home. So if I want to watch Super League on television I have a ready-made excuse to go to the pub and do it. It's quite a noisy pub so I never hear much of what Stevo has to say. Quite a few people say I'm fortunate in this but rugby league fans have always been over-critical of television commentators, as the recent rehabilitation of the late Eddie Waring confirms.

Stevo's autobiography follows a familiar pattern: a couple of chapters about his schooldays and early work experiences before getting on to his real career or, more accurately in his case, careers. He takes us through the lot: player for Dewsbury, player for Penrith, development officer, journalist, restaurateur, radio summariser and finally - after a rapid succession of other jobs, including rugby league museum curator – television commentator and summariser.

I don't know whether or not he would agree with me (I like to think he would) but I think Mike Stephenson's career was at its height in the 1972-3 rugby league season. It was of course the season in which Great Britain won the World Cup and in which no less an authority than the John Player Rugby League Yearbook said, "Dewsbury [captain: Michael Stephenson] could fairly be regarded as the season's top club".

So to me, not surprisingly, the best parts in the book are Chapter 8 on the World Cup Final and Chapter 9 on Dewsbury's great season. In Chapter 8 Stevo is justifiably proud of scoring the most important try in his career and informs us that scrum half Steve Nash played the whole game with three huge boils on his backside. Not quite up there with Alan Prescott's broken arm in that 1958 test match but an impressive feat nevertheless. In the good-humoured way which is typical of the whole book, Stevo is only mildly scathing about the almost complete disregard of Great Britain's achievement when the team returned home.

In Chapter 9 he describes with humour and passion how Dewsbury reached the Yorkshire Cup Final only to be defeated by high-flying Leeds, lost out in the Challenge Cup Semi Final to low-flying Bradford and finally came good to win the 16-team Championship Play-offs after finishing eighth in the League. On the way they beat Oldham, cup-winners Featherstone, league leaders and favourites Alex Murphy's Warrington and in the final Leeds. Stevo comments simply and effectively: "I know many players have won several trophies and teams like Wigan, Leeds, Bradford and St Helens have cornered the market for silverware for years. This was a local team, a bunch of hard workers who combined together and produced the goods. It was a proud moment for team and town."

I'm not knowledgeable enough to judge the reliability of Stevo's memory on rugby league, the television business or any other aspect of his career but one thing I do know about tend to cast doubt on it. On transfer fees in 1973, he says, "In those days £2,000 could buy you a three bedroom, detached house." Well perhaps it could have in Dewsbury but I doubt it. My house in Wigan cost four times that in 1973 and it was only semi-detached. Does this matter? Well, I think accuracy is important when you're talking about key moments in rugby league history – such as did Alex Murphy throw a telephone at Maurice Lindsay – but it doesn't as much if your main aim is entertainment.

There's certainly no shortage of this in Stevo's book. From a number of hilarious anecdotes I hadn't heard before, my favourite is where one of his Penrith teammates tried a bit of sledging to put one of South Sydney's stars off his game - the usual stuff consisting of telling the player how good his wife was in bed. It seemed to be working, so at half time Stevo told him to "keep the bullshit going". He replied, "It's not bullshit at all Stevo, I've been giving his wife one for ages."

If you haven't bought this book you'll have to decide whether or not to invest £17.99 on it. There are plenty of good rugby league books about at the moment and if you just want a humorous autobiography, I think you can't do better than *The Sound of Laughter* by Peter Kay. *Looking Back* is an entertaining book by and about a television personality called Stevo. To me it doesn't reveal much about his alter ego, a man called Mike Stephenson. I would have liked it better if it did.

Published in 2007 by Vertical Editions at £17.99. ISBN: 9781904091233

Bill Lythgoe

Grand Final
100 Years of Rugby League Championship Finals
By Graham Morris

2007 saw the 100th anniversary of Rugby League Championship and Grand Finals. This book nails the myth that the idea of a Grand Final was the idea of the Super League era. As it points out, the idea of an end of season play-off was started by baseball in the USA in 1903, but it was first introduced in Australia by Aussie Rules in 1898. So the play-off is an Australian idea after all.

This book is a tribute to all the teams that have competed during the period and also underlines the fact that the old Rugby League Championship was in some ways the ultimate rugby league competition. In fact if you look at some of the attendances at the finals in the past the gates compare healthily with the Challenge Cup ones.

The origin of the play-offs was, in a typically rugby league way, a solution to the problem of the separate Yorkshire and Lancashire competitions and to produce a genuine champion for the competition. The final had no fixed home, depending on the geography of where the teams came from until 1946 when Maine Road in Manchester was used for 10 years, only for the final to end up across the city when the Premiership final was transferred to Old Trafford in 1987 where it seems to have obtained a permanent home at the moment.

I only attended one Championship Final at Swinton in 1976 between Salford and St Helens. It was a typical Salford no show performance after finishing top of the league, they only managed two David Watkins's drop-goals against two tries for Saints from Eric Chisnall and Geoff Pimblett. Although Salford had finished six points ahead of the Saints in the table the results in the season had been two wins each, the clubs having met in the Challenge and Lancashire Cups.

My other clear memory of the competition was the other occasion in the 1970s when Salford had finished top of the table in 1973-74. The play-off system saw the top 15 sides plus the Second Division champions taking place. Yes, you guessed it Salford as the top side played Bradford at the Willows which, after a Salford lap of honour before the game, finished 16-16. Bradford won the replay.

As I said earlier, the book is a real tribute to the players and teams who have graced this competition, and has a match-by-match report of each of the 100 games. You can relive the successes of Hunslet, Huddersfield, and Swinton as they win the 'four trophies' (Championship, County Cup and League and Challenge Cups).

In some ways, it is the performances of the all-time greats that are most vivid in the book. Billy Batten's late controversial try in 1920 to deny Fartown a second 'four trophies' win at Headingley or Brian Bevan's three Championship Finals between 1948 and 1951. There is also a great description of the Tom van Vollenhoven try for St Helens in the 1959 Final. To show how important was the Championship Final in its hey-day, a staggering 83,190 saw the Wakefield versus Wigan game in 1960, I have been to Maine Road and find it hard to imagine a crowd of that size in the ground. The final pages cover the Super League Grand Finals and show they are truly worthy successors of the old Championship and Premiership Finals.

Published by Vertical Editions in 2008 at £19.99. ISBN: 9781904091226

Dave Farrar

Champagne Rugby
By Henri Garcia, translated by Roger Grime

"My centre is giving way, my right is in retreat; situation excellent, I shall attack"
Marshal Foch

My own Damascus Treiziste moment came at Knowsley Road on a grey autumnal day in November 1958. I had started watching the game as a kid barely out of short pants at Widnes's old Naughton Park the season before.

France versus a Rugby League XIII was my first live taste of international sport. The home side included an all-Yorkshire pack including a goal-kicking prop from York named Vic Yorke. They had two fairly decent wings to in Tom van Vollenhoven and Brian Bevan. What I remembered initially was how the two teams presented themselves. The Select donned a simple plain green jumper with traditional turned up white collar, white shorts & green socks.

The visiting continentals on the other hand looked like royalty. Superb finely cut tricolour tops with laced frontage and cockerel badge. White ankle socks and low cut boots completed the contrast in styles.

If the appearance wasn't enough the action which followed was unforgettable. They played with a lightness and vivacity I had yet to witness. They kept the ball alive seemingly continuously with flowing precise handling at great speed linking forwards & backs alike. I remember their threequarters. Two contrasting wings, the Avignon 'Bison' Andre Savonne and on the other Maurice Voron rapier like from Lyon. Between them the Villeneuve centre pair Andre Carrere and Antoine Jiminez him of the dark features and distinctive white head band. Shee... could they play! Result 26-8 for the visitors.

Its nearly half a century now since that day & the memories have been flooding back to me recently courtesy of Henri Garcia's fine and timely 1961 publication *Champagne Rugby* - the Golden Age of French rugby league" recently translated by Roger Grime. The above threequarter line who I saw at St Helens all those years ago featured centrally in those three epic Tricolour Tours down under of 1951-55-60 when the French game literally ruled the roost.

Getting the game up and running after the Second World War & the indignities forced on the Treizistes by the Vichy Government couldn't have been easy. Additionally, I hadn't realised that although France was liberated in September 1944 it wasn't until July 1947 that the game was finally admitted to the National Sports Committee. Such a time scale must have weighed even more on the ability of the game to get back on its feet and allowed the XV further time to reclaim much of its pre-War losses.

The 1951 Tricolours, the first ever rugby side to tour the Antipodes left Marseilles Marignane Airport on 14 May 1951. Initiated by the legendary administrator the great Paul Barrière, a party of 30 players was led by the manager Antoine Blain and coached by Jean Duhau and Robert Samatan. The comparisons in sizes to modern day players are revealing. Lots of threequarters weighing barely 11 stone and forwards only a couple of stone more.

The player profiles revealed similar occupations to their brothers across the Channel. Tradesmen, porter, market gardener, PE teacher, reps, draughtsman and pharmaceutical student. The average age was over 27 years and people like the tough and highly rated prop Louis Mazon had fought in the Resistance during the War. Interestingly 12 of the team came from two clubs Lyon and Marseille who today hardly feature in the Treize movement.

This was of course a bare few years since the end of War hostilities everywhere so the French arrival in Australia in 1951 was really big news. The tourists soon found out what the game meant to Australians and in particular the Sydney Cricket Ground on the eve of a test match.

"Sydney is the Casablanca of the Southern Seas and the huge palm trees in Moore Park Road barely rustled in the gentle sea breeze. Blain & Duhau went out on to the pavement & lit cigarettes. From the corner, you could see the lights of the city, but their eyes were instinctively drawn towards the Cricket Ground there, below them, on the other side of the street. 'What the hell's that?' Duhau burst out. Had a gigantic swarm of fireflies settled on the stadium terraces? In reality, it was quite simply the thousands of fans who, to secure a good spec, had already taken their places & were smoking to kill time. What an incredible vigil. Just 100 yards away, the French team lay asleep & here, a colossal encampment had formed. Fifteen thousand Australians bivouacked around the pitch with their snacks, beer and whisky."

On the field of play the visitors would have to adapt to the different playing conditions & style of play of the hosts. After the opening games the Tricolours knew what to expect, "for five minutes the Australians launched themselves like demons, battering the French defence like crazed rams. The trial of strength was even harder to win because these Kangaroo devils never lost possession, so there was only one thing to do: let the storm blow itself out and protect the try line at all costs. Arms, legs, backs all ached with the non-stop impact, but they clenched their teeth and nothing got passed."

So it was not just the French flair and 'Champagne Rugby' which went on to making this side immortal. It obviously had a back-bone of size and knew how to defend too. The Australians where still hesitant to garner praise on the visitors but the drawn fixture in Sydney in the fourth match impressed many sceptics. Frank O'Rourke in the *Daily Telegraph* wrote, "The big question about the tourists' quality has been well & truly answered. Sydney has never seen such spontaneous skills as the French displayed in the first half. The pack, solid & speedy, played a perfect game & prompted attacks by their white hot backs."

No one on this historic breaking tour could match the exploits of course of the incomparable vice-captain Puig-Aubert. The Catalan who played at Carcassonne became a legend. He overhauled Jim Sullivan's Australian tour record with a trawl of 236 points but it was his uninhibited carefree style which enthralled the hosts turning certain athletic norms on their heads with his passion for his Gauloises and pastis.

The 1951 French tourists were one of the greatest the game has known with just four losses out of 28 games played. The test decider against Australia produced a sensational winning performance from the Tricolours in Sydney 35-14. The three tests alone drew over 160,000 spectators. This first ever French touring side not only attracted the crowds but also the imagination and empathy of a thirsty sporting public like never before. A Broadway styled parade awaited the tourists on their return home. They turned out in their thousands in Marseille to welcome back their heroes.

In the four years which passed before the next tour down under the Tricolours had played and lost to Great Britain in the inaugural World Cup Final in Paris. It was a much changed side which made the 1955 trip. Some of the great names especially in the forwards where not there like Mazon, Brousse and Ponsinet and they suffered the worse news possible on the eve of their departure when Puig-Aubert broke his arm and had to withdraw. This tour saw the arrival however of some great new names like Gilbert Benausse, Antoine Jiminez, Maurice Voron and Andre Savonne; all free running backs with pace and flair to spare.

This side possibly didn't have the forward hardness and consistency of the 1951 team, losing 14 games but still won the three match series with the Kangaroos.

By the time of the 1960 tour change was definitely in the air. Only two of the 1955 side where still there captain Jiminez and Gilbert Benausse. It is difficult not to over emphasize the effect the all-conquering 1951 side had across the Channel. Antoine Jiminez was the first of a long line of union players - many internationals - who 'crossed-over' even though payments where freely available in the amateur game attracted by aura created by that team. The 1960 tourists called up Lacaze, Mantoulan, Bescos, Quaglio and Barthe all who had played union at international level. In hindsight maybe the game in France like elsewhere followed the wrong path. Not enough may be was done to develop their own junior game and bring through their own players.

1960 saw the Tricolours draw the three match test series, despite losing 11 games in total on the tour. It was no mean achievement taking into account that by then the Kangaroos had started to develop players in numbers of true world standing such as Reg Gasnier, Harry Wells and Johnny Raper. A new world order was heading south and rests there to this day.

For the Tricolours some say that was their end as a true world force. Their 7-5 triumph against the Kangaroos on 15 July 1960 in Sydney was the Tricolours last success against the Green and Gold on Australian soil. That the game across the Channel unravelled at a great rate of knots losing players, clubs and prestige. However even accepting much of that looking at test results the French in typical Gallic unpredictability still produced upsets. They reached the 1968 World Cup Final, defeating Great Britain in the semi-final and a decade later where still good enough to win both tests against Bob Fulton's touring Australians. In 1990 they beat Great Britain 25-18 at Headingley.

After that the arrival of Super League scuppered international football in general and the annual home and away fixtures which France had been involved in since their beginning. Full-time professionalism widened the gap even further and the loss of Paris St Germain after barely two seasons was catastrophic.

The hope must now rest a decade on with what the Catalans Dragons can do now to resurrect the floundering Tricolours' fortunes. It will be a long and slow process back for sure but at least they have made a start. The World Cup in Australia should help and after that 2009 promises a really pivotal year with the expectation that the Tricolours will join an expanded Tri-Nations. Hopefully Henri Garcia may yet see again a Tricolour win against one of the major nations in a meaningful competition. Nous esperons bien.

Published in 2007 by London League Publications Ltd at £12.95. ISBN: 9781903659342

Gordon Derbyshire

No White Flag
By Jamie Peacock with Phil Caplan

Assisted by a respected rugby league writer, the Great Britain captain presents his life so far, complete with striking cover photograph. Yet the subtitle "Autobiography of the

Leeds Rhinos and Great Britain Star" is slightly wrong, or at least misleading, in a couple of ways. This is the story of Jamie Peacock's career as a professional rugby league player rather than an autobiography - the coverage of that part of his life before he signed professionally with Bradford, and of his life outside of rugby league since, is very slight - and the bulk of the book is concerned with his time at Bradford rather than at his current club Leeds. Descriptions of each season follow in turn after an introductory chapter and a few brief pages on Peacock's childhood and adolescence, charting his rise through the ranks to senior professional, concentrating on his and the club's fortunes.

There is, however, more than enough here to interest supporters of other teams. It is perhaps significant that the cover photo shows Peacock in his role as Great Britain captain rather than as a Leeds player, and there is ample coverage of his involvement in the various international series in which he has participated, although the space given to that incident with Willie Mason is slight (and the photograph of the incident included shows the aftermath of the punch rather than the blow landing). Some other anecdotes are also dealt with rather briefly, and some loose ends are left hanging; it would have been interesting to have a little more on how Jamie came to have a fight with one of his best friends at school that led to the latter being expelled, for example.

It is worth reflecting that the current test captain came into the game relatively late, by current standards, and served his apprenticeship in rugby league away from the elite. Amateur clubs can still produce top class players, or at least they could in the 1990s. This is perhaps something that clubs could heed, as should young aspiring players, who might also note how close he came to being cut from Bradford, and the hard work and change in attitude that subsequently enabled him to climb to the top.

There are no real revelations, unless the news that not only are referees human, but at least one of them is actually likeable, comes as a shock. It comes as no surprise to anyone who has followed the game that David Waite was better respected by the players he worked with than he was by the media, or that rugby players like an occasional beer (or more than occasional), or that the players' perspective on moves between clubs is different to that of supporters. The observations on the different coaches' styles, strengths and weaknesses are interesting, as are the description of rivalries between players at the same and different clubs, but again, there's nothing here to really cause controversy. Even the comments about Iestyn Harris's move back to rugby league, which provoked some media coverage at the time of publication, are clearly aimed more at the Bradford club, and by implication its then chairman, than at Harris, whose talents are amply praised. Perhaps this is not entirely surprising. Peacock is still a current player, and the national captain. How far can he afford to offend and antagonise current and potential team-mates, coaches and opponents even if it was in his nature to want to?

The volume is well produced. There is a small section of photographs, mostly in colour. The statistical appendix is also short, but probably comprehensive enough for most readers. There is no index, but its lack is not felt as badly as in, for example, Stevo's memoirs. Nor does the book include some of the traditional sections of a sporting autobiography: there is no "dream XIII" and no chapter ruminating on the state of the modern game. But these are not essential and their absence enables the story so far to finish properly, with Peacock leading his team to triumph in the 2007 Test series against New Zealand, and with a promise that he's not done yet.

In sum, this is reflection of the man himself; nothing too fancy, just a story of hard work and dedication, honestly told in a straightforward manner. A useful insight into the life of the archetypal modern rugby league forward, and an interesting tale of his development as both a player and as a person.

If anyone should wonder why a company named The History Press should be publishing a book about rugby league, they are our old friends Tempus, who have published so many books about the sport in recent years, in a new guise.

Published in 2008 by Stadia/The History Press at £18.99. ISBN 978-0-7524-4612-7

Stuart Leadley

Sculthorpe
Man of Steel
By Paul Sculthorpe with Phil Thomas

This book was first published in 2007 and it has recently been reprinted in a paperback version – a veritable 'best-seller' reflecting the popularity of Paul Sculthorpe within the Rugby League game. Written in a chatty, informal style in conjunction with Phil Thomas of the *Sun*, the book's title is a reference to Paul's back-to-back Man of Steel awards in 2000 and 2001 when he was at the peak of his powers in domestic and international rugby. In fact the only major honour to evade him has been a series win against the Australians at international level, but not for want of trying of course!

So why has Paul been able to carve out such a phenomenal reputation for himself as a player? Perhaps the answer, in microcosm, is provided in the Introduction by the Late, great Eric Ashton, former chairman of St Helens Rugby League Club, who provides an astute analysis of Paul Sculthorpe's attributes as a footballer. Eric leaves the reader in no doubt that he was determined to bring Sculthorpe to Knowsley Road, and in doing so, together with Keiron Cunningham and Sean Long, completed the most potent midfield trio assembled in the Super League era. The rest, as they say, is history!

Although quite a large proportion of the text will not be particularly new for Saints' fans, especially after the Chris Joynt biography *The Quiet Man*, it is an entertaining read nonetheless. A variety of topics are covered in forthright fashion, ranging from the young buck trying to establish himself in the pro game; tales of success and disaster on the international front; battles with younger brother Danny (2004 Challenge Cup final in particular); the different coaches played under and his admiration for Ellery Hanley (a kindred spirit in the Number 13 jersey); various characters in the dressing room and his spin on controversies such as the Sean Long betting scandal; his most formidable opponents and greatest matches and much more.

Indeed Paul comes over as an intelligent, thoughtful person, who strongly believes in the importance of family life and is obviously grateful to the people who have helped him to get to the pinnacle of rugby league. One of three sportsmen to help promote Gillette (Jason Robinson and Beckham are the other two) Scully is a perfect ambassador for the game – a recognisable figure, an excellent role model for youngsters and someone who genuinely wants to promote the many positives of the sport. He is understandably proud of his achievements none more so than his return from some crippling injuries which would have broken the resolve of a lesser man.

There is also plenty of food for thought from this book. It could be argued that his departure from Warrington while still a teenager (together with the sale of Iestyn Harris) probably condemned the Cheshire club to a decade of mediocrity in Super League. He was the one to build a team around in the case of the London Broncos too, had he decided to sign, but the biggest 'what if' surrounds club football in Australia. Many observers feel he would have been sensational in the NRL and the Aussies have always rated him highly with his overall power and dominance, very much in the mould of Brad Fittler. He could have made the same impact as the likes of Mal Reilly, when he took Australia by storm in the 1970s. There is also the admiration from union, but Paul has always remained loyal to the 13-a-side code and St Helens in particular, who have stood by him in adversity.

2008 is Paul's testimonial year at St Helens and hopefully he can begin to re-establish himself with an injury-free run in the team. What of the future? It seems as though this is largely undecided, apart from continuing to play for Saints for as long as he can. We can only hope that his involvement with rugby league continues, however. In fact he will be shortly putting into practice one aspect he talks about in the book, namely rugby league camps for youngsters. Who knows, perhaps he will follow the likes of Ellery Hanley into coaching, but only the future will tell.

So... a fine resume of a career thus far. Mind you... one major 'gripe' from this reader! There are no statistics to back up this marvellous rugby league odyssey. I am not one for 'over-doing' things like this, but some would have been welcome, if only for reference.

Published in 2007 by Century (Random House) at £18.99. ISBN: 9781846051623

Alex Service

Photograph: Paul Sculthorpe with the Challenge Cup in 2004 after defeating Wigan 32-16 at Cardiff – the first time Paul lifted the trophy as captain of St Helens. (Photograph: Bernard Platt)

100 Greats: Huddersfield Rugby League Football Club
By David Gronow

I have to nail my colours to the mast from the outset. Just so we all know where I stand. I seriously question the worth of reviewing 'Greatest players' or 'Greatest matches' or 'Greatest shirt designs' books. And that's not necessarily down to the quality of the writing or the research one tends to find in them. In the main, if the latter is accurate any competent author should be able to piece together 50 players or 20 matches or whatever and come up with something half-competent and semi-entertaining. But are they worth a book review? They do not sell on the ability of the author or the idiosyncrasy of their subject matter. Indeed, if they sell at all it is surely to supporters of whatever particular club might be featured on the cover and it's unlikely that a review will influence the buyer's decision one way or the other. In fact, presuming once more that the author is literate, a review can do little more than act as an unpaid advertisement to supporters of the team in question.

All of which suggests I've got a big downer on David Gronow's latest book of the ilk. Honestly, that's not true. It's fine, perfectly fine – historically accurate and well put together... but, by it's very nature, ultimately similar to many, many other books that have gone before it and are destined to come after.

However, David is a lucky man. As a lifelong Huddersfield supporter I'm in a perfect position the review his particular offering, for perhaps the only controversy that is ever likely to surround books of this kind is the selection made by the author in the eyes of fellow fans. So, gripes out of the way and reservations temporarily suspended, let's take issue or otherwise with the player choices.

Before opening the book I drew up an entirely subjective list (for how can one produce a book of this kind or argue with its choices without being subjective?) of my top 10 Fartown players, based mainly on those I'd seen or whose legend precedes them. In no particular order these were Trevor Leathley, Harold Wagstaff, Johnny Hunter, Lionel Cooper, Ken Loxton, Ian van Bellen, Peter Cramp, Wally Gibson, Ian Hobson and Ken Senior. All of which was good news because now I could pick a fight with the author. He'd left out... oh... bugger... none of them. In that case I needed to posit the inclusion of, erm, how about Ian Hobson and Trevor Bedford? Just for the sake of argument.

Trevor Bedford should be included because, when I first began to be taken to Fartown at the age of six or seven, he was playing full-back and he stood out from the mass of the team because he was standing alone (for what reason, at that point, I had no idea). Then he scored a try on BBC *Grandstand* on a snowy day and a kid was standing behind the posts wearing a claret and gold scarf. At that point I realised I wanted to be Trevor Bedford and wanted a Fartown scarf. Reason enough for inclusion in the book? Probably not.

Then there's Ian Hobson. Certainly he either scored a hat-trick on his debut from the second-row or in one of his very first matches. My friend Jon from school had just started going to matches with me so, in his short rugby league educational period, Hobson was by default the greatest player he had ever seen, sending opponents skittling as he ran head-down for the line. We loved him and to this day sing (a little embarrassedly), 'Ian, Hobson, Ian Hobson, na na na-na-na naaa', when we meet up.

So good cases for both to be included? And so should Dave Hooson (oh, he is), but John Hartley should not have (and, aaaah, he isn't). OK, Gary Senior definitely should not have been in there. In my opinion he caused more trouble than he was worth. If he scored two tries he gave away three through fighting and backchat and being generally a pain in the bum. This is what it's all about... getting the argument going... which is I guess the raison d'etre of any such book.

But all of this leaves me worried, for it this sounds like I'm being critical of the book. I'm not. Loved it, of course. It was aimed directly at me – I was its target audience and I read it in a single sitting in a sunny garden of a weekend afternoon. Perfect. So forgive my flippancy for clearly a lot of hard – and more importantly in such a volume, accurate – work has gone into it. I just question the worth of reviewing it. I think I've just talked myself out a job...

Published in 2008 by Stadia at £12.99. ISBN: 9780752445847

Michael O'Hare

Books round up 1

Four players

As the study of rugby league history develops, there are more biographies and autobiographies being published. Four very different players' stories have landed on my desk in the past few months.

Sean Fagan is one of Australian rugby league's leading historians, and has done ground-breaking work on the game's origins and early history. He has now developed this further with a study of the life of Dally Messenger, *The Master*, written in partnership with Dally Messenger III, the great man's grandson. The story is told in the context of rugby football and life in Australia in the early twentieth century. I hadn't realised that he only played for six full seasons in rugby league.

This is a very thorough study of one of the game's great players. Some of the chapters are quite short, which I found slightly irritating, but the material is excellent. Sadly the book is not easily available in Great Britain, but can be ordered via Sean's website, www.rl1908.com, which is always worth a visit anyway.

The modern equivalent, arguably, of Dally Messenger is Andrew Johns. The *two of me – Andrew Johns* which he wrote with Neil Cadigan, is a fascinating insight into one of the modern era's greatest players, but one who has been plagued with mental health problems, which he kept hidden until near the end of his career. The book also shows the enormous pressures on the top players in Australia, being never out of the spotlight, similar to Premiership footballers here. There is also a chapter on his short time in Super League with Warrington. Although I'm not aware of a British distributor, it is available reasonably priced on Amazon.

Another Australian great, from a different era, is Arthur Clues. He played against the British Lions on the 1946 tour, and then signed for Leeds in 1947. He settled in the city, and lived there for the rest of his life. Maurice Bamford was a young Leeds fan when Clues joined the club, and captures the essence of one of the game's toughest, but skilful forwards. His biography of Clues, *Arthur Clues – Saint and Sinner*, looks at Clues's development as a player, first of all in Australia, and then in the context of Leeds's performances. A particularly interesting chapter is the one on Clues's famous (or infamous) clashes with the French forward Edouard Ponsinet.

Clues never played for Australia again after the 1946 tour, as they would not select players who were not playing their club rugby in Australia, but he did appear for the Other Nationalities team and some other representative sides. The story concludes with his time at Hunslet, and then his life after rugby league. A story of one of the game's greats that is certainly worth reading.

Stanley Gene is one of the greatest players to come from Papua New Guinea. His autobiography, Daydream believer, written with Stuart Wilkin, is a fascinating story. His life at home in his village is wonderfully portrayed, a picture of a society very different from the north of England where he plays his rugby league. The difficulties facing players coming from overseas and having to adjust to life in Britain are graphically illustrated. He also outlines very well his experiences at the different clubs he has played for in British rugby league. After reading this, I'm not sure I would want him to give me a life in his car, or maybe even let him in mine – read the book to find out why!

The production of the book is quite basic, but the material makes up for that. The career statistics are very sparse, and disappointingly does not include his international appearances. Stuart Leadley has done some research on this, which is provided below. Any additions welcome. But despite these faults, all rugby league fans who have enjoyed watching Stanley play, and even those who don't, should read this eye-opening book.

Stanley Gene's playing record for Papua New Guinea in full international matches 1994 to present

Date	Opposition	Venue	Result	Position	Tries	Comments
26/06/1994	France	Port Moresby	W 29-22	sub	1	full debut
16/10/1994	New Zealand	Goroka	L 12-28	sub		
23/10/1994	New Zealand	Port Moresby	L 16-30	sub	1	
10/10/1995	Tonga	Hull	D 28-28	SO	1	World Cup
13/10/1995	New Zealand	St Helens	L 6-22	SO		World Cup
28/09/1996	Great Britain	Lae	L 30-32	SO	1	
05/10/1996	New Zealand	Rotorua	L 8-62	SO		
11/10/1996	New Zealand	Palmerston North	L 0-64	SH		
07/10/1998	Cook Islands	Lae	W 46-6		1	PNG RL 50th Anniversary
11/10/1998	Tonga	Wabag	W 44-28		1	PNG RL 50th Anniversary
18/10/1998	Tonga	Port Moresby	W 54-12		2	PNG RL 50th Anniversary
28/10/2000	France	Paris	W 23-20	SO		World Cup
02/11/2000	South Africa	Toulouse	W 16-0	SO		World Cup
06/11/2000	Tonga	St Esteve	W 30-22	SO	2	World Cup
12/11/2000	Wales	Widnes	L 8-22	SO		World Cup Quarter Final
07/10/2001	Australia	Port Moresby	L 12-54	2R		
09/10/2004	Australia	Townsville	L 22-70	LF		v "Australia Invitational"

Total: 17 appearances, 10 tries

Other Representative Appearance (for PNG Colts)

Date	Opposition	Venue	Result
19/06/1994	France	Madang	W 22-20

Tours
1995 World Cup in England (2 appearances, 1 try)
1996 New Zealand (3 appearances, no tries)
2000 World Cup in France and England (4 appearances, 2 tries)

The Master – The life and times of Dally Messenger
By Sean Fagan and Dally Messenger III
Published in 2007 by Hachette Australia
ISBN 9780733622007

Arthur Clues – Saint and Sinner
By Maurice Bamford
Published in 2008 by Vertical Editions at £11.99
ISBN 9781904091264

Andrew Johns – the two of me
By Andrew Johns and Neil Cardigan
Published in 2007 by HarperCollins Australia
at £19.99 ISBN: 9780732286538

Daydream Believer
By Stanley Gene with Stuart Wilkin
Published in 2008 by TH Media
ISBN 9780955953408

Three centenaries

The centenaries of the game in New Zealand in 2007 and Australia this year have been marked with two massive books. *The Kiwis – 100 Years of International Rugby League* by John Coffey and Bernie Wood is a massive 440 pages, beautifully illustrated, by two of the game's leading New Zealand historians. Covering matches, tours and players, with a great statistics section, it is a fitting book to mark a centenary. The authors are also working on a similar book on Maori Rugby League, which should be available in September 2008 (its advertised on Amazon).

In Australia, Ian Heads and David Middleton have produced *A Centenary of Rugby League 1908 to 2008*. My copy has just arrived, and looks fantastic. Sean Fagan says it "tells the complete, season-by-season story of rugby league's first 100 years in Australia." It covers the domestic game, internationals and Australia's greatest 100 players. Sean concludes that "the search for photographs and memorabilia for this book has been relentless, with countless never before seen and long lost images complementing the rich and revealing narrative." 640 pages - comprehensive indeed.

The Kiwis: 100 Years of International Rugby League
By John Coffey and Bernie Wood
A Hodda Moa book published by Hachette Livre in 2007. ISBN: 9781869710903
(Available on Amazon)

A Centenary of Rugby League 1908-2008
By Ian Heads and David Middleton
Published by Pan Macmillan Australia. ISBN 9781405038300
(Not sure on availability in Great Britain, I ordered one from a bookshop in New Zealand via the internet! I suggest shop around, the price and postage costs varied quite a lot.)

The Second Half
More Funny Stories in Rugby League
By Maurice Bamford

Maurice Bamford has a lifetime's experience in the game as a player and a coach to draw on when writing about rugby league. This format, humorous tales and stories about the game, works well for him. And even if some of them are a bit exaggerated over time, so what! These anecdotes are drawn on the time when the whole game was part-time, players having to balance the needs and demands of work with playing professional rugby league. An entertaining book that particularly older fans will enjoy.

Published in 2007 by Vertical Editions at £10.99. ISBN 9781904091219

The Rugby League Miscellany
By David Lawrenson

This book is one of a series from Vision Sports Publishing. Other titles are mainly football and rugby union, and having found a format, they have applied it to rugby league. Not that there's anything wrong with that. Written by a journalist who knows the game well, it is an eclectic mixture of stories, history, player profiles, statistics, humour and much more. My only problem is that there is no contents list, or index, which makes it not easy to find something specific. But as an entertaining book about the game, one to enjoy. It was published at £9.99, but is now available on the Vision Sports website at £6.49.

Published in 2007 by Vision Sports Publishing at £9.99. ISBN: 9781905326303

Peter Lush

Snuff out the moon
The development of floodlit rugby league
By Tom Mather.

Around the time that I started to write this review, I heard of the decision to rename the St Helens rugby league ground as the GPW Recruitment Stadium. This was not something that I was pleased to hear because Knowsley Road has always meant a lot to me and not just because of the rugby. For five years I travelled along it five days a week to go to Knowsley Road Junior School. I remember watching my first games there, stood in the boys' pen, at a time when there was no tannoy system, no Edington Stand, later opened in 1951, and the main stand was the old wooden one. It was also where I first learned what the word atmosphere meant.

Since 1965, I have lived away from St Helens which probably explains why whenever I hear the words Knowsley Road, it always brings back many good memories. Other fans will have similar ones of their club even though in many cases their original ground has been demolished, just like my old school has now been.

It was with all this in mind that I reviewed this history of floodlights, a subject that at first glance I did not think I would find very interesting. How wrong I was.

Perhaps the most important statement in the whole book is found on page two where Tom Mather states "Today in Great Britain, there is a battle raging within sport, between sport itself and big business that claims it wants to promote it. Nothing could be further from the truth. Business wants simply to promote business and will do so with whatever means it has at its disposal."

What he achieves with this statement is to draw attention to an issue that should be of interest and of concern to all sport and not just rugby league. How many times have we been told that sport itself is now big business and nowhere is that truer than with multi-million pound football? What this book does is to range over the background to the relationship between sport and business and show how it first came into being, around the time when sport was the domain of the wealthy upper classes and the gentry and existed in the shape of horse racing, prize fighting, cock fighting, hare coursing and fox hunting. Ever since then, business has always used sport to its advantage and by tracing the history of floodlights in sport, the author shows how this relationship has developed.

The author has clearly worked hard to put his subject matter into its historical context. He investigates the role of Parliament in dealing with the social problems that the industrial revolution brought about. He explains that as a result of the Ten Hour Act of 1847, which reduced the number of hours that a child could work and the 1850 Factory Act, which banned women and children from working after 2pm on Saturday, many more people had the freedom to play and watch sport on Saturday afternoon.

In the 1860s, there had been a massive swing towards spectator sports with association football and rugby being the most popular, particularly in the industrial areas of the north of England. Within a further ten years more attention began to be paid by those in power to encourage the population to lead a more healthy and moral lifestyle. This had to be done in order to create a more disciplined work force that could fulfil its role as the producers, though not the full sharers, of the growing wealth of the nation.

It was also in response to pressures that were mounting on the governments of the day, particularly from the Chartist movement and early trade unionism. There was also a fear in the minds of many in authority that the French Revolution and its aftermath was still fresh in the minds of the general population. One early response to this was the rise of the works' social club with the main function being to encourage workers to develop a wider loyalty to their company.

The second chapter starts by noting that it was the two forces of business and commerce allied to manufacturing that had driven the Industrial Revolution forward in Britain. These had capitalised upon the original power sources that had kick started the revolution in the first place, water power and then steam, which turned the machinery that drove the revolution relentlessly onward. Later gas helped maintain that momentum. Electrical power came next but the powerful lobbying available to the gas and coal industries produced a situation in which the electrical companies faced an uphill battle to break their stranglehold, particularly for house and street lighting. How did they succeed in doing this? By making available the use of electricity to power floodlights for sporting events!

The first floodlight match was a game of football that took place in 1878 at Bramall Lane in Sheffield, followed eight days later by a game of rugby between Broughton and Swinton. Soon after came Chorley's disaster when tar was painted on the fences to stop spectators climbing over and getting into Dole Park for free and then bad weather forced their game against Swinton to be abandoned.

This was soon followed by a game between Halifax and Birch with over 20,000 spectators in attendance on a field near to the old Thrum Hall farm. Unfortunately the game only lasted for 10 minutes at which point the enormous crowd encroached onto the field and made further play impossible. Not everybody had come to watch the match though as by now there was much fascination throughout the land with anything to do with electricity.

Comparing what was then just rugby with its major spectator competitor, the author reminds the reader of the formation of the Football Association in 1863 and the Rugby Football Union in 1871. This period of time is well covered by such writers as Tony Collins in *Rugby's Great Split* and Trevor Delaney in *The Roots of Rugby League*. *Snuff out the Moon* adds more to what they have written and leaves the reader with a good feel for what it was like living in those times.

The book moves on to cover a period which some of us will have our own personal knowledge of. In 1955, with the arrival of the Independent Television Authority there was the launch of the Associated Rediffusion Rugby League Trophy. Featherstone,

Huddersfield, Hunslet, Leigh, Oldham, Wakefield, Warrington and Wigan all played mid week floodlight games at various venues in London. Ten years later the BBC2 Floodlight Trophy was introduced, with the first final being won by Castleford beating St Helens 4–0 at Knowsley Road in December 1965. The last winner was Hull in a local derby beating Hull KR 13-3 at the Boulevard in front of 18,500 spectators in 1979.

In recommending this book, I am in agreement with Dave Hadfield who has penned the foreword. In it he states that "It is good to see Tom back in print, shining a beam into an aspect of the game that would otherwise be neglected". He recommends it and not necessarily because it is light reading.

I also liked the photographs of five former grounds, along with the front covers of programmes for various floodlit games including Wales versus New Zealand in December 1951 and Bradford Northern versus Cardiff in January 1952, both games played at Odsal. Another good feature was the drawing of the internal workings of the Serrin lamp that was once used in lighthouses spread all along the British coastline and photographs of a Jablochkov Candle and a Siemens dynamo, but then I was for years an electrical draughtsman.

Published by London League Publications Ltd in 2007at £1195. ISBN: 9781903659335

Geoff Lee

Books round up 2

Champions!
The Story of the 2007 Leeds Rhinos
By Phil Daly and Leanne Flynn

A fine and comprehensive review of the 2007 season from the perspective of the champion club. Reports and statistics for all their matches (but for some reason, possibly space, no statistical summary), along with snippets of news and plenty of photographs, all in full colour. The authors of the match reports are perhaps a bit forward with criticism of referees, but no more biased towards Leeds than might be expected in an official club publication. As it says on the back cover, this probably is "a must for any Rhinos fan" although "an essential addition to any Rugby League collection" is pushing it a bit.

Ignition Publications, no ISBN. Paperback, 96pp, £9.99

Just Jacko
The autobiography of Lee Jackson, with Mark Chestney

It is interesting to compare and contrast Lee Jackson's autobiography with that of Jamie Peacock, which was published at roughly the same time. Just Jacko is shorter and smaller in format, but it does provide much more information about its author/subject's life outside of rugby league. Peacock's book was published as a well-finished hardback by a national company, Jackson's by a local, essentially private, publisher as a paperback, with those little things which identify its production - occasional printing errors, page numbers on the preliminaries, contents page without page numbers. This is not intended as a criticism of Jackson or Mark Chestney, but it is a bit of a shame that such an influential recent player for more than one major English club who represented Great Britain in seventeen Tests and England eight times could not attract a national publisher. Perhaps partly as result though, we do get the more or less unexpurgated Jacko, complete with language that some (though not anyone who ever attended a match at the Boulevard) might consider a bit strong, putting forward his views on the game in an honest and straightforward, if not always very eloquent, manner. As he puts himself, he's "a kid off Bransholme".

As well as a fair bit of background to Jackson's life and an interesting account of his professional career, the early days of which, even though relatively recent, belonged to a different age - how many of today's Super League players would need to catch two buses to travel to their day job - there are some sections of especial fascination. The full itinerary for the 1990 tour of Papua New Guinea and New Zealand is included, along with comments on the hotels used. Jackson's various transfers are covered in some detail. There is also a selection of tributes from team-mates and various Hull rugby league notables, and a selection of photographs, and the inevitable statistical appendix.

Published in 2008 by Hull of a Game Publications at £8.99, No ISBN.

Four Cups to Fame
By Bryan Smith

An account of Hunslet's 'All Four Cups' season, which remains one of the great feats by a team in the history of rugby league (or Northern Union) football. The progress of the season is covered in some depth, with (fully referenced!) excerpts from contemporary match previews and reports and short notes on each of the players that appeared during the campaign. The match details include the Hunslet teams and scorers, but not the opposition's (these can be found, along with an alternative selection of illustrations, in Les Hoole's 1991 *We've Swept the Seas Before Boys* booklet, whose existence, oddly, is nowhere mentioned by Bryan Smith). A history of the Hunslet club and the rugby game in Yorkshire more generally up to 1907 is included, along with a section on the history of the area, which makes for a nice rounded read and adds context to the main narrative.

Privately published in 2008 at £12.95, No ISBN.

Kangaroos, Kiwis and Roughyeds
By Michael Turner

Oldham are well served by their historians, even if their fortunes on the playing (and administrative) front have not been so great in recent years. This is another superb volume to add to Michael Turner's previous *Oldham RLFC The Complete History 1876-1997* and Brian Walker's *Roughyeds The Story* the latter of which is arguably the finest history of an English rugby league club. This latest book is more than just an account of Oldham's matches against touring Australasian sides (not to mention their various encounters with French club and representative teams and full coverage of the 1997 World Club Championship); a splendid selection of contemporary illustrations and other material is also included. Lots to look at, informative and well-written text, and sufficient statistics to keep the inner anorak happy. Recommended, and not just for Oldham fans.

Published by the Oldham Rugby League Heritage Trust at £20.00. ISBN 9780954639310

Celtic Crusaders Rugby League Football Club Official Yearbook 2008

A handy yearbook and season guide from Celtic Crusaders, similar in format and contents to that produced for 2007. This booklet is more than just a Crusaders' book, with plenty of information about the game in Wales, and for Wales, generally. The practical information as regards directions to and facilities at the grounds of all their opposition for the season should also prove useful for any supporters of the other teams in National League One. The other striking feature is the list of club officials and backroom staff at the beginning - it's a good job Leighton Samuel is reputed to be very well off, if he's paying all of these.

Published by Celtic Crusaders RLFC at £4.99. No ISBN

Telegraph & Argus 100 Years of the Bulls
By John Downes and Martin Bass

The blurb in the dust jacket flaps proclaims this as "a definitive history of the club". It isn't. About half of the book is given over to a history of Bradford rugby league (most, it should be noted, as Northern rather than as Bulls), but the font is large, the line spacing generous, and the margins wide. There are some nice photographs, but it is disappointingly insubstantial. The other half of the book is a round up of the 'Team of the Century', although, unless I missed it, the actual 'team' is not named. Instead there is some inconclusive discussion about the great, the good, and the slightly obscure players who have turned out for Bradford over the years. And some more nice photos.

If you can find a copy of Phil Hodgson's *Odsal Odysseys*, buy that instead. Same number of pages, but much more content.

Published by Breedon Books at £16.99. ISBN 9781859836040

Rugby League Where Are They Now?
By John Huxley

A mildly amusing, funny in a groan-inducing rather than side splitting sort of way, little book, with fascinating new facts, mostly fairly trivial, about former players. Something new for everybody. Probably best read in small chunks. It's difficult to escape the impression that perhaps this might work better as a weekly column in a newspaper rather than in this book format. Also, I'm not sure why Eddie Waring and Clive Sullivan are included as they are both dead.

Published by yfp publishing at £9.99. ISBN 9780954533366

Stuart Leadley

Obituaries

Robert Gate writes about some of the players lost to the game over the past year. Mike Gregory and Duggie Greenall were both well covered in the rugby league press, and Robert decided that there was little he could add to what had already been said about them.

Eric Ashton
Born 24 January 1935 – Died 20 March 2008

Eric Ashton was one of those rare men whose careers were so replete with success, interest and incident, who was such a significant player on rugby league's stage and whose name resonates so loudly down the last half century that any obituary can merely skim the surface of the landscape of his life and times.

The bare facts tell some of his tale:

Representative rugby league
* 26 tests (1957 to 1963), 15 of which were as captain
* Ashes-winning tours in 1958 and 1962, the latter as captain, plus a home Ashes winning series in 1959
* World Cups in 1957 and 1960, captaining the winners in 1960
* 10 Lancashire caps, five of which were as captain

Club rugby league with Wigan, 1955 to 1969
* 497 appearances, 231 tries, 448 goals, 1589 points
* Captained Wigan 1957 to 1969
* Captained six Wigan sides at Wembley. Winners in 1958, 1959 and 1965, losers in 1961, 1963 and 1966
* Captained Wigan to the Championship in 1959-60
* Captained Wigan to Lancashire Cup Finals in 1957 (lost) and 1966 (won)
* Captained Wigan to Lancashire League Championships in 1958-59 and 1961-62

Coaching career 1963 to 1980
* Player-coach at Wigan 1963 to 1969
* Coach at Wigan 1969 to 1973
* Coach at Leeds 1973-74
* Coach at St Helens 1974 to 1980
* England and Lancashire coach 1978 to 1980
* Great Britain coach 1979

Other achievements and honours
* 1966 awarded the MBE, becoming the first rugby league player to be honoured
* 1966 Record Wigan benefit of £1,677
* 1977 Inaugural winner of Man of Steel Coach of the Year
* 1982-2007 Board member at St Helens, becoming chairman from 1993 to 1997, and Life President in 2003

* 2000 Elected a Life Member of the RFL
* 2005 Elevated to the Rugby League Hall of Fame
* 2006 Awarded Tom Mitchell Lion of the Year trophy
* 2007 Inducted into Wigan Hall of Fame

The above is a mightily impressive *curriculum vitae*, an eloquent testimony to one of the game's monumental careers, but the facts and figures can never adequately encapsulate the player and the man. Talk to anyone with any depth of knowledge of rugby league and never a bad word will pass his or her lips concerning Eric Ashton. As a centre threequarter he was a paragon, as a captain he led by example, with quiet but absolute authority and as a man he conducted himself with modesty, friendliness and dignity.

The cover of Eric's 1966 autobiography *Glory in the Centre Spot* gave as good a description of him as any: "Ashton is the dark-haired, slim and elegant destroyer who has loped across the stadiums of two continents – and left their rugby league idols clutching and gasping after his elusive shadow. Ashton is the egg-head in the middle. He is the master planner, who can coax and soothe the brawn and brashness of the game's hard-bitten rank and file into something that gets close to genius."

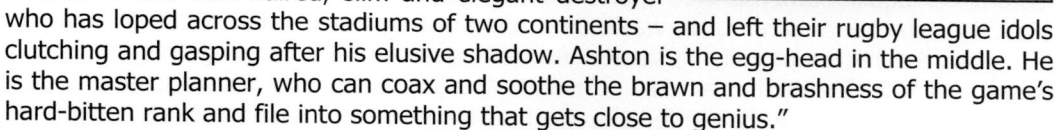

Vince Karalius, in his own autobiography *Lucky 13,* published in 1964, wrote: "Ashton is the perfectionist. He can 'read' a game and be streets ahead of his own team-mates – and sometimes of the opposition – with moves he simply plucks out of his sleeve... That's Ashton, the star who can keep his play ice-cool when tempers are at boiling point, the star whose centre play is deceptively fast and smooth as silk; the star whose captaincy will eventually lead him to the top coaching job in Rugby League." Who would contradict The Wild Bull of the Pampas or Neil Fox, who, 44 years later, on Eric's death, wrote to the *Daily Telegraph* saying, "He was one in a million... He was a gentleman, both on and off the field, and a great captain, probably the best international captain that I played with... Eric was always a hard man to beat but never did anything nasty or dirty... He was a great person."

Mike (Stevo) Stephenson regarded Eric as a hero in his childhood and was in awe of him when he first played against the Wigan maestro for Dewsbury. Stevo recalled the occasion in *League Express*: "His stature and balance were amazing: he seemed to glide past you with so much ease. I recall our coach at half-time suggesting I should perhaps try and tackle him, rather than look on dumbstruck... Believe me, I tried good and hard, but I couldn't get anywhere near him. It was as though he was on roller skates."

That was one of the most striking things about Eric's style. It all seemed so effortless, so smooth, so simple. There was never a hint of panic, his brain seemed to be constantly in a silent whirr and he would invariably come up with the right decision, the match-winning move, the telling pass, the subtlest of kicks.

Yet it could have all never happened. After starring in schoolboy rugby for Rivington Road School, St Helens schoolboys and Lancashire schoolboys, he gave up rugby league when his hometown club showed no real interest in him. He had begun to play for St Helens 'B' at under-16 level but was constantly overlooked for matches and decided life held other pleasures. When he was called up for National Service he was stationed in

Scotland and began to play rugby union. He represented Scottish Command but, contrary to some sources, he never did play for The Army in the Inter-Services tournament. He did, however, attract the attention of Wigan and signed for them for £150 after being called out of the crowd at their pre-season public trial at Central Park. Wigan was clearly not his first choice as a Sintelliner, while his father Ernie had briefly been a three-quarter for Warrington from 1926 to 1928.

He made his debut at left wing on 20 August 1955 in a 52-5 home thrashing of Dewsbury, scoring 14 points from two tries and four goals, but was upstaged by the other winger, Billy Boston, who crashed over for seven to equal the club record. Almost 14 years later Eric pulled on the cherry and white for the last time, when he was again among the try-scorers in a 26-21 home defeat to Salford on 3 May 1969. In between he and Billy Boston had formed one of the most celebrated and dangerous centre-wing partnerships of all time. The pairing first saw the light of day on 13 October 1956, when both were try-scorers in a 17-11 win at Leigh. No one who ever saw the two in tandem is likely to forget the spectacle.

Eric had few, if any, weaknesses, although even he could occasionally be put off his game by over-vigorous opponents. Mostly, though, even that type of play failed to disturb his equilibrium. He was quick, he was clever and he was clinical, capable of creating chances for others. He was also a fine finisher, as his total of 320 tries in 572 first class fixtures graphically illustrates. Add 481 goals and his career points tally finally stood at 1,922. Those figures do not include the 25 points (five tries and five goals), which he bagged in a game for the Northern Hemisphere against New Zealand at Auckland during Great Britain's World Cup tour in 1957.

Among his other impressive scoring feats were 11 goals in a Challenge Cup-tie against Leigh Miners Welfare in 1969, 24 points (four tries, six goals) against Hull KR in 1961 and 26 points (four tries, seven goals) against NSW North Coast and 21 points against Perth on the 1958 Lions tour. His most prolific try-scoring season as a Wigan player brought him 37 in 1957-58, while in 1956-57 he piled up 244 points from 18 tries and 95 goals for Wigan and reached the 200 points mark in 1959-60 with 24 tries and 64 goals. Eric stands alongside just five other players who have performed the feat of scoring 300 tries and 300 goals – James Lomas, Jim Leytham, Neil Fox, Ike Southward and Garry Schofield.

Among all the triumphs and honours there were, of course, some disappointments. A broken leg caused him to miss the New Zealand section of the 1962 Lions tour, for example, and his trip to Australasia as Lions coach in 1979 saw his team become the worst performing British touring squad up to that time. Such setbacks were few and far between, however and it will indeed take a remarkable man to match Eric Ashton's achievements in the triple role of player, coach and administrator.

Photo: Eric Ashton leads out Wigan at the 1960 Championship Final.

David Royston Bevan
Born 2 January 1928 - Died 16 April 2008

Few top class wingers have been better known for their impregnable defence than for their attacking skills and propensity to pile up tries. Dai Bevan was an outstanding exception to this rule.

David Royston Bevan was born in Penycraig, Tonypandy in 1928 and played rugby union for the local grammar school before migrating north. Although he was a good enough football player to have had trials for Manchester United, his rugby union career continued with Oldham RU Club from where he joined the old, lamented Belle Vue Rangers as a 20-year-old wingman. He made his debut at right centre in Belle Vue's 10-7 home defeat by Wakefield Trinity on 18 December 1948 and spent four years with the Rangers, scoring 48 tries in 130 games. He made his last appearance as a Ranger on 22 March 1952 in a 10-6 home win against Castleford.

Wigan recognised his talents and paid Rangers £2,000 for his signature in 1952. His debut on 2 April saw Wigan lose 20-7 to Leigh at Central Park. He arrived in time to help them win the Lancashire League title and take the Championship, although he did not play in the Final against Bradford Northern.

In 1952-53, his only full season at Central Park, Dai scored 38 tries in 43 games and won caps for Wales against Other Nationalities at Warrington and for Great Britain against Australia, coming in for the third test at Odsal when Arthur Daniels dropped out. The following season he helped Wigan reach the Lancashire Cup Final, scoring their only try in the semi-final against Leigh, but again did not figure in the Final. Further international honours came his way with selection for Great Britain against France at Lyons on 24 May, 1953 when he bagged two tries in a 28-17 defeat, while he won a second Wales cap against England at St Helens on 16 September 1953. Unfortunately for Dai all four of his international appearances resulted in defeats. His last game for Wigan was a desperate 8-7 victory over Keighley at Central Park on 10 October 1953.

Halifax had a problem filling their left-wing spot following the retirement of Terry Cook and decided that Dai Bevan was an ideal replacement, despite the fact that almost all of his games had been played as a right-winger. They paid Wigan £1,700 for his services in December 1953 and he played his first game for them in a 14-3 win over York at Thrum Hall on 12 December. He arrived at a good time as Halifax ended up top of the league, won the Yorkshire League Championship and contested the Challenge Cup and Championship Finals in 1953-54. Dai played in the historic Halifax versus Warrington trilogy – the 4-4 Challenge Cup draw at Wembley, the Odsal replay, a cruel 8-4 defeat, and the Championship Final at Maine Road, which was an even crueller 8-7 defeat.

Dai had the satisfaction of snuffing out Warrington's major threat, the incomparable Brian Bevan, who failed to score in any of the matches. Indeed many pundits thought Dai the best defensive wingman in the game. He certainly became a sore trial for Brian Bevan, who was unable to score a solitary try against Dai in eight direct confrontations between 1949 and 1955. On the other hand, Dai had managed just one against Brian – in Wigan's 13-9 loss at Wilderspool on 19 September 1953. Brian finally broke the spell when the pair clashed for the last time on 24 September 1955, zipping over for two tries in Wire's 24-9 success against Halifax at Wilderspool. Dai attributed his defensive prowess to his ability to give opposing wingers the outside but still being quick enough to take them into touch – practicable enough against straight, powerful runners but decidedly risky against such a quirky mover as The Great Bev.

Halifax had not bought Dai for his tackling – he was very quick and determined and had scored almost 100 tries for Belle Vue and Wigan – but it took him nine games to score his first try for Halifax, against Hull KR on 27 February 1954, and he only claimed three in 23 games in his debut season. His rate picked up in 1954-55 when he scored a dozen and he was in Halifax's Yorkshire Cup-winning team against Hull. Opposing three-quarters had a hard time scoring against Halifax's left-wing pairing of Dai and Peter Todd, another tough tackler.

Dai's final season was 1955-56 when he had a new centre partner in Geoff Palmer. Dai scored 19 tries, including a hat-trick in a 44-7 romp against Castleford at Thrum Hall. He played in Halifax's thrilling 18-17 victory over the Kiwis and claimed important tries in Yorkshire Cup-ties against Wakefield Trinity in the second round, Castleford in the semi-final and in the drawn Final against Hull at Headingley, picking up his second winners' medal after Halifax's 7-0 victory in the replay at Odsal. He also collected a second Yorkshire League medal and runners-up medals for the Challenge Cup and Championship, although the emerging new star Johnny Freeman was preferred for the finals against St Helens and Hull. Dai's last game, his 101st, for Halifax saw them vanquish Batley 10-8 at Mount Peasant on 17 April 1956. He had scored 34 tries for the club, bringing his career tally to 129 tries in 294 first class fixtures.

Dai would have been a real conundrum for modern coaches. Although a games teacher by profession, Dai was a heavy smoker and a light eater, standing 5 feet 9 inches and weighing around 12 stones. He always reckoned he was never 100 per cent fit and never really reached his full potential as a player. Around 1952 he did give up smoking for a time and was rewarded, he believed, by winning his test cap.

Note – This obituary is an extended version of the profile of Dai Bevan in Robert Gate's book *Thrum Hallers: Halifax Heroes 1945-1998* (Tempus 2004)

Billy Blan
Died 11 April 2008, aged 86

Billy Blan was one of the game's outstanding back-row forwards of the immediate post-war decade, as adept in the second-row as he was at loose-forward, where he played most of his career. He was one of a trio of brothers, who all had distinguished careers in the game. His older brother Jack played anywhere in the pack in a seven year stint from 1940 to 1947 with Wigan before moving on to Salford and Swinton, while younger brother Albert played for Wigan 'A' before moving on to Swinton, captaining the Lions to consecutive Championships in 1962-63 and 1963-64. The brothers hold the unique distinction of all playing in Roses matches for Lancashire.

Billy began his playing with the wonderfully named Squirrel Hornets, a team from Scholes, which joined the Wigan Intermediate League before the war. He was serving in the RAF when he trialled for Wigan in the Wardonia Cup against Warrington in August, 1945 and subsequently signed for the club for a fee of £50. He made his official first team debut on 29 September 1945 on the right wing, when Wigan beat Oldham 19-0 in a first round, second leg Lancashire Cup-tie at Central Park. Wigan went on to lose to Widnes in the Lancashire Cup Final, but Billy had not yet established himself as a regular by then. By the season's end, however, he had earned a Lancashire League Championship medal and had played in Wigan's dramatic 13-12 defeat by Wakefield Trinity at Wembley. He had also gained a League Championship medal after figuring in Wigan's 13-4 victory over Huddersfield at Maine Road. In both finals he had played at loose-forward, while brother Jack played at hooker.

The 1946-47 season provided Billy with winners' medals for the Championship, the Lancashire Cup and the Lancashire League, as he established himself as a regular at second-row, while the following season he added further winners' medals from the Lancashire Cup and Challenge Cup to his collection, the latter after an 8-3 Wembley win against Bradford Northern. The 1947-48 season also saw him score a try against the New Zealanders and his only appearance at full-back in a 6-3 home victory over Leigh. The 1948-49 season provided fewer highlights – a third Lancashire Cup winners' medal and a 16-11 triumph over the Kangaroos being perhaps the most notable.

In 1949-50 Billy experienced his *annus mirabilis*. Hitherto he had been variously described as "a tireless worker", "a good dribbler and safe handler" and he had always been a mighty cover tackler. In four seasons he had scored 23 tries in over 120 appearances – a fair return by most forwards' standards. Suddenly, however, he could not stop scoring tries, his rangy, muscular frame (6 feet 1 inch, 13 stone 12 pounds) tearing opposing defences to shreds. At the season's close he had bagged 34 in 46 games. He was the game's fourth highest try-scorer behind his team-mate Brian Nordgren (57), Huddersfield's Lionel Cooper (46) and Halifax's Arthur Daniels (36) and he actually pushed Brian Bevan (33) into fifth place. In four consecutive games in January and February he scored 14 tries (4, 2, 4, 4) – all against Liverpool Stanley and York – which must surely be a unique occurrence for a forward. He touched down in the big games too, claiming tries in the Lancashire Cup Final victory over Leigh and in the Championship Final rout of Huddersfield. He also pocketed a winners' medal for the Lancashire League. His 34 tries came close to breaking the record of Hull's Bob Taylor, who rattled up 36 in 1925-26. Taylor had scored four of his tries for England so Billy had in fact set a new record for tries scored for a club by a forward. Subsequently, Taylor's record was shattered by Leeds's Bob Haigh, who amassed 40 in 1970-71.

Amazingly, Billy's scoring extravaganza failed to excite the representative selectors and he was overlooked for any honours, including the 1950 Lions tour. He was finally recognised in the following season when he played in Lancashire's games against Yorkshire at Fartown and Cumberland at Barrow. His scoring rate for Wigan fell dramatically to 13 tries in 42 appearances but he earned a fifth Lancashire Cup winners' medal when Warrington were pulverised 28-5 in the Final at Swinton. The season's end also brought him a third Challenge Cup Final appearance and his second winners' medal after Barrow were defeated 10-0 at Wembley. Wigan captain Ces Mountford took the Lance Todd Trophy but some thought Billy had come close to winning it. W.E. Riley, of the *Sporting Chronicle*, for example, wrote, "The greatest danger to the Furness defence came from the brainy play of Billy Blan. Skill in avoiding the tackle and speed in exploiting the advantages gained or by his trickiness made him the most consistent figure in the match".

The 1951-52 season was a real curate's egg for Billy. He made his international debut for England, scoring twice in a 35-11 victory over Wales at St Helens on 19 September. He bagged another try in a 42-13 loss to the French in Marseilles on 25 November. On 6

October he was awarded his first test cap figuring prominently at loose-forward in Britain's 21-15 win against New Zealand at Odsal. He played in the second row in the following two tests, which yielded victories at Swinton, 20-19, and Leeds, 16-12, where he was a try-scorer and also won his third cap for Lancashire against Yorkshire at Leigh. At a domestic level he earned three more winners' medals with Wigan, for the Lancashire League (his fourth), the Lancashire Cup (his sixth) and for the Championship (his fourth). However, he did not play in the finals of the latter two competitions and all his 20 appearances for Wigan were in the second-row, as Wigan had forked out a world record fee for Dewsbury's test loose-forward Harry Street.

Billy played three times for Lancashire in 1952-53 and won a third and final England cap in a 31-12 loss to Other Nationalities at Fartown on 18 October 1952 and they proved to be his last representative honours. There were no trophies for Wigan in 1952-53, although they did reach the Challenge Cup semi-finals. Billy made his 255th and last appearance for them in a 9-5 home win against Workington Town on 8 April 1953, having contributed 77 tries and four goals.

Leeds were quick to sign Billy, who was by then as much admired for his constructive ball-playing as for his powerful, running, tackling and vigour. After playing for them in a Lazenby Cup win over Hunslet, he made his official debut on 15 August 1953 in a 23-14 reverse at Hull. Leeds restored him to the loose-forward berth and they reached the Challenge Cup semi-final, losing 8-4 to Warrington, a game Billy missed because of a thigh injury. In 1954-55 Billy earned a Yorkshire League winners' medal but reluctantly left Headingley for domestic reasons to join St Helens. He made his debut in a 27-3 home victory over Leigh on 8 January 1955. His stay at Knowsley Road was short and concluded on 31 August 1955, when he kicked a couple of goals in an 11-10 defeat at Salford. He made 17 appearances, with two tries and seven goals for the Saints.

Billy then agreed to help Leeds out again, as they struggled with an injury crisis and he reappeared in blue and amber on 3 September 1955 in a 24-12 success against Bradford Northern at Headingley. He played 11 games for them in this period, including a desperately close encounter against the New Zealanders, who won 18-16. His three-month stint for the Loiners ended on 3 December 1955 with a 23-9 home loss to Leigh. Ironically, the arrival of Harry Street at Headingley heralded Billy's departure. In his two spells at Leeds he had totalled 57 appearances (12 tries, 4 goals).

A final move followed to Rochdale Hornets, his debut being a Christmas Eve home fixture against Workington Town, which was lost 26-5. His 10th and final game for the Hornets on 10 March 1956 also ended in defeat, when Barrow triumphed 30-14 at The Athletic Grounds. Billy only played in two winning sides for Rochdale and did not trouble the scorers as a Hornet.

Billy's first class career encompassed 351 appearances, 96 tries and 15 goals. In his playing days he had been a motor engineer but many of his later years were spent in the pools office at his beloved Central Park, where he worked as Wigan's lottery manager. Billy was deservedly a member of Wigan's Hall of Fame.

Alan Buckley
Born 23 October 1941 – Died 12 March 2008

One of the classiest and most constructive centres of the 1960s, Alan Buckley played his entire club career for Swinton and was one of the original inductees into the club's Hall of Fame. Fair-haired and beautifully balanced in his running, he formed a deadly left-wing partnership with John Stopford for many years, the pair totalling almost 400 tries between them for the Lions, as well as playing together in five test matches and three county games. Alan had pace, an eye for the gap and the precision passing to despatch supporting players to the line. He stood an inch under six feet and weighed 13 stone 7 pounds. Ray French in *League Weekly* described him as "majestic on attack, solid in defence... Alan Buckley was a wonderful stylish centre of the old school but he was more than that – he was a fair opponent, modest man and a gentleman, who earned the respect of all who played against him."

Alan, a native of Ardwick in Manchester, was playing rugby union for Broughton Park Colts when Swinton signed him in 1959. He made his first team debut at left centre in a 5-0 home win against Barrow on 9 January 1960. He did not play in the first team again that season, but became a fixture in the side in the 1960-61 season, when he scored 25 tries in 38 appearances, including three hat-tricks, while his winger Stopford bagged 30 tries. Swinton served notice that they were a rising force by taking the Lancashire League title, losing the Lancashire Cup Final to St Helens and contesting the Championship semi-final.

There was a desperate setback for Alan, however, when he suffered a shoulder injury in the Charity Cup match against Salford at Station Road on 12 August 1961 and was put out of the game for the entire season. He was back for the 1962-63 season to help Swinton to a third consecutive Lancashire Cup Final, although it resulted in a third consecutive defeat by St Helens. The campaign ended gloriously, however, as Swinton emerged from the Big Freeze to outclass the rest of the First Division and win the Championship by six clear points. On a personal level Alan had broken into representative football with appearances for Lancashire against Cumberland and Yorkshire in September, 1962. Over the following nine years he would win ten Lancashire caps, including six Roses matches. His county appearances yielded him just two tries and a goal. Bizarrely, that solitary goal was scored in the Roses match of 1965 and was the only goal he ever kicked at Station Road. He did kick three goals for Swinton, but they were all away from home – at Hull KR, Wigan and Leeds.

Alan repeated his feat of scoring 25 tries for Swinton in 1963-64, equalling the club record with five in a Western Division Championship match against Salford, who were squashed 47-0 on 8 April. Swinton went on to contest the Western Division Final at Central Park on 16 May but lost again to St Helens, 10-7, and Alan missed the Final through injury. Swinton took a much bigger prize, though, by retaining the Championship with another clear six point margin.

The 1963-64 season brought Alan test recognition for the first time, when he was brought into the Great Britain team for the third test at Headingley on 30 November after Britain had been pulverised in the first two Ashes tests. The new-look British team rose to the occasion to win a torrid match 16-5. Alan had earlier been in the Lancashire side, which had beaten the Kangaroos 13-11 at Wigan and in the Swinton team, which held them to a 2-2 draw the week before the third test. His test career stretched to seven matches, with one try, against France in 1964, and he won selection for the 1966

Lions tour, playing in the first and third tests against Australia at the Sydney Cricket Ground and in the first test at Carlaw Park against New Zealand. Alan played 16 games on tour, scoring tries against Northern Territory, Queensland, Balmain and Wellington. He also played for England against Wales at Salford on 7 November 1968, when he went on as a 25th minute substitute for Mick Shoebottom in a 24-17 defeat.

In domestic rugby Swinton continued to be a force. In 1964-65 Alan got another Lancashire Cup runners-up medal against bogey side St Helens and experienced the despair of defeat in the Challenge Cup semi-final against Wigan. In 1965-66 he top-scored for Swinton with 21 tries and the team finished second in the league but crashed out of the Championship play-offs, 33-2 at home to Halifax. The following season he picked up another runners-up medal after Swinton lost the BBC2 Floodlit Competition Final 7-2 to Castleford at Wheldon Road.

Subsequently Swinton occasionally threatened to break back into the game's elite and Alan continued to score tries prolifically into the 1970s. They had steadily lost their great players of the early 1960s, however, and never adequately replaced them. Alan finally acquired a Lancashire Cup winners' medal in 1969. After scoring five tries in the first two rounds against Blackpool Borough and Oldham, he created the only try of the final at Wigan, where Leigh were defeated 11-2. In 1972 he collected a fourth Lancashire Cup runners-up medal after local rivals Salford beat Swinton 25-11 at Warrington. At the close of the 1972-73 season Swinton finished 21st in the league table and were consigned to the newly instituted Second Division for the following campaign. Alan played on in the Second Division but finally called a halt to his career on 24 March 1974 when he played on the left wing in a 16-5 win at Barrow. His first class career had stretched to 494 games and he had scored 199 tries, 192 for Swinton, and four goals.

Norman Field
Died 13 January 2008, aged 71

Norman Field was a powerful, direct winger, who amazed almost all the rugby league fraternity when he won selection for the Great Britain team in the first test against Australia at Wembley in 1963. Those were the days when players from lowly clubs could still catch the eye of the international selectors and such an occurrence would be unthinkable today.

Norman was born and bred in Huddersfield. He attended Hillhouse School and played in the same team as Maurice Oldroyd, now the Patron of BARLA, although he was a year younger than Maurice. He went on to play amateur rugby league for Lockwood before signing for Batley on 7 January 1954. He also played rugby union in the army while on national service. He made his debut on the left wing at Odsal in a 24-0 defeat against Bradford Northern on 20 February 1954. He remained at Mount Pleasant for three and a half years, scoring 15 tries in 72 appearances. In his last season, 1956-57, he became established as the regular left-centre.

At the start of the following season Norman went to Featherstone Rovers in an exchange for Yorkshire centre Mick Hirst. He made his debut for Rovers at left-centre in a 25-18 home victory over Leigh at Post Office Road on 17 August 1957. The move did not work out and he made just six appearances, scoring one try, for Featherstone in the course of barely a month. He subsequently returned to Mount Pleasant and by coincidence his second debut for Batley again ended in a 29-15 defeat at Bradford on 28 February 1959. In his first three seasons back at Batley he played only 21 games and missed the entire 1960-61 campaign. His luck began to turn, however and in 1962-63 he bagged 19 tries in 27 appearances, an exceptionally good return for a team with limited resources.

Even so, there was a certain amount of surprise when Norman was picked for the Roses Match at St Helens on 11 September 1963. He scored a try but Yorkshire were hammered 45-20. He had impressed sufficiently, however, to retain his place for the game against the Australians at Craven Park, Hull the following week. Only Norman and forwards Ken Bowman (Huddersfield) and Fred Ward (Hunslet) survived from the Roses debacle. Yorkshire proceeded to inflict the first defeat of their tour on the Kangaroos, winning more easily than the 11-5 score-line suggested. Derek Marshall in the *Daily Mail* commented: "Field again impressed with his limited chances on the wing". A week later Norman scored his second try for Yorkshire but the side were beaten 15-13 by Cumberland at Wakefield. Interestingly, Norman had different centre partners on each of his county appearances – Terry Major (Hull KR), Neil Fox (Wakefield Trinity) and Frank Smith (Castleford).

His performances in the Yorkshire matches prompted the selectors to elevate him to the test team for the Wembley game on 16 October 1963. Norman was then 27 years old and stood 5 fee 11 inches tall and weighed 13 stone 7 pounds, according to the match programme. The game was a disaster for the Great Britain boys who crashed 28-2 to a rampant Australian team. Norman never got another chance to play test rugby and retired prematurely a few months later, his last game being a 14-6 loss to Hunslet in the second round of the Challenge Cup at Mount Pleasant on 29 February 1964. His second spell at Batley had brought him 38 tries in 95 appearances. His first class career record comprised 177 games and 56 tries.

He retired from the game to concentrate on a garage business he ran with his brother Reggie on Bradford Road, Huddersfield but in later years he migrated to Torquay, where he became an hotelier.

William Brian Radford
Died 15 August 2007

Brian Radford, a Welshman from Kenfig Hill, who had played his senior rugby union with Aberavon, joined Bradford Northern in December 1948. At that time Northern were in their pomp, a team full of great players accustomed to winning trophies and frequently appearing before massive crowds. Eleven years later Brian was still at Odsal but the club was in freefall and heading for the oblivion of 1963. Brian's 333rd and last game for them, an 18-10 home defeat by Hull on 19 December 1959, drew a record low post-war crowd of only 1,200 to Odsal. In the circumstances his loyalty to the club was laudable but perhaps his name, B Radford, pre-ordained that he should remain an Odsalite.

When Brian arrived at Odsal it must have felt as if he was entering an enclave of Wales. The man who sought his services, manager-coach, Dai Rees had brought a huge Welsh influence to bear. Of the 25 players used in the Bradford team in 1948-49 Willie Davies, Alan Edwards, Trevor Foster, Ron Greaves, Bill Jenkins, Gwylfa Jones, Sandy Orford, Emlyn Walters and Frank Whitcombe hailed from the valleys. Brian pushed the Welsh quota into double figures.

His debut ended in a 17-3 defeat at York on 22 January 1949 when he appeared as a second-rower. He established a place in the side immediately and within five months had a Challenge Cup winners' medal to credit. However, after playing in all the rounds up to the Final, he was controversially left out of the side that played in the 12-0 victory over Halifax at Wembley. Fearing that underdogs Halifax might monopolise possession though their great hooker, Alvin Ackerley, Dai Rees recalled giant prop Frank Whitcombe to the front row for his scrimmaging expertise, despite the fact that he had practically retired. Rees' strategy certainly worked as Northern won the scrums 42-13 and the match 12-0 but it must have been a major disappointment for Brian Radford to have missed the Final.

Brian was 23 years old when he arrived at Odsal. He stood 5 feet 11 inches, weighed around 14 stones and he was a sound all-round forward. The 1949 Challenge Cup Final programme described him thus: "Splendidly built, he is an ideal man in the loose – fast, strong and a sure tackler". Subsequent pen pictures of him included the following in a *Rugby Favourites* (ca 1951) booklet, "Equally useful in defence or attack, he is a powerful unit in a powerful pack", while the 1952 Championship Final programme marked him out as "a very strong scrummager and useful in the loose". In his earlier years at Odsal he was predominantly a second-rower, sharing that job with that other "Mr Bradford", Trevor Foster, but he also frequently packed down at blind-side prop and deputised at loose-forward when Ken Traill was missing. His pace was considerable and Northern played him on the wing in emergencies. Of his 333 appearances, 193 were as a second-row, 119 as blind-side prop, 18 as loose-forward and three as a winger. His try tally for Northern was 47, his best haul being 11 in 1957-58.

Brian played in Northern's Challenge Cup semi-final defeat by Widnes in 1950 and earned Yorkshire Cup winners' medals in 1949 and 1953, although he again missed both finals. Northern topped the league in 1951-52 but Brian's ill luck in finals continued when Wigan beat them 13-6 at Leeds Road, Huddersfield, when he turned out at prop. The following season Northern finished third but went out 18-16 in the play-off semi-final at Halifax with Brian in the second-row. After 1953 Northern began their downward spiral. There were still appearances in semi-finals of the Yorkshire Cup in 1954, 1955 and 1957 for Brian but as the old stars retired they were not adequately replaced.

There was no shortage of excellent Welsh forwards playing rugby league in Brian's days but he did gain a Welsh cap on 17 September 1952 when he appeared in Wales's second-row alongside St Helens's George Parsons in a 19-8 loss to England at Wigan.

In 1959 he was granted a joint testimonial year with fellow Welshman Bill Jenkins, who retired in August of that year. The pair shared a benefit match with Keighley's Ernest Redman, which took place in teeming rain under the Odsal floodlights on 26

October. A crowd of 1,500 paid a shilling each to watch Northern beat Keighley 40-34, with 18 tries being recorded. By that time Northern's crowds would have been barely a tenth of their halcyon years and when Brian and Bill finally received their testimonial cheques they amounted to a mere £175 each.

After his rugby league career ended Brian returned to Wales. He died after a long struggle with cancer in Kenfig Hill, aged 81. It says much for his love of his adopted game that his order of service funeral card bore a caricature drawn by Ken Adams in 1950 of Brian in his Bradford Northern kit.

Note - I am indebted to Tony Lewis for help with this obituary. Tony wrote, "Brian, who I had known all my life was a true gentleman and a sportsman of the finest order. In addition, he was one of the most powerful and strongest men I have ever seen. He will be sadly missed by everyone".

An appreciation

Jeffrey Murray Stevenson
Born 15 May 1932 - Died 13 October 2007

It was a miserable afternoon in February, 2006, when the phone rang. When I answered it, you could have knocked me over with a feather. It was Jeff Stevenson. I had never met or spoken to him before. I had, however, cursed and admired him since childhood. Jeff had lung cancer and was very emotional. He was trying to raise some money for a children's charity and I was his last resort, apparently. He wanted a picture of the Great Britain team which won the Ashes in 1959, when he was the captain. He was going to get the surviving members of the team to autograph it and raffle it but he had drawn a blank with all his enquiries. I told him I could provide him with one – it would be a lot easier than winning Lance Todd Trophies and avoiding kamikaze Kangaroo forwards. Jeff was thrilled to receive the picture and later told me it had raised £1,000 for the charity. He also told me he had no pictorial souvenirs of his career and dearly wanted to leave some record of his career to his youngest grandson. The upshot was that over the next year or so I dug out all sorts of photographs and articles for him. In return I got lots of stories about his career and a great deal of enjoyment from listening to one of my boyhood heroes. I considered it a fair swap.

Jeff was one of those players who made rugby league so fascinating to me. He was so slightly built that he would be immediately told to go away by any modern coach. In comparison Rob Burrow, arguably the current incarnation of Jeff, both for Leeds and Great Britain and England, is built like a brick wall. Jeff's vital statistics were 5 feet 5 inches and his weight varied between 9 stone 2 pounds and 10 stone, according to various pen pictures, and some of us thought they were probably exaggerating. Yet such a tiny figure could captain Great Britain and make monkeys of any number of rough, tough forwards and strapping backs.

As a schoolboy at Buslingthorpe National School he played stand-off and in 1945-46 represented Leeds City Schools and Yorkshire Schools. Leeds were interested in him and local teacher Ken Dalby organised their 'B' team for 14 to 16 year olds. He was keen that Leeds should sign up good local players, as well as bringing in star players from everywhere on the planet. He invited Jeff to play for the Leeds 'B' team. Jeff duly played his first game for the side at Featherstone. He told me: "I was kicked to bits. So I told Ken that I couldn't take such punishment and was giving up rugby league." So Jeff played football as a winger for a local Leeds side. The famous Leeds United manager Major Buckley came to see him play but told Jeff that he was just too small to make it at professional level. Jeff took great pleasure in telling me, "When I got my first Great Britain selection I felt 10 feet tall. In the dressing room I was given a jersey and put it on. I stood in front of a mirror, looked at myself and then started talking to myself. I said, 'Well, Major Buckley, what do you make of that then? Too small?' I think the other players thought I was mad. That was also the first time I ever wore shoulder pads – so I could fill out my Great Britain jersey."

Jeff did his National Service as a Leading Aircraftsman in the RAF, where he took up rugby union as a scrum-half, even though he appeared incapable of putting on any weight. It was this elfin appearance, which misled so many people, who doubted his durability. In his wonderful book *The History of Royal Air Force Rugby 1919-1999*, John Mace tells of an incident involving Peter Yarranton and Bob Weighill. Both were England rugby union forwards and distinguished RAF officers. Yarranton was the President of the RFU in 1991-92 and was knighted in 1992 and became chairman of the Sports Council. Weighill won the Distinguished Flying Cross in 1944 and was secretary of the RFU from 1971 to1986. Mace relates one of Yarranton's memories: "Bob Weighill and I shared another great experience when we travelled to Birkenhead Park in the knowledge that our regular scrum-half had slipped and pulled a muscle getting into the train. Luckily, before we left, the chairman of selectors, David Strong, had managed to get a message to RAF West Kirby asking them to find us a replacement. The dressing rooms had huge log fires and standing beside ours was a pale-faced slim young airman, forage cap in the centre of his head. David thanked him for tending the fire and asked him if he'd like a ticket for the game. 'I'm your scrum-half, sir', replied the young man. A hastily convened committee meeting outside was just about to make other arrangements when three coach loads of supporters arrived from West Kirby carrying banners and placards upon which were emblazoned 'Up Stevey', 'Good old Steve', and other similar devices. 'Dim' Strong wavered, but then said: 'We'll have to play him, but do what you can to protect him'. It was only after 'Stevey' had scored two brilliant, early, individualist tries – and converted them himself without being asked – that we realised we had someone rather special in the side. The man concerned was Jeff Stevenson who went on to play 19 rugby league tests for Great Britain and was reckoned by many to be on a par with the great Alex Murphy. I immediately became aware, and have never forgotten, that appearances mean nothing. It was a golden moment."

A little while later, on 16 February 1952, LAC Stevenson was chivvying the RAF pack along in the Inter-Services tournament against the Royal Navy at Twickenham. Captain of the RAF side from the back-row was Squadron Leader Bob Weighill, while Flight Lieutenant Yarranton was in the second-row. If Stevey was big enough for games like that, Leeds decided he was big enough for them and signed him four days later.

Jeff made his first team debut on Good Friday, 11 April 1952, when he dropped a goal in a 12-9 home win against Castleford. The following season saw him firmly ensconced in the first team despite the claims of Johnny Feather, Frank Watson and Billy Pratt for the Leeds number seven shirt. Ken Dalby summed up Jeff pretty succinctly in his book *Nothing but the Best* (1989): "sudden flashes of fork-lightning brilliance; the eye for an opening; an excellent pair of hands; the outrageous dummy that suckers couldn't resist; the flickering sidestep at speed, that left forlorn tacklers clutching thin air; the quick brain, ever alert to possibilities and, by no means least, tiger-like tenacity in the tackle."

Leeds began to challenge for honours reaching the Challenge Cup semi-final in 1954, the Yorkshire Cup semi-final later that year and the Championship semi-final in 1955. Jeff gained his first winners' medal when Leeds lifted the Yorkshire League Championship in 1954-55. The following season saw him break into representative rugby. He made his Yorkshire debut on 26 September 1955 against Lancashire at Oldham, partnered by his club stand-off Gordon Brown. He would go on to represent the county a dozen times between 1955 and 1961.

He gained his first test cap on 8 October 1955 in a 25-6 success over New Zealand at Swinton, scored his first test try in the next test, a 27-12 win at Odsal and proceeded to play in 15 consecutive tests for Great Britain between 1955 and 1958. His half-back partners in that period were Ray Price for six games, Dave Bolton on four occasions, Gordon Brown twice, Lewis Jones twice and Austin Rhodes once. He played in winning series against the Kiwis in 1955 (2-1), Australia in 1956 (2-1), and France in 1956-57 (2-0, with one draw) and 1957-58 (3-0). His only disappointment at that level was the 1957 World Cup in Australia, when Britain beat France but lost to Australia and New Zealand. He played in all 10 games on that tour, which also included games in New Zealand and South Africa.

On the domestic front Leeds won the Yorkshire League in 1956-57, beat the Kangaroos 18-13, Jeff figuring at stand-off, and reached the Championship semi-final. Most importantly, however, they got to Wembley, courtesy of Jeff's miraculous 40-yard drop-goal out of the Odsal mud against Whitehaven, enabling his side to win the semi-final 10-9. The final produced a 9-7 victory for Leeds over Willie Horne's Barrow and Jeff played one of the games of his life to win the Lance Todd Trophy. Jack Bentley wrote in the *Daily Express* "Barrow never, never subdued... scrum-half Jeff Stevenson. This 9 stone stripling, who looks more suited to a jockey's job, was a darting, scheming terror, his dark, crew-cut head bobbing up in every worthwhile move... His tackling was terrific, his running and distribution of the ball exemplary."

Jeff was in prime form again in 1957-58, rattling up a personal best 17 tries for Leeds, including the only hat-trick of his career in a 25-25 draw with Salford at Headingley. He was unsurprisingly selected for the 1958 Lions tour as first choice scrum-half along with the up and coming Alex Murphy. However, he withdrew for personal and business reasons, having just started a new job and having played for virtually two continuous years without a break because of the 1957 World Cup tour. Oldham's Frank Pitchford took his place and Alex Murphy went on to establish himself as Britain's number one scrum-half, at least for a while.

Jeff acknowledged Alex's quality but told me, maybe tongue in cheek but maybe not, "Murphy was good but not as good as me. I used to give him a crack early on and he would lose his rag. Once when I played for Yorkshire against Lancashire he was in the car park when we arrived. I was first off the bus and he greeted me by shouting, 'F****** hell, Stevey. Are you still playing?' Well I scored twice and so did Alan Kellett, my stand-off. Yorkshire won 38-28. After the game I shouted at Murphy, 'F****** hell, Alex. Are you still here?"

Alex played in six straight tests in 1958-59 but got the chop along with several others after Britain lost the first test against the 1959 Kangaroos at Swinton. Jeff was recalled for the second test at Leeds on 21 November and was made captain. It is now part of rugby league folklore how he conjured up the winning score with a masterly back-flip to Johnny Whiteley from a close-in scrum. Neil Fox converted the try and Britain won 11-10. Jeff then led his side to an 18-12 victory in the decider at Wigan and Britain have never since won an Ashes series on home soil – a totally inconceivable prospect for anyone involved in playing or watching the game at that time. Jeff's test career was extended to 19 tests, when he skippered the side in the two games against France in March 1960. They proved anti-climatic, however, with a 20-18 defeat in Toulouse and a 17-17 draw at St Helens.

Jeff's last season at Headingley was 1958-59, when he led them to a 24-20 victory over Wakefield Trinity in the Yorkshire Cup Final at Odsal, claiming one of his side's six tries. Just over two months later he played his 226th and final game for the Loiners on Christmas Day 1958, when Featherstone Rovers won 12-11 at Headingley. He had scored 67 tries for Leeds and four drop-goals.

It was not an amicable parting. Jeff explained to me that he wanted Leeds to award him a benefit, especially as they were constantly paying big signing-on fees to rugby union men. His original contract had given him £150 on signing and a further £150 after he had played 20 first team games. County and international recognition would eventually make the contract worth £1,000 but that was in the lap of the gods and, as events proved, would not materialise for three years. Ces Mountford had offered him £1,000 up front to sign for Warrington but Jeff was keen to play for his hometown team. He recalled that his father went mad when he heard that Jeff had turned down Warrington's offer. The Leeds chairman, Sir Edwin Airey told Jeff, "No Leeds player will get a benefit while I'm chairman". In those days players who requested a transfer were not entitled to any share in the transfer fee. So Jeff simply told Leeds he had retired. York eventually came in for him and paid out a club record fee of £7,500 to Leeds. Jeff gleefully recalled how he got £800 from the move and even more gleefully that when he later moved from York to Hunslet he pocketed £1,000. He was very unflattering toward the Leeds chairman. His view was that "Edwin Airey was a pillock – with a capital P".

Lewis Jones was Jeff's best man at his wedding to his first wife, Dorothy, whose death left him as a widower before he married Judith, who survives him. Jones and Stevenson were both unquestionably stamped with genius and it is a common misconception that they formed a wondrous half-back partnership. However, the pair only played half-back together once for Leeds – in a 22-10 home victory over Batley on 16 November 1955, when winger Drew Turnbull was the main beneficiary with five of the six Leeds tries. The only other occasions they combined at half-back were the 1957 World Cup games against France and Australia at the Sydney Cricket ground.

Jeff made his debut for York on 7 February 1959 in a shock 8-3 defeat at Bramley. He remained a York player for three years, forming a potent half-back combination with Stan Flannery and later developed a fine understanding with loose-forward Fred Ward. It was as a York player that Jeff won his final four test caps, while seven of his Yorkshire appearances also came in this period. In 95 games for York he claimed 25 tries and dropped a solitary goal. His last game for them was in an 18-2 home loss to Leeds on 20 January 1962.

A week later Jeff was in Hunslet's side, which lost 22-17 at Warrington. Hunslet failed to qualify for the newly formed First Division for the 1962-63 season but under Jeff's inspiration and Fred Ward's captaincy they won the Second Division Championship and lifted the Yorkshire Cup with a 12-2 triumph over Hull KR in the final at Headingley. On the way to that final Hunslet met Halifax at Thrum Hall in the semi-final and I was one of the 8,100 in the crowd. I had a bad feeling because the previous night I had dreamed that someone dropped a goal against Halifax to put us out of the competition and no, I am not making this up! Well, of course, Jeff Stevenson turned out to be the culprit and his drop-goal won the match 7-6. I still resent that drop goal and so when I asked Jeff about it I was flabbergasted when he swore he had absolutely no recollection of it. He only dropped 13 goals in his entire career, seven of them in the 1962-63 season. I didn't bother to ask him about the two he dropped against Halifax later in the season, when Hunslet beat us 16-3 in the second round of the Challenge Cup at Thrum Hall. Jeff continued to play for Hunslet, partnering the talented Brian Gabbitas, until 4 September 1964 when he made his finale in a first round Yorkshire Cup-tie at Leeds, who beat Hunslet 25-8. He had made 64 appearances, with 17 tries and eight goals, for the Parksiders.

The little man who was once deemed to be too fragile for both professional rugby and soccer enjoyed a 12-year career, which yielded him 427 appearances, 122 tries, 13 goals and precious few serious injuries. I have seen and admired many great scrum-halves yet none, even Alexander the Great Murphy and the sublime Peter Sterling, impressed me more than Jeff Stevenson. Harry Street, Jeff's loose-forward in the 1957 Wembley Final, wrote in the *Yorkshire Evening Post* in 1958, "I think Jeff Stevenson is the biggest match-winner I have known".

The second picture of Jeff Stevenson is the presentations at Wembley in 1957.

David Topliss
Born 29 December 1949 – Died 16 June 2008

David Topliss's career spanned 20 years during which he always played the game in the way it should be played – competitively, entertainingly and sportingly. It could be argued that Toppo was the last of the great old-style British stand-offs – small (5 feet 8 inches and barely 11 stones), marvellously elusive, eye-catchingly quick, capable of going through gaps and of creating them for his colleagues. His play was at once intuitive and instinctive yet calculating. In other words as an attacking player, he had it all. He did his share in defence too and his temperament was ideal, enabling him to become a splendid and respected captain.

As an amateur he played for Normanton, from where he won Yorkshire and England under-19 caps before signing in 1968 for Wakefield Trinity, just at the point when the club's golden era ended. His debut, on the right wing, ended in a 15-6 loss to Halifax at Thrum Hall on 2 September 1968, when the incumbent Trinity stand-off Harold Poynton was sent off four minutes from time. It spoke volumes for David that he seamlessly took over the position from Poynton, one of the great men in Trinity's history, without the invidious comments and comparisons often directed at young players supplanting such icons.

David played for Wakefield for 13 seasons, racking up 408 appearances, with 11 at centre, eight on the wing and one at scrum-half, the rest at number six. His ability as a try-scorer was reflected in 193 touchdowns for the club, which included seven hat-tricks and five four-try feats. His best return for Trinity was 29 in the 1972-73 season, while he also passed the 20-try mark in 1970-71, 1971-72, 1974-75 and 1976-77. His final tally of 595 points for Trinity included 16 drop-goals, 14 of which were one-pointers.

In David's time at Belle Vue Trinity struggled to match the exploits of the scintillating team of the previous decade and there were no winners' medals in his cabinet when he left in 1981. There had been some near misses, however. He had been a try scorer in the inaugural John Player Trophy Final in 1972 but Halifax had beaten Wakefield 22-11 at Odsal. In 1973 and 1974, the latter as captain, he had to settle for runners-up medals in Yorkshire Cup Finals against Leeds, 7-2, and Hull KR 16-13. In 1979 he realised his ambition of leading Trinity to Wembley. His performance in a dire and dour Final was outstanding and brought him the Lance Todd Trophy but just another runners-up medal as Widnes triumphed 12-3. Widnes ultimately deserved their victory but, like many another of Trinity's opponents, used questionable measures to bottle up the brilliant Topliss. Paul Fitzpatrick, of *The Guardian*, wrote, "Dave Topliss, an inspirational captain, won the Lance Todd Trophy... but at the afternoon's end all his running, weaving, ducking, all his creativity and boundless energy had achieved less for Wakefield than a single explosive [try-scoring] run by Wright had achieved for Widnes."

David soldiered on as Wakefield skipper for a couple of years after that Wembley loss but made his final appearance for the club in a 25-8 home defeat by Castleford in the Premiership play-offs on 26 April 1981. By that stage he was 31, a veteran with 15 Yorkshire caps, a couple of England appearances and three Ashes tests to his credit. Hull believed he was the man to lead their expensively assembled team to glory and snapped him up for a transfer fee of £15,000 – an absolute bargain, as it transpired.

He made his Hull debut on 16 August 1981 in a 19-15 home defeat by Leeds in a Yorkshire Cup-tie, a rare occurrence in his time on Humberside. He remained as captain at The Boulevard for four seasons, during which Hull contested 10 major finals and were Champions in 1982-83. Most notably, Toppo led his side to victory in the Challenge Cup Final in 1982, winning the man of the match award, scoring two tries and playing superlatively against Widnes in an 18-9 replay victory at Elland Road after a 14-14 draw at Wembley. He made a third Wembley Cup Final appearance in 1983 but Featherstone Rovers spoiled his day by winning 14-12, while he was left out of the side which lost 28-24 to Wigan in the epic 1985 Challenge Cup Final, Fred Ah Kuoi playing in his place. Hull lost the Premiership Finals of 1982 and 1983 to arch rivals Widnes but lifted the Yorkshire Cup in 1982, 1983 and 1984, while the Players Trophy Final was won and lost to even archer rivals Hull KR in 1982 and 1984 respectively.

His 120th and last game for Hull ended in a 46-12 trouncing at Wigan in a Premiership play-off match on 28 April 1985, in the course of which he claimed his 56th and last try for the club for whom he had also dropped a couple of goals to finally amass 189 points. His most prolific season as an Airlie Bird was 1982-83 when he ran in 24 tries in 37 matches.

A transfer to Oldham saw him make a try-scoring debut in a 30-14 home loss to Leeds on 8 September 1985. Injury restricted him to 15 appearances during the 1985-86 season but Oldham were clearly on the rise and reached the semi-finals of the Challenge Cup. The 1985-86 season was a real roller-coaster for Dave and his Roughyeds, who ended up being relegated to the Second Division but knocked Wigan out of the Challenge Cup having lost to them in the Lancashire Cup Final, when David's opposing stand-off was Ellery Hanley. In 49 appearances for Oldham David added another nine tries to his tally, making his finale for them on 20 April 1987 in another defeat by Wigan at Watersheddings.

Fittingly David returned to Wakefield for the 1987-88 campaign as player-coach. His return saw Carlisle hammered 56-8 at Belle Vue on 30 August. Dave added another dozen appearances and a try to his Trinity statistics before finally calling it a day after playing at Featherstone in a 20-16 defeat in a Division 2 Premiership play-off fixture. Trinity finished third in Division 2 to gain promotion. On retiring as player-coach David carried on as coach at Belle Vue until April 1994 helping to keep Wakefield in the First Division throughout that period and taking them to Yorkshire Cup Finals in 1990 and 1992, winning the latter against Sheffield Eagles in the last ever competition for that trophy. In 1988-89 he coached Great Britain under-21s in their two fixtures against France.

At representative level David did not really reap the recognition he deserved. It was both his great good fortune and his misfortune to play at a time when there were plenty of fine stand-offs operating and, of course, almost 100 per cent of them were genuinely British. His county career began with a 32-12 rout of Lancashire in 1970, when Mick Shoebottom was his scrum-half. It ended 10 years later with his ninth Roses match, a 17-9 defeat, when Gary Stephens was his partner. He scored five tries in winning his 15 Yorkshire caps and picked up five County Championship winners' medals. His test career was restricted to a measly four appearances – all in Ashes tests. He enjoyed a wonderful debut in the first test of 1973 when Australia were beaten 21-12 at Wembley but endured a 14-6 defeat at Headingley in the next game. In 1979 he was flown out to Australia as a replacement for the injured Roger Millward and played seven games on tour with two tries including a 28-2 drubbing in the final test at Sydney. Leeds's John Holmes filled the stand-off berth in all the remaining tests and it was also Holmes and Dennis O'Neill (Widnes) who shared the stand-off role in Great Britain's magnificent World Cup triumph in France in 1972, leaving Toppo as the only non-playing member of the squad. In 1975 he partnered Roger Millward in England's 11-9 victory over France at Perpignan and later in the year came on as a 66th minute substitute in England's 25-0 loss to Australia at Leeds in a special challenge match following the World Championship tournament.

Toppo's wonderful performances with Hull brought him a surprise swansong at representative level in 1982 at the ripe old age of 32. On 31 July he skippered Great Britain in an 8-7 loss to France in the unlikely arena of the St Elena Stadium in Venice in a game designed to help prepare the national XIII for the series against the incoming Kangaroos. History knows that Australian party as *The Invincibles*. David was overlooked for the first two massacres, Leigh's John Woods and John Holmes winning the selectors' approval. He was, however, recalled from holiday to lead Great Britain in the final test at Headingley on 28 November, which probably surprised him as much as everyone else in the sport. There was no fairy-tale ending, however, as the Australians swept Britain aside 32-8.

David travelled to Australia for summer seasons in 1976 and 1977. Like the rest of his career, they provided both grave disappointments and heady successes. In 1976 he joined Penrith, playing in a dozen games but, amazingly for so prolific a try-poacher, he failed to register a solitary try. Coach Barry Harris failed to utilise him properly and at one stage dropped him to reserve grade saying "He was hard to coach because when he played he just went and the rest had to try to follow him". Mike Stephenson was the Penrith hooker at the time and, according to the Penrith history *Bound for Glory* (1992), declared "It was the biggest disgrace of all time. Topliss was already an international and, yet, he was put into the background... I said: 'This kid's the best thing since sliced bread!' A year later he was blitzing them with Balmain."

Balmain coach Ron Willey certainly got the best out of David and fellow Englishman Brian Lockwood. Toppo earned constant rave reviews and rediscovered his scoring touch with ten tries and a drop-goal in 18 appearances, as Balmain charged through to the final play-offs after finishing well down the table the previous year. In one astonishing display Dave equalled the Balmain club record in claiming five tries in a 43-12 win against Newtown at Henson Park.

Including his stints in Australian club rugby, David's career record stretched to 647 first class matches. His points tally was 876 with 266 tries and 17 goals. David Topliss – unquestionably top class.

The photo of David Topliss was taken in 1972.

All the photographs for this feature were provided by Robert Gate.

RUGBY LEAGUE JOURNAL

FOR FANS WHO DON'T WANT TO FORGET

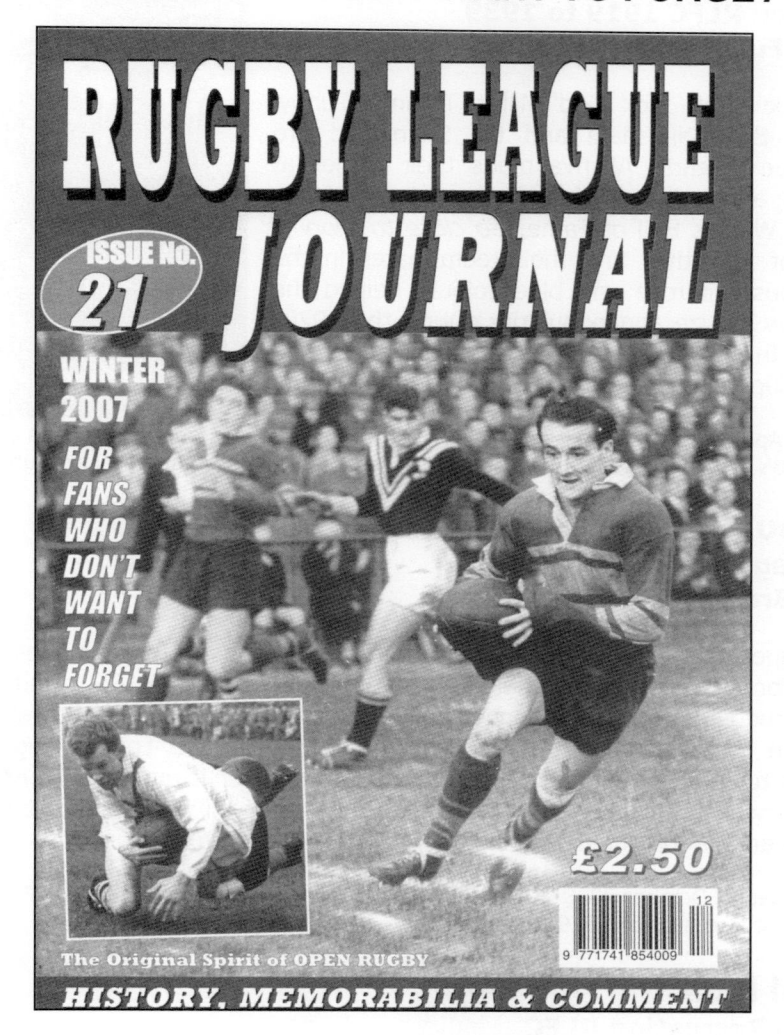

Published quarterly

History, Memorabilia and Comment with every issue packed with wonderful old black and white photographs.

www.rugbyleaguejournal.net

For more details:
e-mail: **rugbyleague.journal@virgin.net**
Or write to: "Rugby League Journal," P.O. Box 22, Egremont, Cumbria, CA23 3WA.

New books from London League Publications Ltd

So close to Glory
Warrington RLFC 1919 to 1939
By Eddie Fuller and Gary Slater

Big Jack Arkwright, Jack 'Cod' Miller, Tommy 'Tubby' Thompson, Billy Dingsdale and Bill Shankland are rugby league legends. All five made their names at Wilderspool and are now founder members of the Warrington Wolves Hall of Fame. *So close to Glory* is the story of how they and their team-mates in the club's famous primrose and blue colours helped the club to grow in size and popularity during the 1920s and 1930s. In this period the team played in three Challenge Cup Finals and three Championship Finals.

Published in April 2008 at £12.95. Available direct from London League Publications Ltd for £12.00 post free. ISBN: 9781903659373. Available at full price in the Warrington Wolves club shop.

Liverpool City RLFC
Rugby league in a football city
By Mike Brocken

Rugby league in Liverpool has a long history. Older fans have memories of visits to watch Liverpool Stanley before the war and Liverpool City in the 1950s and 1960s. This history of rugby league in Liverpool covers from the 1850s to the present day. It includes the first Liverpool City RLFC, Wigan Highfield and London Highfield - the forerunners to Liverpool Stanley RLFC, and the club after it moved to Huyton in 1969 until it was wound up in 1997. This fascinating story will be of interest to all rugby league fans and people interested in Liverpool's sporting history.

To be published in October 2008 at £14.95. Available direct from London League Publications Ltd for £14.00 post free. ISBN: 9781903659403

All local lads
St Helens Recreation RLFC
By Alex Service and Denis Whittle

The full story of the only works team ever to play in professional rugby league. From their early days in rugby union, to association football, St Helens Recs and then the post-war amateur Pilkington Recs, a fascinating tale of triumph, tragedy and survival against the odds.

To be published in November 2008 at £13.95. Available direct from London League Publications Ltd for £13.00, post free. ISBN: 9781903659434

To order from London League Publications, go to www.llpshop.co.uk to pay by credit card.
Cheque payments to PO Box 10441, London E14 8WR.
All our books can be ordered from any bookshop at full price.